NO VISIBLE WOUNDS

Identifying

nonphysical

abuse of women

by their men

MARY SUSAN MILLER, PH.D.

CONTEMPORARY
BOOKS

A TRIBUNE NEW MEDIA COMPANY

Library of Congress Cataloging-in-Publication Data

Miller, Mary Susan.
    No visible wounds : identifying nonphysical abuse of
women by their men / Mary Susan Miller.
        p.   cm.
    Includes index.
    ISBN 0-8092-3546-3 (cloth)
    1. Abused women—Psychology—Case studies.
2. Psychological abuse—Case studies.   3. Abusive men—
Psychology—Case studies.   I. Title.
HV1444.M55   1995
362.82'92—dc20   95-23227
                                                                                    CIP

Published by Contemporary Books, Inc.
Two Prudential Plaza, Chicago, Illinois 60601-6790
Manufactured in the United States of America
International Standard Book Number: 0-8092-3546-3
10   9   8   7   6   5   4   3   2   1

*To abused women the world over in the belief that
knowledge will bring understanding;
and understanding, rebuilt lives*

Contents

Acknowledgments

I WANT TO THANK the people whose help was invaluable while I wrote this book:

The hundreds of battered women I met, who must remain anonymous but whose lives are forever interwoven with mine

The many professionals whose caring and insights have enabled them to heal abuse's invisible wounds and to broaden my understanding through both pain and hope

Doris Feitelson, whose guidance continues to lead me and whose friendship supports me in working with abused women

Michael Pugsley, whose computer expertise rescued eight chapters and my life

Victoria Pryor, whose faith, hard work, and discriminating eye always turn possibilities into print

My family, for sharing the suffering I encountered during this study and for knowing, as I know, the need for American society to encounter it too

The names of authors I have referred to or quoted in this book are real. The names of professionals I have interviewed are also real. The names of abused women and their abusers are not real. I have changed their names; the names, number, and sex of their children; the places where they live; and at times the circumstances surrounding their abuse to maintain their anonymity. The horror they have endured and/or still endure is real.

That reality is what the book is about. To have the world acknowledge that reality is why I wrote the book.

Introduction

THIS IS THE STORY OF ELLIE—Eleanor Ames, living in New York, born in Norwalk, Connecticut, daughter of Martha Lapone, a housewife, and Jonathan Shattuck, a lawyer. It is simultaneously the story of all the other Ellies and Sarahs, Lorrie-Anns, Corishas, and Rosas in America and truly throughout the world.

Ellie: graduated fifth in her class from Norwalk High and in 1944 from Pembroke College with a B.A. in English, a Sigma Psi pin from her boyfriend, and very little in her head. She worked as a gofer in her dad's law firm for three months before marrying that Sigma Psi brother, Roger Ames—second lieutenant shiny-fresh from a three-month stint in Officers' Candidate School, about to embark overseas for a destination unknown.

Two years later he was back in Ellie's arms, discharged and unscathed, and with his wife in tow headed for a studio apartment in New York with a one-year lease and a job as third assistant to the second assistant of an editor at *Time*.

Forty-nine years later they are still married and still have a studio apartment in New York but have added a ten-room Tudor in Mamaroneck, four children, nine grandchildren, and two dachshunds. Ellie became a paralegal after her second child, then worked on and off until the last one entered junior high school. It was then that Gloria Steinem and Company raised her consciousness, and she worked full-time for three feel-like-somebody years, until Roger's complaints about TV dinners and late work nights turned every evening into a dirty political campaign. She conceded his victory like the good wife she was brought up to be, quit her job, and settled down to home and husband with quiet resentment.

Ellie looks back:

"I walked into marriage like Cinderella into the ball: Roger was Prince Charming, all-knowing and all-powerful, and I the adoring chosen subject. I had no doubt that we'd live happily ever after; with his wise leadership and my eager submission, what could go wrong?

"You know, I wasn't really a moron. Everyone was like that. It was 1946: the war was over; our men had come home alive; we were lucky to be married; and we knew our place. But soon it was the 1950s and 1960s. If the prince treated me with a little less charm, I refused to notice. So what if he wouldn't let me have a checkbook? He assumed that I was dumb in math and would bollix it up—which wasn't true because I had gotten the highest mark in the class in calculus—but he said men should handle the money. My dad did, so it sounded all right to me. It killed me having to ask for a few dollars to go marketing or buy the kids shoes—like a beggar. But that's the way it was.

"I tried not to notice how he made fun of opinions I expressed on anything, whether it was politics or an author we'd read or something as stupid as the weather. As for mak-

ing decisions, forget it. I wasn't even allowed a say in where
the kids went to school or what we did on vacation. He
always knew best. He knew everything. At a teacher conference once he actually told me to shut up because I didn't
know anything about education; I think the teacher was as
embarrassed as I was.

"He took charge so completely that he even started
telling me what clothes to wear—said I looked like a hag in
red, which he knew was my favorite color—and I kidded
myself into believing he was right and wanted him to be
proud of me. Until one morning when I couldn't find the
red suit I continued to wear once in a while. I was hunting
in every closet while he followed me. 'You're wasting your
time,' he finally said. I can still see him leaning against the
open doorway, smirking. 'I gave it to the Salvation Army.'

"Can you believe it? I couldn't then, but I can now when
I begin to look back and realize that our whole marriage
had been leading to this. From the very beginning, if Roger
didn't get his way, he would make me pay. Sometimes he
wouldn't talk to me for weeks or wouldn't eat, even when I
cooked his favorite dinner, and believe me, I tried. Oh, how
I tried! And there were weeks when he wouldn't have sex
with me unless I pleaded—naked on my knees—and
promised I'd do whatever he wanted."

Roger Ames was behaving in a way that kept his wife in
full submission, and Ellie Ames was doing everything she
could to please him. What neither of them was able to realize, though, was that she could never do enough. Just as a
desert traveler can never reach the mirage oasis toward
which he staggers, so Ellie could never meet Roger's
demands, which on the verge of attainment forever moved
further from her reach.

Roger was a wife abuser. No one knew it, though—not
even Ellie—since he was not recognizable from news stories

and pictures of bloodied and broken women. Nonetheless, he was an abuser, who controlled his wife through fear, isolation, emotional and sexual withdrawal, and humiliation. He didn't have to lay a hand on Ellie; he made her submit to his will without a fight, and neither labeled the relationship abusive.

It is difficult for a man who punches a woman or throws her into a wall to not know that he is an abuser. It is equally difficult for a woman who sustains a black eye and body bruises not to know she has been abused, although both of them find rationales to avoid reality. However, the subtle manifestations of nonphysical abuse usually escape acknowledgment—at least for a long period of time. Although a man can't help being consciously aware of depriving a woman of money or social contacts or of drumming into her that she is stupid and crazy, he can be consciously unaware that what he is doing is legally abusive. Similarly, a woman, cognizant that she is systematically being made miserable, may not recognize what is happening as abuse. The netherworld environment in which they both live, therefore, keeps abuse alive and thriving until—and if—the woman steps into the reality of the real world by demanding a halt.

Ellie wouldn't have denied her unhappiness—even her parents saw that; nor would she have denied her confusion over Roger's behavior or the hurt that poured out in frequent tears over his coldness and the distance he kept. However, the word *abuse* never entered her mind. "He's under stress, and I have to be patient," she'd tell herself, or "I expect too much." And then she would try still harder to please Roger and fail again . . . and again . . . and then again.

Although her Cinderella dreams had long since reverted to pumpkins and ashes, she never lost hope because she knew that if she could just make Roger happy he would become Prince Charming again. Having embraced Roger's teaching that she was to blame for the problem, she accepted the fact that she was also responsible for its solution. Leaving him wasn't the answer; after all, she was his wife. What she had to do was wave the magic wand that would enable her to do things right so that Roger could love her again. But Ellie could never do things right because for Roger there was no right.

Ellie continues:

"Roger is the one who made me quit work. He said I wanted a job only to pick up men, which couldn't have been further from the truth. I loved work—it's the only place I felt I was worth anything. After I was stuck at home, he'd call my friends to see if I'd gone out with them. When they said no, he called them liars. I tried to keep up some sort of social life, but Roger turned everyone off. When he'd finally let me invite a few couples for dinner, he'd sit like a statue, and wouldn't eat anything or take a drink or say a word to our guests. I was so embarrassed and tried to cover up, but after a while I stopped trying.

"Naturally the kids saw all this and asked questions. 'Daddy's upset,' I'd tell them, but it became even more than I could take when he started in on their grandparents—my mom and dad; fascists, he called them, and said the world would be better off without them. I know it's hard to believe, but he once told me in front of the kids that he couldn't wait to dance on my father's grave. He was so hateful about them that I started sneaking off to pay them visits so he wouldn't know. My own parents—can you imagine?"

Ellie broke into tears for the first time as she spoke. She sat for a long time staring into space, then turned to me and asked in a chillingly calm voice, "I've done everything I could to be a good wife. Why does he hate me?"

Roger doesn't hate Ellie. He abuses her, but he doesn't hate her. He loves her—as far as he is able. What he hates is himself because Roger, like many abusers, sees himself from a deep-down view as a loser. Raised in a home with a sternly authoritarian father, Roger received the message in hundreds of ways daily that he was too stupid to have opinions and that his achievements fell far below the required mark. With strict rules of discipline and orders issued by his father, he was punished severely for any infraction and punished doubly if he put up an argument. As a result, Roger grew up seething with pent-up rage and with self-loathing at his helplessness.

Then he met Ellie, shaped by the sexual stereotypes of the thirties and forties, the perfect wife who vowed to love, honor, and obey. And she did. As Ernest Andrews writes of an abused woman in *The Emotionally Disturbed Family,* "She serves as a foil for his disillusioned anger . . . he serves as the embodiment of her accepted fate." And so the marriage lasted: Roger the controller he never could be as a child, Ellie the submissive enabler she grew up to believe in.

Eleanor Ames is not one of the millions of women who report severe battering at doctors' offices and hospitals each year, not one of more than quadruple that number who keep quiet about it and hide their blood and bruises at home. She is one of a number so much greater that statistics haven't even been estimated, one of the women who have no visible wounds. Their husbands, like Roger, batter their wives but come away with clean hands because they land more refined blows; they undermine the wife's self-esteem and break her spirit and knock supporting pins out from under her. They know what matters most to her—her dog, her car, her friends, maybe her red suit—and destroy it.

They manipulate her into thinking she's to blame and, as a result, into trying harder and harder to please. For a long time they keep her believing that things will get better by allowing her occasional moments of compatibility, but after a while they leave only the ceaseless pain of hope and excuses and wishful thinking: "He didn't mean what he said . . . his behavior is just a phase . . . he'll change." But he does mean it, it's not just a phase, and he won't change. He can't. He needs it: power, control.

Until about twenty-five years ago there was no such term as *battered woman*. Men were expected to keep women in their place by whatever means necessary, and if it took battering, she had better shape up. In recent years, however, physical abuse has been dragged from the closet with books and TV films like Faith McNulty's *The Burning Bed*, well-publicized court cases like Hedda Nussbaum's, and research findings that give women new awareness and, as a result, new strength to resist:

- According to former surgeon general C. Everett Koop, battering is the single major cause of injury to women, greater than accidents, muggings, and rape combined.

- FBI figures indicate that a woman is beaten every fifteen seconds.

- Twenty-one percent of all women who use hospital emergency surgical services are battered.

- Up to four thousand women are beaten to death annually by a family member—about a third of all female homicide victims.

- Fifty-nine percent of the women who killed a so-called loved one were abused at the time.

- In half of all marriages there is at least one violent incident; in almost a third the violence is severe.

Physical battering in all its enormity and horror is no longer a secret. Nonphysical battering, however, remains in the dark closet corner where few want to look. The silence seems to indicate that researchers and writers are blind to wounds that leave no scars on the body and that nonphysically battered women are afraid to look at the wounds that scar their soul. "But not looking doesn't mean it's not there," a woman told me after thirty-four years of abuse that she had just allowed herself to confront.

Yes, it is there, nonphysical abuse, in shapes so subtle that women fail to recognize it—emotional abuse, psychological abuse, social abuse, and economic abuse . . . with results so damaging that its victims become the walking dead . . . with escape doors so bolted that until recently its prisoners surrendered hope.

As a court aide, counselor, and writer, I have connected to abuse from the outside. I have been able to analyze it, divide it into components, and explain it through its characteristics and categories. However, those who know abuse firsthand—both the men who inflict it and the women who are victims of it—experience it holistically. The man does not select one form of nonphysical abuse with which to control and shun the other three; he uses what is available and effective. For instance, while social abuse against a woman close to her family and friends is a powerful weapon, so may be economic deprivation, psychological mind games, and the ego pummeling of emotional abuse. The abuser sustains dominance by using them all.

Similarly, the anguished woman makes no effort to label the various kinds of abuse her man heaps on her; her concern is survival. Nonphysical abuse by any name is the overlapping destruction of a woman's emotional, psychological, social, and economic well-being. My reason for classifying four specific kinds of nonphysical abuse in this book is my hope and belief that it will help the reader gain greater understanding of the abuse syndrome.

The Battered Women's Task Force of the New York State Coalition Against Domestic Violence, along with organizations in other states, has made great strides in helping women identify nonphysical abuse so as to offer support and guidance. The first step is asking women to study the following list of questions that identify nineteen abusive behaviors.

Does your partner:

1. hit, punch, slap, shove, or bite you?

2. threaten to hurt you or your children?

3. threaten to hurt friends or family members?

4. have sudden outburts of anger or rage?

5. behave in an overprotective manner?

6. become jealous without reason?

7. prevent you from seeing family or friends?

8. prevent you from going where you want, when you want?

9. prevent you from working or attending school?

10. destroy personal property or sentimental items?

11. deny you access to family assets such as bank accounts, credit cards, or the car?

12. control all finances and force you to account for what you spend?

13. force you to have sex against your will?

14. force you to engage in sexual acts you do not enjoy?

15. insult you or call you derogatory names?

16. use intimidation or manipulation to control you or your children?

17. humiliate you in front of your children?

18. turn minor incidents into major arguments?

19. abuse or threaten to abuse pets?

At the bottom of the list is written "If you answered yes to one or more of the above . . . you might be abused." Note that only one of the nineteen behaviors is physical. The other eighteen identify four different kinds of nonphysical battering.

As a Family Court counselor and aide, I show this list regularly to women applying for orders of protection, most often against men who have physically attacked them. As they read down the list, they are appalled, nodding their heads in recognition. "Why, he's been doing all of those things for years," they say, "but I never knew it was abuse till he hit me."

Abuse never—and I use the word *never* fully aware of its pitfalls—goes away of its own accord; it escalates. Name-calling grows into public humiliation, isolation, and eventually threats, at which level a union may continue until death do them part; on the other hand, threats may become the reality of beatings and murder.

I am not surprised that every woman who comes for a protective order against the beatings, stabbings, or chokings that endanger her life has had, in addition, a long and painful history of nonphysical abuse. What surprised me at first, however, was that as many as one woman in five or six who seek help from the court has suffered no physical abuse at all; she comes pained and frightened for protection against the unbearable controls of nonphysical abuse that have destroyed her life. Even as recently as five years ago a woman would have been unaware of a need for that kind of court protection.

Yet women who suffer nonphysical abuse, while unaware of the need for protection in the past, have known full well its anguish. Even those women who regularly cower under beatings tell me, almost without exception, that the battering that touches their bodies is far worse than the day-to-day diminishing they endure. The broken bones mend; the bruises disappear; the blood stops flowing, but the crushed sense of self is never made whole again. As one woman put it, "It wasn't being hit or thrown against the wall that hurt most. It was having to live like a nonperson."

Born and raised at a time when a woman's sex role called for acquiescence and submission, I decided to try an experiment on a group of my old college friends—most of them upper middle class, married for forty years or so, a little on the conservative side, perhaps, but far from reactionary. I gave them the Battered Women's Task Force list of abusive behaviors and asked, "What do you think?" They were stunned at what was identified as abuse because many of them had been living with it all their married lives. Certainly they were angry at the inequality, hurt by the lack of empathy, and ashamed over their powerlessness. Certainly they felt isolated—"more lonely than if I lived alone," one woman told me. However, they had entered marriage at a time when society expected husbands to dominate and wives to submit. As one of the wives said, "Aren't *all* husbands like that?"

Like that: authoritarian, emotionally withholding, overprotective, unresponsive to your feelings. Like that: controlling the family finances, demanding your attention when he wants it, expecting your compliance. Like that: using sex as his husbandly right, blaming you for problems, manipulating you into accepting his decisions. Like that: making you live like the same nonperson I see in court. And with it all, charming at the office, socially acceptable with friends, a good husband in the eyes of the world, who might also ask, "Aren't all of us like that?"

No, not all of you, but more than anyone knows, more than anyone suspects, more than even your wives admit. My closest friend, Irene—college roommate, next-door neighbor, confidante throughout my life—lived like that for forty-two years with a good man, an intelligent man, a respected man, a hardworking man, a man who cared for his family, a man she loved. Hardly a day passed when I didn't see Irene—in my kitchen for coffee or over the privet hedge in the backyard or in town on our daily chores—yet not until her husband died did she reveal a secret she had not dared to share: her husband Sam had been an abuser. I, along with other friends, had seen him rise from a young attorney on the bottom rung of a prestigious law firm to a sought-after senior partner. We had shared with Irene newspaper reports of Sam's achievements and read his articles in law journals. With Sam as the model of success, Irene hadn't told anyone of his abuse, not even herself, because she felt ashamed, as if she alone of all women suffered this indignity.

It was almost a year after Sam died that Irene told me. I had been working for about three months with abused women in the Family Court and, agonized over the hurt and humiliation their husbands or boyfriends inflicted on them, I kept pouring it out on her. One day, not crying or choking back sobs as I would have expected, but in a flat monotone, she began the story of her marriage, long years during which her husband battered her not with physical blows but with the systematic undermining of her sense of self and her sanity. Throughout this book I quote Irene *verbatim* with her permission. She who suffered nonphysical abuse in dark silence for so many years exposes her invisible wounds in the hope of healing those wounds of other women through visibility.

Irene: "To this day I do not know what Sam earned, what he saved, what he invested in; he kept his desk locked and answered no questions. I never had a checkbook, never had a monthly sum to spend; instead I would find a twenty-dollar bill on the windowsill from time to time and have to, like a child, ask for and account for more if I needed it.

"I never had a heart-to-heart talk with him—not over coffee in the morning or at dinners out or in bed—not about anything we felt, like love or fear or sex or hopes or difficulties or hurts or beauty. I tried for years, pouring out my heart and my thoughts, inviting his with no response but sullen silence. 'You act like an adolescent,' he kept telling me, so I gave up. Our conversations, when he agreed to communicate at all, focused on business, and I lived alone with my feelings.

"Sam never wanted people in the house and reached a point where he wouldn't go out. Having no friends of his own, only co-workers at the office, he found fault with my friends: they were stupid or talked too loud or tried to use him or were boring or weird or owed us a dinner first. When we did go out, he would silently seethe if a man paid attention to me; several times he actually grabbed my arm and pulled me out the door with everyone watching. Since he walked away when I attempted to discuss our social life, which I felt was a serious problem in our marriage, for a long time I pretended it wasn't there. I accepted invitations and had people in, and though he never voiced objections, he withdrew in stony silence.

"Since he rarely agreed to go on vacation, I began to go with the children. We took some wonderful trips, which they remember as outstanding parts of their childhood—boat trips and camping and car trips. He never objected or asked us not to go; he even drove us to the airport occasionally. When the children grew up and went their own ways, deprived of my traveling companions, I took off alone or

with my mother. Remember? Twice I went with you. He still
wanted to stay home, but apparently he now wanted me to
stay home too—not that he ever told me so or even discussed
my trip. No, but the day after I left he would begin calling
the children daily with stored-up complaints about me;
if a friend of mine phoned, he would detail years of my
neglect. You probably got an earful more than once. Several days into my trip he usually developed psychosomatic
illnesses—a cold or stomach pains or an allergic reaction;
twice one of the boys had to rush him to the hospital with
heart palpitations.

"Painful as all this was, my greatest hurt was the lack of
affection. Sam never looked over and smiled at me, never
surprised me with a flower, never gave me a compliment.
He didn't read the poems I wrote or respond to the love
notes I left him on his pillow or in the refrigerator or under
the windshield wipers when I was away. I never heard 'Thank
you'—everything I did was his due. I never heard 'I love
you.' As I look back, I think he may have loved me but was
so fearful of his vulnerability, so needful of control, that he
couldn't admit it even to himself. When I cried into my pillow at night, longing for a touch on my shoulder, a whispered word, he turned his back, leaving a mile-wide abyss
between us. Reaching out for affirmation one day, I asked
him point blank, 'What do you feel about me?'

"I should have known better. 'I like you all right,' he said,
turning back to his paper."

After months of listening to my horror stories about
Ellie and the women in Family Court and my college friends,
Irene began to realize that she was not alone and stopped
feeling ashamed. "I am one of them," she was able to say. "I
lived with a man who systematically isolated me, undermined
my sense of worth, kept me dependent. He controlled me
through manipulation, and though I raged in silence and

wept in the dark, like those other women, I assumed that's the way husbands were. During my childhood, my mother had repeatedly told me, 'It doesn't matter how you feel; put a smile on your face.' For many long married years I wore that smile before I understood I could scowl. Even then it was hard to think of myself as abused. Sam never understood and, were he alive today, would shrug off my unhappiness, much less an accusation of abuse, with 'You're being a child again.'"

There's a difference between a bad marriage and abuse. While every marriage in which abuse takes place is obviously bad, not every bad marriage is abusive. A marriage may be bad because of incompatibility or philandering or immaturity or any number of factors for which courts of law grant divorce. An abusive marriage is one in which a spouse (the man in more than 95 percent of cases) uses his power—be it muscle or subtler manipulation—to control his partner. The irony is that he doesn't control himself.

The question of why men don't control the behavior that injures and often destroys women they claim to love probably has as many answers as the number of abusive men themselves. The underlying reasons for such behavior, however, become more understandable if we classify the abusers in three main groups. First, there are men for whom abuse is the everyday method of conflict resolution. Many, as we have learned in court, were raised in abusive homes, where one or both parents served as models, not only beating their spouse, but also threatening, belittling, name-calling, and seeking revenge whenever disagreements arose. "Bottoms were put on kids for two purposes," a man lectured me professorially a few weeks ago, "for sitting and for beating."

"And wives?" I asked.

"Oh, you can keep them in their place easier," he tossed off. "Get them to know how stupid they are, and they'll obey like a dog." This type of husband has adopted verbal abuse as his *modus operandi* as the result of such a philosophy.

A second group of men don't intend to abuse their women—or rationalize that they don't—yet find themselves doing so periodically. With a low frustration level and minimal coping skills, these men lash out whenever thwarted: if dinner is late, if an unwanted in-law visits, if the kids make too much noise, if their wives defy an order. Afterwards with apologies, flowers, and promises, they succeed in convincing their wives and themselves that the aberrant behavior was brought on by outside forces such as problems at work or one too many drinks or—more pointedly—by their wives' actions. A man in this category doesn't see his behavior as a real problem, however, because he is convinced that he has the solution: he will handle work stress and drinking if she'll stop annoying him. Unfortunately, neither partner can live up to this decree because the man continues to lay blame outside himself, and no matter what she stops doing, it's not enough to appease him. Eventually she may catch on that the abuse is not going to end and either seek court protection or abandon the controlling relationship. Women married to men in this group often end up in court when—and if—they realize what is actually happening.

The third group of abusers don't wait to be thwarted before hurling abuse but use it daily to exert dominance. Control is their tool, a vise whose pin they consciously and deliberately turn in order to tighten their power. What may begin as mere correction—"I think you should eat fewer sweets"—escalates until the woman is so drained of ego strength that she can only agree, "I am a fat, ugly slob whom nobody else would put up with." Women so ego-battered need a great deal of support before taking the first step to court for protection.

The aim of all abuse, unlike that of sadism, is not the pleasure of inflicting pain, but the need to control: domination is the end in itself. While a man may explain his actions by saying: "I lost control," in fact what he did was *gain* control. His degree of awareness of his behavior and its results is determined by the group into which he falls. Men who use abuse as the normal way to settle disputes and eradicate irritations know full well what they are doing, do it matter-of-factly, and see nothing wrong in their behavior. In fact, they do not view their behavior as *abuse* at all. To these men, such actions are entirely normal and are the "natural" way husbands and wives relate. They are guilt-free. Men who turn to abuse when frustration grows greater than their ability to cope with it, though aware of their actions, tend to remain (often by design) oblivious to the control factor. They berate themselves from guilt, but only long enough to pinpoint the blame elsewhere and begin the buildup anew. Men who keep their women in an ever tightening grip of control tend to know full well what they are doing: weakening their wives in order to strengthen themselves. However, despite the deliberately planned program, their self-righteous machismo eliminates guilt.

Irene told me that when her husband died, despite the abuse she had endured, she wept—and still weeps today—not for what she and Sam had together but for what they could have had. Despite his brilliant mind, his success, his stature, despite the professional legacy he left, she saw Sam as a lost soul groping for a way out of himself. "I weep for the closeness he never touched, for the fun he never had, for the joy he never felt," she explains. "I weep for the little boy he was long years ago in a home that knew no closeness, no fun, and no joy and for the self-hating man he became. I weep for the dominance he sought in the hope of easing his pain, and I weep most for the grimness etched on his gray face in death."

At a small memorial service that only Sam and Irene's children and I attended, they remembered him and the unique gift he bestowed—unknowingly—on each: honesty at any price, said one son; commitment to work, said another; support in times of need, said his daughter. "People show their love in different ways," Irene added and for the first time choked back sobs, "and sometimes they're too afraid to acknowledge it."

In the several years that I have been working as a counselor/aide to battered women in Family Court, I have counseled perhaps two hundred women—weeping, enraged, or benumbed. They bare their arms and breasts to show me bruises; or straight from the hospital emergency room, they come with bandages or splints; or unscathed, they begin, "He didn't hit me, but. . . ." There follow the details of threatening, demeaning, isolating, and depriving with which their husband or, in growing numbers, their live-in partner has assaulted and controlled them.

Is there any counsel for them to ease their pain? To allay their fear? To restore their hope? I question this each day, and still I try. I give them options: get an order of protection; change your locks; stay at your mother's or sister's or friend's for a while; report any violation; ask the police to issue a warrant for his arrest; get a lawyer; don't let your child out of your sight. Most of all, I tell them, "Here in this office we care. We're here for you. Call us."

I return home each night, a receptacle overflowing with both their pain and mine. And I know, as the judge before whom they stood that day may not know, that their invisible wounds are every bit as life-threatening as the breaks and bruises and blood the judge's eye cannot avoid.

To recognize and understand nonphysical abuse is not easy, for as Ginny NiCarthy writes in *Getting Free,* "A woman who has a black eye or broken bone knows something has been done to her, but emotional abuse is sometimes so complex and bewildering it is difficult to name. If it can't be identified clearly, the person it's directed toward may believe she's imagining it."

The secret, unidentified, unacknowledged nonphysical abuse of women must end. Not until men and women can face it squarely, however, as they are beginning to face physically violent abuse, will they reach the goal. And only then will any man and woman be able to enjoy a truly equal and loving relationship.

PART I

What Is Nonphysical Abuse?

CHAPTER 1

"I don't do anything right."

The Humiliation of Emotional Abuse

BARBARA WAS A GOOD COOK. She knew it, and Sal knew it. When they were first married, not a week went by when he didn't bring friends home for dinner and brag about her fettuccine Alfredo and cheesecake. One night almost a year into their marriage, when after announcing that she had made a date with a girlfriend she explained that his dinner was in the microwave ready to be heated since she wouldn't be home to cook, Sal flew into a rage. "You damn well *will* be home to cook. You'll have my dinner on the table when I come home, not in the microwave." Barbara broke her date.

A few weeks later, while she was serving him and his friend, Sal spit out a mouthful, shouting to her in the kitchen, "What are you trying to do, poison us?" He made her recook the dinner, which tasted good enough to her, while he and his friend polished off two bottles of wine. Three days later his truck broke down, and when he walked

23

in two hours late, Barbara began reheating his dinner. "I don't eat cold slop," he said slowly and deliberately. "Give it to the dogs or eat it with them, bitch."

That night began eight years of emotional abuse that ended only when Barbara went to her mother's with a case of shingles so severe that she couldn't move and then never returned. Sal had focused on the one thing in which his wife took great pride—her cooking. What had once been a joy to her as she discovered new recipes, grew herbs on the windowsill, and created her own dishes became a source of terror. One night when the neighborhood had lost electricity for about twenty minutes, Sal stormed out of the house because dinner wasn't on the table when he came home. Another night he threw his plate across the floor because she had used beef left over from last night's roast in the stew.

No matter what Barbara did, she couldn't please her husband. What began with her failed cooking escalated into her "dumb" conversation and her gaining weight and her poor performance in bed. As surely as if Sal were grinding down one of the rocks he hauled in his truck, he wore down Barbara's self-esteem until she was flattened. Sal made her feel not only worthless for doing everything wrong but also guilty for making him angry. After all, he convinced her, wasn't it her fault she couldn't cook the way he wanted? And her fault she couldn't talk intelligently with him? And her fault she embarrassed him by getting fat? And her fault she couldn't please him in bed?

Sal is like any abuser: he manipulates the relationship into the perception that no matter how hard a woman tries, her inability to satisfy him is due not to his unreasonable demands but to her own faults and failings. The mistakes she makes, which the man stages in growing size and number, for him add up to success: complete control. Like Kate at the end of *The Taming of the Shrew*, the abused woman submits to her man's will, saying in effect,

> *Thy husband is thy lord, thy life, thy keeper,*
> *Thy head, thy sovereign, the one that cares for thee.*

Emotional abuse takes many different forms en route to the goal of domination, all of which undermine a woman's self-respect and sense of worth. A man may begin with a complaint and slide into constant criticizing and name-calling before she even senses a problem. He may embarrass her in public by putting her down or screaming. He may accuse her of having lovers and begin watching her every move, stalking her when she meets a friend. He may walk away when she tries to talk to him or pout and not speak to her for days at a time. He may throw accusations and curses at her parents and other relatives with whom she is close. He may forbid her to make decisions or offer an opinion in family matters and even in her own affairs.

The emotionally abused woman lives in a state of fear: what will the man do next? Her life becomes a living hell, like a dissident under Stalin wondering moment to moment when the KGB will pounce. Afraid to let her guard down, she can't even enjoy calm times together—a movie or an evening with friends—wary always, aware what he might do with the least provocation.

As if it were a thundercloud, the imminence of danger threatens should she say a wrong word or give a wrong look or laugh when she shouldn't or not laugh when she should.

At her job she may forget for a while: the work she does is important, and she does it well. Her boss respects her; she works hard, and she joins in the camaraderie of the office. Thank God, she thinks each morning, for her job, and pity the woman without one! However, the nonworking woman finds a release valve too in the home her husband leaves as he heads for work each morning. Eight wonderful hours of peace! She can watch "The Morning Show" and take her time with the newspaper, finishing the pot of coffee. She can concentrate fear-free on any of the things she enjoys— a book, sewing, painting, exercise. She can meet friends or shop or just walk and be herself. Life stops sobbing and sings.

Then evening comes for both women: the office closes, the friends leave, the open space in the house is invaded. Women tell me that emotional abuse begins before he even comes home or before she returns from her job, begins with the memory, begins with the dread. As for Cinderella, the magic of the ball ends, and as the man opens the front door or the woman heads home to the enslavement of abuse, she withers, knowing there is no glass slipper to leave behind.

My friend Irene says she was different and probably worse because she was unrealistic. She couldn't get herself to believe even after forty years that when she returned, home would be the same cheerless, stress-filled place she had left. She says she can still feel the soaring expectation each time she turned the key in her door lock, thinking this time it would be different; something wonderful would have happened—he would have changed! "What a fool I was," she exclaims. "With my first cheery 'Hello, I'm home,' the heavy winding-sheet from which I had escaped once again smothered me. It takes the eternal optimist a long time to abandon hope, doesn't it?"

For many women the upper edge of middle age brings the joys of social security checks and the togetherness of retirement. I know couples in their midsixties and seventies taking up tennis together, traveling as they never could before, enjoying each other in a newfound romance. For others, however, it brings a greater dread: he won't have work to go to, his office buddies to pal around with, or business problems to occupy his thoughts. He will be home, and all he will have is his wife.

When an emotional abuser finds himself at home full time, he tends to escalate abuse for two reasons: one, because he has more time for fault finding, and two, because with his job status gone he has only one focal point for bolstering his ego, domination at home. "I dreaded the day when Harry would retire," a friend told me, "and it's even worse than I feared." She is at his beck and call, forced to surrender any decision making she previously had for fear of a scene, ordered around and humiliated, and deprived of the peace and freedom she had enjoyed on occasions as mundane as marketing. So fearful is she of failing to please Harry that she refused to join a class reunion dinner in case Harry had planned something for that evening.

"Why don't you ask him?" I suggested.

"He likes to surprise me at the last minute," she answered, not realizing that Harry's euphemism for *control* was *surprise*.

Each woman ensnared in emotional abuse is caught before she is even aware. She doesn't expect it. Even if she has heard of emotional abuse, which many women have not, like an airplane accident, it happens to other people, not her. Not her husband. At first she has easy explanations and rationales for his behavior. If he becomes jealous, it's that he finds her desirable; she is flattered. If he insists on making all the decisions, it's that he wants to protect and shelter her; she feels cared for. If he won't communicate, it's that he is the strong silent type; she understands. If he embarrasses her or calls her names, it's that he just lost his temper and didn't mean it; she forgives. By the time she realizes he does mean it and she no longer feels flattered, cared for, or understanding—and certainly not forgiving—she finds herself in a relationship so skewed that she can't see a way out. Edith Wharton, as read by Irene Worth in her one-woman show, was no stranger to the feeling, expressing it in a single metaphor. "I heard the key turn in my prison lock," she wrote one time as her husband landed another emotional blow.

Older women, like my friend Irene, may not know their unfulfilling relationship is abusive, and even if they did, they wouldn't expect a way out. Having been raised in a home where the husband ruled as unchallenged boss—facsimiles of the play *Life with Father*—they have been conditioned to a submissive role. They don't like it, but they accept it. "What am I going to do?" a seventy-year-old friend of mine asked. "Give up a nice home and comfortable living just because Jim treats me like dirt? No way. I'm miserable, but I live with it." She lives with it, as Irene did and as thousands of women her age do, not by pretending it's not there—it *is* there—but by numbing their feelings. They are survivors, these older women—not happy, but strong. Had they been able to choose or even envision a more equal relationship with their husbands when they were younger, they might not have developed the fortitude required to exist with an abusive spouse. Given a choice, they might not have become so strong, but they would certainly have been far more fulfilled.

To keep emotional abuse at an endurable level, as Irene did and as many of my friends still do, a woman has to numb not only her feelings but her will as well: the obeisance, the humiliation, the sense of failure. Whether it's worth it or not is up to each individual. Should she weigh the pros and cons and decide to stick it out, she must abandon the option to talk back, for it is in response to a woman's challenge that a man escalates abuse so he can hold on to power and control. Studies show that a far higher number of older women live with abuse than younger women. That's understandable:

having grown up before Betty Friedan et al. shattered the old sexual stereotypes, they don't challenge his domination. He remains secure in his macho role.

The cases of emotional abuse we hear from friends or endure personally on a daily basis can slide by unnoticed by the outside world when a woman wears the smile her mother insisted on and covers up with long-practiced playacting. The cases that come to Family Court, however, are so flagrant that the woman seeks deliverance from brutality that is about to break her. The following sampling illustrates what might be called the last straw:

- One husband refused to let his wife turn the heat above fifty-five degrees, even in January after she came home from the hospital with a new baby. When she asked a neighbor to explain the danger to her husband, he screamed, "You want heat? OK, I'll give you heat," and turned it up as high as it would go—over eighty.

- Another made his wife sleep on the floor if she cooked a dinner he didn't like—and he never liked it. Even after she developed back trouble, he did not relent.

- One man, a prison corrections officer, continues to take great delight in playing with his gun in front of his woman if she does anything to annoy him. "You can't be sure I won't shoot you, can you?" he taunts with a smirk.

- One man, who is unemployed, flies into a jealous rage when his wife comes home from work, calling her a whore and a bitch. Often the neighbors call the police, not only angry at the close-range disturbance but also fearful of what he might do.

- A policeman, his mind twisted with jealous possessiveness, has two officers from his precinct follow his wife in a prowl car when she leaves the house, hoping to catch her with a lover. Once, seeing a man in the car with her, they pulled alongside to question who the passenger was. It was her father.

- A former lover calls the woman up to twenty times a day, shouting obscenities or leaving them on her answering machine when she doesn't pick up the phone.

One quality emotional abusers have in common is the ability to zoom in on a woman's weak spot, to use as a weapon what matters most to her. In many cases it is her children. One divorced man chopped off his daughter's long hair on a visit because his ex-wife took such pains with it. Another would return the children after a visit only if his ex-wife appeared in her best clothes and pleaded with him seductively. One husband found the best way to batter his wife was to threaten to punish their children; another kept saying he would run off with their two daughters and that she would never see them again. One called his wife into the den to watch him teach their thirteen-year-old son to drink beer and smoke, two of his own habits that she detested.

When screaming and name-calling no longer humiliate a woman as they originally did, some men give their abuse a new twist and begin hurling their obscenities in front of the children, whose tears and pleas serve as further distress to the woman. The most extreme example of child abuse as a means of wife abuse was the case of a man later indicted as a sex abuser. "You found the perfect weapon," the judge said at a visitation hearing, "the children. By your own admission, you played sex games with them to get at your wife." The result was that the judge restricted him to two hours a week with the children, under professional supervision.

Pets are another weapon of emotional abuse for a man too "law abiding" to attack a woman. Like one man brought to court, he may wrap a cord around the cat's neck and threaten to strangle it. One man teased and tortured four kittens his girlfriend had before drowning them. Another plucked all the feathers from the body of his wife's pet canary. One hid her miniature poodle in a closet and told her it ran away. More than one emotional batterer has lit a match to her dog's tail.

A woman's property, particularly her car, in which she takes great pride is another handy weapon for abuse. One man cut deep scratches along both sides of his wife's beloved Thunderbird. Another set the front seat of her Plymouth on fire, while still another drove her Subaru into a wall, caving in the whole front end. Men have systematically smashed vases and chairs, have burned cigarette holes in prized couches, gouged holes in the tops of antique tables. The damage is not only a heartbreak to the woman but also a threat of what might befall her.

Men have mocked the Ph.D. their wife is studying for, clipped buds off the rosebushes she nurtures, cut up her favorite dress, smeared feces on the bedroom wall she just painted, slandered her parents. Anything that hurts. Any way to degrade her. Among the most vulnerable women, lawyers tell me, are Asians, to whom family is so important that a single accusation of infidelity is cause for abandonment; they dare not even look up on the street or in an elevator for fear of meeting the eyes of a man and thereby losing their husband.

Immigrant women living with men who refuse to legitimate them through marriage are an equally vulnerable group, the threat of a report to the Immigration and Naturalization Service holding them in virtual bondage to the abuser. The saddest of all, perhaps, are addicts—women held under the domination of men who will withhold drugs for even the slightest challenge to their control. The irony is that in a high percentage of cases it was the men who led them into drugs to begin with.

Emotional battering, then, runs the gamut from a steady grinding down of a woman to emotional trauma. While her bones are never broken, her flesh never bruised, her blood never spilled, she is wounded nonetheless. With self-confidence and self-respect gone, she lives, empty, with no self left to assert. She cedes control of her life to her abuser. She is helpless.

Joan Zorza, director of the National Center on Women and Family Law, feels that emotional battering is far worse than physical battering because it goes to one's basic essence. "I have seen shelter women talk unabashedly about broken noses and swollen cheeks," she says, "but when they start talking about emotional battering, they break down and fall apart." The resilient body mends with ointments and splints—physically battered women know that in their pain. But so deep is the wounding of emotional battering, so down-reaching the anguish, so hopeless the mending that, as the Spanish maxim says, "He that loseth his spirit loseth all." The emotionally battered woman loses herself.

CHAPTER 2

"I think I'm going crazy."

The Madness of Psychological Abuse

IN THE OLD MOVIE *Gaslight,* Charles Boyer, determined to find and possess four precious jewels hidden in a house by its former owner, whom he has strangled, plots a scheme that almost works. Marrying the heiress, Ingrid Bergman, he persuades her to move back into the house and then proceeds to eliminate her by driving her insane. With protestations of concern, he convinces her that she stole his watch, hid a picture from the wall, lost the brooch she placed in her purse, until she believes she is losing her mind. He forbids guests in the house and refuses invitations in the guise of worry over her health; he humiliates her in front of the servants and grows jealous when she smiles at a stranger—all, he explains with the famous Boyer suave solicitude, because he wants to protect her. In the course of the film the viewer sees Ingrid Bergman degenerate from trust to terror, from love to submission under the tightening grip of her husband's control. Finally she *is* insane because she *believes* she is insane, and in the required happy ending it is the "insanity" he has foisted on her that does him in.

The film is notable not only for winning an Oscar but also for bringing a new word into our vocabulary. *Gaslighting*—the planned process of steadily convincing someone she is crazy. Gaslighting, one of the major forms that psychological abuse takes, is a subtle way to corrode the foundations of logic on which a person has learned to make decisions and take action.

For example, Ingrid Bergman knows she has not removed the picture and hidden it or lost the brooch or taken his watch, but Charles Boyer convinces her that she has. "You have forgotten, darling," he comforts her lovingly, convincing her that she is fatigued and not well. Tension builds: is she losing her mind?

Real life has its drama too. A woman who had sought refuge in a temporary shelter after many years of varying kinds of abuse told me a story not unlike *Gaslight*. Her husband loved a special chocolate nut cake she made, so much so that she often made it to appease him when he got angry at her or the children. One night when he didn't even appear angry, she gave him a piece for dessert, only to hear him tell her, "What are you serving me this for? You know I hate chocolate nut cake." Like Ingrid Bergman, she asked herself, am I losing my mind?

A man can devise endless kinds of mind games with which to psychologically abuse his woman. A common ploy is to call her during the day with instructions—pick up dry cleaning, buy stamps, have the car tires rotated, etc. When upon his return home that evening she proudly announces, "Mission accomplished," he looks confused. "What are you talking about? I didn't call you." He can also reverse the procedure: *not* call her with instructions and then fume when he gets home because she hasn't carried them out.

The husband of a woman at a New York shelter observed the meticulousness with which his wife arranged her shoes in the closet—color-coded with all the blacks together, the shades of brown, whites, creams, and pastels. His abuse took the form of breaking up the color codes by moving a few shoes, and because it never dawned on her that he could invent so diabolical a scheme, puzzled by the mismatched shoes, she too assumed she was losing her sanity.

Another man worked in tandem with his best friend, who resented the abuser's wife for "putting ideas" in his own wife's head—threatening ideas like equality and respect and sharing. The husband got his friend to call his wife night after night and hang up as soon as she answered the phone. When the wife expressed concern over who was making the calls and why, her husband told her, "The phone didn't ring. You must be imagining it."

The ultimate in psychological abuse is to drive a woman over the edge of sanity. A man used to be able to put his wife in a mental institution—an insane asylum as it was called then—merely on his word that she was insane. Today, however, it is more difficult since new laws demand that a person be proved a danger to herself or to others to warrant institutionalization. Actually, most abusers, unlike Charles Boyer, don't want to put their wives away because then they would have to turn control over to the institution. With domination their goal, they even fight hard against divorce proceedings their wives set in motion, to keep them "where they belong"—in subjugation to their abuser. "I love her," they insist to the judge and to the woman, possibly even meaning it. What love means, however, is so subjective that it defies definition. While an abuser and a caring mate may both identify their feelings with the words "I love her," no one is in a position to read their hearts. Clearly legible, though, is behavior, and it is difficult for most of us to believe a man loves the woman he batters, despite his claims. The truth lies closer to—"I love what she does for me." What she does for him is grant him control.

As varied as the preceding examples of psychological abuse are, they all accomplish the same end—to undermine a woman's security in the logical reasoning on which she has relied all her life. With psychological abuse, cause no longer leads to effect. The physiologist Ivan Pavlov, followed by behavioral psychologists like B. F. Skinner, has demonstrated the efficacy of a cause-and-effect system. Established on the principle of punishment for wrong and reward for right, it accomplishes two ends.

First, it motivates a person to do what the controller sets up as right, which may be ringing a bell to bring on dinner or resolving an interpersonal conflict without force to gain peace. Children are motivated by this system every day in school, where "right" is an answer to which the teacher gives an *A*. The reward makes effort worthwhile, especially with punishment held out as the alternative—dinner withheld, a reprimand, an *F* on a test.

Second, repeated use of reward and punishment has been shown actually to alter a person's behavior. Even when the bell isn't rung, the dog will salivate on time; even when no one is around to praise, the person will mediate his conflict; even when there is no *A* to receive, the student will study.

So dependent are most of us on this system that, expecting it to work, we structure our behavior accordingly. Our lives take the shape of our driving patterns: if we stay on the right side of the road, we arrive home safely; if we choose to drive on the left, we get killed.

An abused woman learns, as it were, to drive with the traffic, in the right lane. Although the result may be ulcers or a nervous breakdown, she is conditioned to anticipate what will please her husband—and more important, what will not *displease* him—and to act accordingly. As long as cause and effect hold firm, so does she, not liking, but at least *knowing* what for safety's sake she must and must not do.

However, should her husband distort the system of cause and effect under which they live, she will, like Lewis Carroll's Alice, find herself in a senseless wonderland. The psychologically abusive man seems to know this instinctively and uses it demonically. He will emotionally batter her for weeks, reinforcing the patterns of humiliation and worthlessness he has established, and then suddenly for no reason he will switch. He will come home one night with flowers and take her to dinner at a nice restaurant. Since she hardly dares talk or smile, he chides her gently, "Come on, we're having fun, aren't we?" and she begins to think maybe they are.

Until the next day or the next week or the next. Then, with no provocation, he screams at her, reestablishing the same old pattern of abuse. Now she is confused: why was he suddenly so good to her? What has she done to make him mad again? Her husband continues to play the good guy-bad guy role in this way with no logic—no reason for the sudden kindness and no reason for the reversion to abuse. With neither change attributable to her actions, there exists no cause for the effect.

Lacking a way of knowing what to do to please her husband and what to avoid so as not to displease him, the woman is in a quandary. As the Cheshire Cat says to Alice when she balks at visiting the Mad Hatter or the March Hare because both are mad, "Oh, you can't help that; we're all mad here. I'm mad. You're mad. . . . You must be, or you wouldn't have come here." Before falling down the rabbit hole, life made sense to Alice; now it is topsy-turvy.

Similarly a psychologically abused woman feels she has entered an upside-down world in which the logic on which she has built sanity no longer applies. She feels like Alice trying to make sense of Wonderland's time schedule when the Red Queen describes it: "Here we mostly have days and nights two and three at a time, and sometimes in the winter we take as many as five nights together—for warmth, you know." Her abuser has, in effect, altered her state of consciousness since she has passed through the framework of the looking glass into a world where nothing is as it should be. In this mind warp she is more dependent on him than ever, a realization that enabled one man to tell his wife, "Nutty as you are, you're lucky to have me, or you'd be in the loony bin."

Some abusive men use drugs to achieve this effect. One man forced the woman he lived with to drink with him at night until she was drunk. He would then get his friends to have sex with her, describing the act to her in detail the next day. He always wound up his lurid report by reminding her she was a slut that any other man would throw out. Although she didn't feel like a slut, she believed him because she didn't know what else to believe.

As a counselor to prison inmates some years ago, I spoke with many women who had landed in federal prison through the drug manipulation of their men. In the words of an attractive magazine illustrator, "He got me into a world I thought existed only in pulp magazines until I became one of the denizens. I didn't know myself anymore. He didn't beat me, but he kept me so high that I felt like a robot controlled by buttons he pushed. When the police dragged me to jail, I didn't even know I'd been in a drug bust." A man who turns his woman into a robot has surely won the mind game of psychological abuse.

Brainwashing as Abuse

A second major form of psychological abuse added another word to our vocabulary although it did not originate with women. It came to our attention when American prisoners of war in Japan and jailed dissidents in China were shown confessing the errors of their behavior and reciting the liturgy of their captor's creed. *Brainwashing.* This is the method by which a captor, through coercive control, bends the mind of his captives to his will.

With the advent of television, brainwashing was honed to a sharp cutting edge. No longer did it have to rely on the captor's voice on radio or his words quoted in newspapers; now a world audience could see and hear the broken and bowed converts firsthand. Few who watched the evening news can forget Communist prisoners in Russia, zombies lined up before the television cameras, admitting their crimes and their guilt before being executed. More recently and more painfully remains the scene of American hostages in Iran marched blindfolded through jeering crowds, apologizing for the sins of America and pleading for the president's acquiesence to Iranian demands to secure their release.

In the early 1970s I, as an educator, was invited by the Reverend Sun Myung Moon to a dinner at New York's Waldorf Astoria. Hundreds of guests sat at tables of eight or ten in the grand ballroom, dining on filet mignon and listening to propaganda speeches on the good works of Moon's religious community and to the reverend's two-hour keynote speech delivered unbelievably in Korean. Although many people with shorter boredom fuses than mine got up and left midway, I am glad I hung on, for when it finally ended, we were encouraged to ask questions—not of him but of the cult-member seated at each table for that purpose.

These were attractive young men and women of different nationalities, squeaky clean, as my children would have described them, who looked at us with toothpaste smiles and spoke in emotionless tones. Their answers were obviously put in place like WordPerfect in my computer, because whenever a guest pressed a button, the answer came out flat and verbatim. Having worked with young people most of my life, I can recognize spontaneity. These young people had none. They responded to us like Ken and Barbie plastic creations, and all I could think of was *The Stepford Wives*. This was my first face-to-face encounter with brainwashing.

Since then, both I and the rest of the world have become familiar with the technique as it is used by cults. More than a hundred followers of Jim Jones were so drained of will in 1978 that they submitted to drinking poison and giving it to their children. In 1993 almost eighty members of the Branch Davidians followed David Koresh to death by fire. I spoke at length to one cult member, a young Yale graduate I met on a talk show, who had written a book about his experiences entrapped by the Moonies. So roboticized had he been, he said, that his beard had stopped growing like a man's and, even more to his horror, he had lost the protective mechanism of pain: at one time he had continued to shovel and hoe on the Moonie farm for eight to ten hours a day with a suppurated hand that previously would have sent him to a hospital emergency room in dire pain.

"What had they done that got you to this state?" I asked him. His answer explained a method of thought control at that time unimaginable to those of us who had not undergone it:

First, they undercut his health and strength, depriving him of adequate sleep and giving him only enough food for survival. In addition, they worked him for long hours.

Second, they isolated him by making him sever all contacts with his former life—friends and family—so that only the Moonie community was left as his support group.

Third, they subjected him to repeated propaganda from the cult leaders and from peers who, while propagandizing, wrapped him in the batting of acceptance and love. He snuggled in their beliefs and their lifestyle as if of his own accord.

Finally, they kept him in a constant state of anxiety. As supported as he felt by the community, he knew that should he question or break a rule it would turn on him en masse with severe punishment, and he knew too that there was no escape.

Years ago an American celebrity made headline news and became the subject of books, a movie, and a TV show by being kidnapped from her palatial California home and held captive by the Symbionese Liberation Army. Patty Hearst. The downpour of fears and tears showered on her by the public during her weeks of captivity dried up soon afterward in a thunderous shock: Patty Hearst was photographed with a semiautomatic carbine in her hand along with her former captors holding up the Hibernia Bank in San Francisco. She escaped with them and for weeks after was in hiding, a wanted criminal. When she was finally brought to justice, the facts of brainwashing were brought to light. Like prisoners, hostages, and cult members, she had been worn down, not through punishment but through thought control. Her kidnappers had transformed the debutante daughter of the Hearsts into a mirror image of themselves just as the Moonies had transformed the young Yale man:

- They kept her exhausted.

- They smothered her with propaganda on the exploitation of the poor by the power-hungry rich like her father and on the need for violence to overthrow the system and establish justice.

- They held over her head, like the sword of Damocles, threats of beatings and rape if she challenged them.

Like police investigators eliciting information from a suspect, they alternated verbal abuse with gentleness, wrath with caring, to throw her further off balance. Soon, with her will bent to theirs, she devotedly became what her captors intended—one of them.

Psychologically abusive husbands adapt brainwashing methods to manipulate their woman's will. Similarities are difficult to ignore:

Captivity

Psychological abusers hold their women captive—not by the bars of penitentiaries or hostage cell walls, not even by the hypnotic trance of cult members. They chain them by what many call *learned helplessness*—a mental state in which women are unable to resist the manipulative pressure of their men— and others see as just plain fear. Even those professionals who oppose the learned-helplessness theory admit that a psychologically abused woman often falls into a clinical depression that produces similar symptoms: loss of initiative, resignation, inability to handle even the simplest daily chores. One woman with whom I spoke, now two years away from her abusive marriage, recalls opening the closet each morning and being unable to decide what to wear. "I mean really unable," she explains. "I'd put on and take off three or four skirts or slacks, not conscious of what I was doing."

Other women express similar changes in attitude as well as in behavior: "being out of it," "in a fog," "like I was drugged." Psychological abuse so disorients a woman that she staggers as if she were in the fun house at Coney Island, floors tilted to topple her. As she gropes for a wall to keep from collapsing in the darkness, she leans on the only wall she can reach—the man who led her into a world askew.

Psychiatrists say that depression is a survival technique in which the mind, clinging to life during suffering too intense to bear, escapes. Years after her escape from both a psychologically abusive relationship and depression, a woman in her midfifties told me that at the time she had actually thought she was dead. She had seen herself, risen from a deathbed, walking around without feeling or thoughts, often deaf and blind to what went on around her. That's how the world of a psychologically abused woman ends—in T. S. Eliot's words, not with a bang of resistance but with a whimper of submission.

Deterioration of Health

A psychological abuser undermines the health and strength of his woman too, just as brainwashers do. Statistics indicate that abused women are up to three times more likely to be in poor health than other women. Sleep deprivation is common. Just the other day a woman at Family Court told me that when her husband comes home from his job at 2:00 A.M. every day, he wakes her up to cook dinner and makes her sit with him while he eats. "He doesn't like to eat alone," she explained acceptingly, despite the fact that he sleeps all day while she gets up at 7:00 to go to work.

Other men don't just wake their woman to cook but force sex on her throughout the night. Some keep her pregnant year after year, refusing to use or let her use birth control. "That's what God put you on Earth for," one man told his wife after the birth of their eleventh child.

An old Arab proverb says that he who has health has hope and he who has hope has everything. For a while as an abuser plays out the good days of affection and the bad days of abuse, the woman is able to raise hope; in time, however, as he depletes her health and strength, hope fades with exhaustion, and she is left with nothing.

Since physical health and mental health are twins in a symbiotic relationship, the psychological abuser works on each to undermine the other, and which came first is no more important than the chicken-and-egg controversy. A woman convinced she is going crazy loses her appetite, can't sleep, and develops any of a hundred psychosomatic illnesses doctors need to treat. Ingrid Bergman did in *Gaslight*; so do the long line of women I see in court with stress-related health problems such as asthma and migraines.

On the other hand, a woman weakened by sickness is far more vulnerable to the machinations of an abusive husband trying to drive her near-crazy. One woman complained that her husband wouldn't get the medicine prescribed by her doctor for pain relief after a leg operation that immobilized her. A close friend of mine, desperately sick with the flu, begged her husband for some cold ginger ale, the only thing she felt she could keep down. From the next room, taking care of her two children, I heard him tell her, "I'll get it later. You can wait." I bundled the children up and drove the quarter mile to get it myself.

Isolation

A psychological abuser, like the cult leader with his followers, isolates his woman from the rest of the world so that she has no input but his own. He banishes her friends, who would serve as real-life measurements of her own phantasmagoric condition, and allows contact only with his friends. He severs connections with her family, whose concern would reflect her deterioration, and pulls his own family close around her. He forbids her a job, which would provide self-esteem and communication with associates, and confines her to the house. Like Peter Peter who had a wife and couldn't keep her, he puts her in a metaphorical pumpkin shell, and there he keeps her very well. (Isolation will be discussed fully in the following chapter.)

Propaganda

A psychological abuser also wears down his woman through propaganda. Day in, day out he calls her a slut, a bitch, a whore, often refusing even to use her name. He maximizes any mistake she makes, and if there aren't enough, he creates others to plant in her mind. Over a period of time he transforms her into the woman she sees in the mirror of his eyes—the inadequate slut, the bitch, the whore who does his will.

A middle-aged woman who came into court one day had been living with an abusive husband for thirty-four years. She had lost one of her four children to leukemia, held two menial jobs to make ends meet since her husband was professionally unemployed, and struggled to meet all his demands. Still he demeaned her constantly. "I know I'm stupid, but I do the best I can," she told me apologetically. "A smarter woman would be able to please him, I think." As hard as I tried, I could not make her see the enormous strength and many skills she exhibited every day of her life, nor could I convince her that *smart* was what brought her to court that day. Her husband's propaganda was too deeply embedded.

In another case a man had convinced his young, attractive wife that she tried to seduce his friends. It was true that some of the men had made passes at her from time to time, which she had parried with a laugh to avoid a scene. Although her husband knew the predatory nature of his friends and had often laughed with them about it, instead of blaming them he chose to accuse his wife. When I met her, she had stopped using makeup and was wearing a shape-less jumper, convinced by her husband that, as she said, "I used to act like a tramp."

Anxiety

Finally, a psychological abuser keeps his woman in a constant state of anxiety. Since consistency would stabilize her expectations, he makes certain to keep her riding a roller coaster—not like Thunder Mountain in Walt Disney World, where riders anticipate the crashing fall as they climb upward, but like a demon drive in which ups and downs follow no law of gravity. He sees to it that she is never sure whether he will hurt her, never sure whether her efforts will please or enrage him, never sure that she can follow his orders properly.

Psychiatrists tell us that most children can survive parental abuse if it is consistent, since they learn what to expect: Mother will get drunk, or Dad will come home frustrated and scream at them tonight. However, if Mother and Dad suddenly shift gears one night, kissing them instead of screaming, the children's stability is undermined. What can they expect tomorrow night?

Women in psychologically abusive situations react similarly. A bride of less than a year explained to me that when her husband stopped to drink with his pals after work he usually came home raging at her for no reason. She dreaded hearing his key in the lock but steeled herself for his abuse. Occasionally, though, he came home bringing flowers, kissing her, wanting to make love. "It would have been lovely," she explained with a sigh, "if I'd known, but I was a nervous wreck expecting the worst." Sometimes, she said, she would purposely be out of the house on a trumped-up errand so that she could telephone him to size up his mood and prepare herself.

Another way the psychological abuser creates anxiety is through the use of threats. He may be obvious and verbally threaten to hit the woman should she step out of line. If he has in the past physically abused her, his threat has sharp claws. On the other hand, he may be more subtle and more menacing by holding a fist to her face or toying with a gun before her without saying a word.

Many abusers use threats against a woman's parents, hurling them either at her parents personally or vicariously through her, or they frighten her by aiming threats at a friend whom they see as a rival. The expert abuser chooses the most lethal weapon of all, a woman's children, threatening to beat them, kidnap them, have the court remove them from her custody. Whenever his wife challenged his power by daring to disagree with him, one man grabbed their two-year-old daughter and drove off, often not returning until two or three in the morning while she paced and worried whether they would ever return.

After he and his wife were divorced, the same man often had the children roll around on the New York sidewalks during visits so that when returning them he could alarm his ex-wife with their filth and with possible diseases they may have picked up. So little concern did this man have for the welfare of his children that, regardless of the law, he refused to let them use car seats or wear seat belts during visits so he could intensify his ex-wife's anxiety.

The Effect of Mind Games

Professionals who work with battered women report that the damage from psychological abuse is far more difficult to eliminate than that from physical abuse. Being beaten or kicked down the stairs certainly arouses fear and anger in a woman; however, these are emotions she can recognize and call by name and, with professional support, can deal with. On the other hand, having her world upended and her mind set askew obliterates the trusted guidelines on which she has previously lived her life. As a result, she is left dangling. Dr. Joanna Landau, who runs programs for abused women at Four Winds Hospital in Cross River, New York, is quick to correct anyone who asks about her treatment. "Treatment is for the sick," she explains. "Abused women don't need treatment, because they are not sick—mentally, that is. They need affirmation and support." Affirmation of their sanity. Support to stand again on solid ground.

Even amid her bewilderment, Alice was eventually able to shout to the Wonderland world, "You're nothing but a pack of cards" and wake up in her evenly balanced home. Some of the woman mentioned here were eventually able to do the same; they left their husbands or lovers, having some-how kept in touch with reality enough to be able to tell them-selves, "He's the crazy one. There's nothing wrong with me." With help they rediscovered themselves. Many, however, were too mind-twisted, had gone too far over the brink, had grown too dependent. All they could tell themselves was "I can't handle life alone." They stayed.

Alice Miller in her profound study of self-esteem, *The Drama of the Gifted Child*, defined a healthy self-feeling to mean "the unquestioned certainty that the feelings and wishes one experiences are a part of one's self." The psy-chological abuser creates a mise-en-scène that precludes a woman's own experiences, denying her her own thoughts and feelings. To be told what to *think* deadens the mind; despairingly we see results of this in the miseducation of chil-dren who are forced in school not to think but to memo-rize and play back by rote. However, to be told what to *feel*, or not feel is even more damaging, for it challenges sanity: if we are made to believe that we should be happy when we're miserable or should count ourselves lucky when we are cursing fate, we begin to believe there's something wrong with us.

The mind of the psychologically abused woman is brutally played with. Her abuser does not stop at ordering her to think prescribed thoughts and feel prescribed feelings; no, instead he deposits himself inside her brain and persuades her that the thoughts she thinks and the feelings she feels are truly hers. Like Dr. Frankenstein, he makes the person of his creation think with someone else's brain.

If the implant were 100 percent, the woman might live out her life in the calm of a programmed automaton. However, bits and pieces of her old self give rise to opposing thoughts and feelings: What does she really think? What does she really feel? She spins in a maelstrom of disorientation.

Gloria, a woman who left her boyfriend and came to court for protection after two years of abuse, explained that he was driving her crazy. She suddenly stopped when she said it and reflected for a minute. "You know," she went on, "I never thought about that expression before—driving someone crazy—but it means just what it says. Curt *did* drive me crazy." He may have tried, but the fact that she walked out proves her wrong.

Oliver Wendell Holmes called insanity the logic of an overtaxed mind—a defense mechanism, in fact, to survive what a sane person cannot endure. Gloria and the thousands of others whose abusers are driving them crazy are not insane, for if they were they would withdraw from their ominous reality to float happily in the safety of fantasy; like Blanche DuBois in *A Streetcar Named Desire*, they would depart with a radiant smile. That is not the abused woman's way, however. It is her abuser, not she, who is insane in a self-created world of power; and it is she, not her abuser, who clings to sanity in the real world of her anguish.

Why I'm feeling pain & he's not.

CHAPTER 3

"If only I could visit my folks."

The Isolation of Social Abuse

JOAN WAS RAISED IN A middle-class suburb of New York, the youngest of two girls and two boys. "We fought a lot," she says, "but boy, let anyone else look cross-eyed at us, and we'd solidify!" Their mother taught math in the local high school; their father commuted to his middle-management job with a New York advertising firm. After graduating from the state university, Joan got a lowly job in a publishing company in New York that paid so little that she moved in with her brother, taking him up on his offer to foot the bills.

Then she met Irwin. Waiting in line at the supermarket, they began a conversation, carried their groceries with them for a cup of coffee, and became a couple. The fact that none of her family liked him only added to the attraction. She puts it this way: "I felt so damned middle-class till I met Irwin. He was different from anyone I'd gone with—you know the conservative suburbs. He dressed like a 1960s hippie and was sort of a Communist, always railing against the rich. I didn't tell my dad, but Irwin referred to advertising as 'poison for the poor.'

"Both my brothers warned me against Irwin, felt he was a freeloader, since he held a job only long enough to collect unemployment insurance, and my sister was repelled because he wasn't very clean and smelled a lot of the time. 'How can you sleep with him?' she'd ask. Well, I did sleep with him, got pregnant, and married him. The biggest mistake of my life. Not getting pregnant—I have the greatest little girl in the world—but getting involved with Irwin in the first place.

"He knew how close I was to my family and was so jealous that he did everything he could to keep me away from them. He'd tell them I was out when they called and wouldn't give me their messages. It got so he wouldn't let me invite them over for dinner—not even for a cup of coffee. Whenever I went out, he'd quiz me to make sure I wasn't going to see them.

"Things got so bad that he wouldn't even let me see friends I'd known since I lived at home or with my brother. Heaven help me if I called them! Somehow he'd know—probably from the phone bill. He'd scream at me and threaten to have the phone disconnected. It was awful. I hated him sometimes and felt like he'd locked me up in an ice cube."

Joan was lucky: she could leave Irwin because she had strong family ties. She knew that her parents, her sister, and her brothers all stood behind her and would be her support through what turned out to be a harrowing divorce. Today she and her daughter are on their own. She's working at a somewhat better-paying job in the same field, studying to be a lawyer, and letting her family help out with money and baby-sitting. She laughs, "With Irwin, I was living on borrowed time. Now it's borrowed money!"

Maureen, with a similar story, can't laugh at the end. There is no end. At thirty-one, when she met David, she loved the idea of having a man to take to the social gatherings at which she had previously been a single. She didn't have to fight off wolves or invent credible excuses to avoid the bores any longer; she had her man, who guarded her zealously. Proud of his tall good looks, she showed him off at family gatherings and exuded charm for his family and friends when he included her in his circle. She cheered him on the tennis court Saturday mornings and at the bowling alley Thursday nights, and she cooked creative Sunday dinners each week for his parents and hers. When her mother kissed David and said she felt she was gaining a son, Maureen saw a bright and beautiful future.

After they married, however, what had been an active social life ground down to a halt: no more parties with her friends, no more two-family Sunday dinners, no more cheering at tennis and bowling. David still got together with his friends, but it was "man stuff" that excluded her, and he cut both of them off from her family's gatherings. Most painful of all, they now sat down to Sunday dinners at his parents' house with her parents being noticeably uninvited. The only word Maureen could think of to describe how she felt was *amputated.*

David is the prototype of a social abuser. He set the trap so skillfully that Maureen easily rationalized the hints he unwittingly dropped. For instance, had she been mindful, she could have noticed that he guarded her not zealously but jealously, and she might have pondered the maneuvering that led to her accompanying him to tennis and bowling instead of going out with her friends. But since she wasn't and didn't, the change came as a shock. What he was doing Maureen didn't see until she was solidly walled in, and why he did it she didn't understand until his control had tightened around her like a vise.

The purpose of social isolation is control. If a man can keep his woman out of contact with the outside world, she will be dependent on him and him alone. She will therefore be forced into compliance, forbidden outside resources from which to gain support, and drained of inner resources from which to build strength. Solitary confinement remains one of the most effective disciplinary measures for recalcitrant prisoners because by depriving them of social contact it deprives them of the power to resist. Fingernail scratches on stone walls in medieval dungeons and the Tower of London and Alcatraz speak of the desperation within those lone cells. The scratches of socially abused women leave no marks on the walls of their homes but wear away the straight-backed will until, like an ancient Christian prostrate before God, they swear, "As Thou wilt, what Thou wilt, when Thou wilt."

The most common way a man isolates a woman is through manipulation, arranging situations—or rearranging them—until she is cut off. For instance, when David decided that Maureen was seeing too much of her family, he terminated the dinners Maureen looked forward to hosting every Sunday. It's too much work, he convinced her, with assurances that his mother would gladly have the weekly dinners at her house—of course with invitations for her parents as well. Although disappointed and hurt, Maureen acquiesced, and the dinner locale was switched—minus her parents.

He inched away from social gatherings with her friends by having other engagements when the invitations came and eased her into spending more time with his friends by accusing her of becoming antisocial. Several times he called off plans she had already made by phoning her friends to say she was sick and lying to Maureen that an emergency had made her friends cancel. Before she knew it, she was seeing nothing of her friends, very little of her parents, and far too much of those who peopled David's world.

When manipulation fails to gain the day, the social abuser resorts to dictatorship and issues a command. As hard as David tried, he couldn't persuade Maureen that her mother and father exerted a bad influence on her. "They baby you too much" didn't work. "They take up too much of your time" didn't work. "They don't listen to you" didn't work. So David, no longer beating around the bush, got to the point with "I won't have you seeing your parents any- more." Shocked by David's edict, Maureen stood her ground. "I'll see my parents when I want to," she insisted. "You don't have to be there, but you can't stop me."

"No?" David knew otherwise. The first time she pre- pared to visit them, David hid her car key. The next time he locked her in the bedroom, saying her parents got in the way of their lovemaking and that he wanted to be alone with her more often. When he locked her out of the house one night, Maureen knew that David meant business and she grudgingly obeyed.

When in resentment she balked at his insistence on hav- ing his bowling buddies for dinner every Thursday before their league match, David at first attempted to persuade her: they'd have fun; he wanted to show off what a great cook she was; wasn't a wife supposed to be there for her hus- band? "No way" was her only answer.

David turned livid with rage. "What did you say?" he shouted. "Come on, you don't have to yell at me," Maureen attempted to reason. "Can't we just talk to each other any- more?"

"I'm talking," David insisted in anger. "The trouble is you're never listening." Maureen turned and walked into the kitchen, unable to hold back tears of hurt and puzzlement over her husband's sudden metamorphosis. Like all women in the face of unrecognizable abuse, she asked herself, "What have I done?" Deciding the answer lay in her refusal to

please David, she fixed a bowling league dinner every Thursday and made a point of saying yes more often.

But not always. When they had a baby and David considered their house too small, he decided to build on the
corner of his parents' lot. Horrified at being even further
absorbed by his family, Maureen offered every excuse she
could fashion. None worked. Determined as ever to have
his way, David issued a flat order that they would build
where he wanted, and that was that; she might as well
shut up.

When Maureen continued to argue on the grounds that
she had to live in the house as well as he and should therefore have an equal say, David looked at her coldly but didn't
go into his usual shouting routine. She wondered why, thinking maybe she had proved her point, until, still not raising
his voice, David snarled, "We'll build there. Get that straight.
If you mention it once more, you won't have to live there,
because you'll be out on the street. I'll live there." Maureen
started to draw the line with threats of divorce until David
added, "with the baby."

The ultimate argument: the baby. He would do it too,
she had come to realize; with his family like a stockade
behind him and she alone and jobless, she would have little
chance of winning custody. Since the outcome was too
unspeakable to risk, she acquiesced.

When manipulative ploys and strict orders fail, a nonphysical abuser can still resort to intimidation to exert his
power. He threatens to beat her, kill her, kidnap her children, burn her parents' home, crash her car, do any harm-
ful thing his mind can conceive—and he need never act on
any of them. The fear his threat arouses, like a murderous
blunt instrument, beats his woman into submission. Thus
he maintains control, and thus he is able to isolate her as
he will.

The social abuser employs a variety of means to achieve his goal, although he rarely limits himself to one:

Banning Family Contact

He finds his woman's family a ready weapon. He may begin, as David and Irwin did, by cutting off lines of communication—no phone calls, no visits, no letters. If she disobeys by sneaking a visit or phoning from an outside booth, he sharpens his attack—no contacts with friends of the family. To one young woman this meant cutting off midmorning coffee dates with a longtime "aunt," her mother's oldest friend. To another it meant refusing dinner invitations from a couple whose friendship she and her sister's family shared.

If a woman is a dog or cat lover, the man classifies her pet as family, cutting it off as well. One woman had to find a home for a ten-year-old sheltie to which her husband had had no objections prior to their marriage. Another tried to keep her cat, but her husband's daily stream of invective against her wore her down to the point of giving it away. If a man allows his wife to keep a pet, his abusive behavior may extend far closer to cruelty than it could with her human family. For instance, I know a husband whose wife dares not displease him because he will take revenge on her dog with a kick or a swat. Another husband had the veterinarian put his wife's cat to sleep while she was away because he didn't want to clean its litter box.

In addition to cutting off the lifeline to family, the social abuser intensifies the hurt through denigration. "Did the bitch try to call you today?" was Irwin's inquiry when he suspected Joan's mother might have phoned. When he saw Joan reading their three-year-old daughter a story about a bunny's sweet old grandma, he interjected, "Not your bitch grandma, babe."

When name-calling isn't enough, the abuser often turns
to harassment. He may dial his in-laws and hang up when
they answer—not once or even twice but in one case 130
times in one day. Middle-of-the-night calls are effective,
especially when spaced evenly to assure sleeplessness. In the
past a telephone hang-up provided no proof of the caller,
so people were loath to take the man to court; today, however, with caller identification, they are able to present fool-
proof evidence.

Not all abusers hang up; some remain on the line to
shout obscenities and threats at their wife's family: "You
whore," "You fucking idiot," "I'll get you one of these days."
Irwin was content to yell "fascist" into the business phone
of Joan's father every day. It is not difficult to empathize with
a woman's fear and powerlessness when she learns that her
abuser has turned his venom on her parents.

To social abusers family-bashing is a triple-edged sword.
First, it makes the isolation of his wife or girlfriend even
more painful; second, the depreciation of her family further
depreciates her; and third, it gives him an extended realm
of power. All three bolster his shaky self-esteem, which is
not an uncommon practice among the insecure—from the
sixth-grade bully in a school yard to the gang of bullies in
a subway car. Like them, the social abuser hurls his obscenities, unaware that they are projections of the loathing he
feels for himself, for the bigger the bully, the greater is his
own unmet need for importance.

Often the social abuser uses his own family to pour salt
into the wounds he has inflicted through the exile of his
wife's family. Like David, he insists on frequent family visits
and on lavish entertaining of them at home, for which his
wife prepares with fear and trembling. In addition, he may
give his mother and father free rein, even encourage them
to criticize his wife: her cooking, her housekeeping, the way

she raises the children, her clothes and hairstyle. By building a team that joins him in denigrating her, he reinforces
her aloneness within the confines that wall her off from the
family she misses even more.

Irwin used his willing mother to attack Joan's family on
the telephone. Sometimes the message she left was funny:
"Irwin is so wonderful, if he were Catholic, he'd be a saint."
Other times it was menacing: "I hope you all die of strokes."

Banning Work and School

For many abused women work is their single link to sanity.
As devastating as the night before may have been, when the
alarm wakes them at six or seven in the morning, instead
of groaning like the rest of us, they breathe a sigh of relief—
eight wonderful hours of freedom! Whatever they do at the
office or door to door or on the assembly line or in the store,
they are in control: they make their own decisions. They feel
good about themselves: they earn a salary and have lunch
with associates and mingle in a large world. They have an
identity. Of course, five o'clock inevitably arrives, and they
shed the real person and crawl back into their shell, timo-
rously facing home and husband and abuse.

Tuned in to this scenario, many abusive husbands refuse
to let their wives work. Although some keep them at home
under the guise of protection—"No wife of mine has to face
that hassle"—others do it under no guise at all: "You can't
work, and that's that." The result is the same for the woman:
her one lifeline is severed, and she is ensnared more securely
in the isolation of her abusive relationship.

School is another off-limits area to socially abused wives.
One reason is that it affords her an opportunity to make
friends and exchange ideas that break down the wall of isolation her husband has built. Another, more threatening

reason is that it offers her a way over the wall: with the acquiring of skills, she becomes capable of getting a job and supporting herself and her children. Education means independence, a state her abuser will not allow. It is significant that in the book *The Burning Bed*, based on Faith McNulty's real life story, the battered wife complies with every one of her husband's demands until he destroys her books and insists she quit business school. At that she refuses, taking the near-death beating that motivates her murder of him.

Not only does an abuser force his woman from the fellowship of school or from her job, but he also forces her into an exploitive partnership in his job. While forbidden to keep in touch with her friends, classmates, and former co-workers, she has to be at the beck and call of his business associates, looking and acting the role he demands that she fill. One man made his wife take a correspondence course so she "wouldn't sound so dumb" when they entertained his associates. Another, with a high-profile position, bought the clothes she had to wear when she accompanied him on business trips because her taste was "low class."

At the opposite extreme, I know one victim of social abuse who, after she has prepared and served dinner to her husband and his weekly ball game buddies, has to stay in her room until he rings a bell to order beer refills. He then humiliates her with lewd references to what we would call her "full" figure. One of the most hurtful situations of social abuse I have encountered was a top executive in a large firm who made his wife drop close friends she had known since high school—a woman and a man whose nonaggressive manner had kept him in a low-level job—"because they're not the kind of people I should be seen with." He, like other abusers, permeated his wife's life as if by osmosis until her own life was so diluted as to be indistinguishable from his.

Locking Her Out—or In

Perhaps the strongest weapon of isolation a social abuser has at hand—and *in* his hand—is a key. With a key a man can lock a woman out of the house and frequently does if she has broken a rule and visited friends or family; one woman came to court after spending the night in her car because she took her sister a birthday present and stayed for coffee and birthday cake. Another drove his wife into the street in the middle of the night after an argument; in bathrobe and slippers, she ran half a mile to her parents' apartment for shelter.

With a key an abuser can also lock her *in* the house or in her bedroom or in the bathroom or in a closet, and sometimes the lock with which he imprisons her is not tangible— a threat to be carried out should she dare go out. There are women kept under lock and key from the time their man leaves until he returns. One man justified it by telling me, "I don't want anything to happen to her."

Fire escapes have been used as paths to freedom by some women brave enough to venture a fall but have also been used to imprison them further. One man, realizing that his wife had outwitted her fourth-floor bedroom confinement by creeping down the fire escape, locked the window so she couldn't return until the next day, when he greeted her with a new dead bolt in his hand.

Even greater than a fire escape, the real road to freedom lies in an automobile. One has only to watch car ads in magazines and on television to realize the joy of flight by auto—flight from drudgery, from boredom, from isolation, flight toward friends and laughter. One has only to know an elderly person living in fear that her driver's license will be revoked to understand the escape her car offers from dependence and immobility. To an abused woman, her car is the most readily available escape hatch, affording her the com-

panionship of friends or the choice of privacy. To an abuser,
since a woman's car is a threat to his control, one of the most
common acts of revenge for real or imagined disobedience
is to deprive her of it.

Hiding the car keys is the easiest trick but not always the
surest, since she might find them. Taking the keys to work
with him is effective unless, having planned ahead, she has
a second set. The men of a good number of women I see
forbid them to get a driver's license, a sure ploy to keep
the car in the garage. A good friend of mine, previously married to a highly successful gynecologist, used to go to her
car only to find that it wouldn't start. Upon inspection by
the AAA repair man several times, she learned that someone had disconnected a switch or cut a wire. Someone—her
husband.

One woman to whom I spoke explained that her husband would siphon the gas tank dry. Another said that, running late to a club meeting one day, she found the car with
a flat tire. Frustrated, but philosophical about Murphy's
Law—everything that can go wrong will go wrong—she
switched into her blue jeans, changed the tire, redressed in
her skirt and blouse, and raced to the meeting. Several days
later, when she found two flat tires, although she couldn't
change the tire with only one spare, she did change her mind
about Murphy's Law, renaming it after her husband, who had
invented a new "everything" to go wrong.

Joan's husband, Irwin, found a menacing way to play the
car abuse game: he deprived her use of the car by keeping
her prisoner inside it. The first time it happened, she had
driven the children to the social agency where he visited
them once a week under supervision. That day, however,
since the supervisor was not waiting for them outside and
Joan was informed that he would not be there, she refused
to drop the children off with Irwin alone. Despite the court

order of supervision, Irwin demanded his visit, standing firm on his "rights." As Joan started the engine, he flung himself against the hood, blocking her way. When she switched into reverse, he raced to the rear of the car, standing arms outstretched, a barrier to her departure. In that way he imprisoned her, yelling and cursing, for almost an hour, until the superintendent of the building ordered him away under the threat of arrest.

Irwin used the same technique on Joan's mother one hot August day as she attempted to drop the children off for a visit. With the agency closed and no supervisor in sight, she kept the children in the car. Blocking it with the width of his arms in front and having his friend block it behind, he kept Joan's mother and the two children virtual prisoners in a hot box. Terrified, the children hid under the dog's blanket, sobbing, until finally their grandmother opened a window to give them a breath of air. As they emerged from beneath the blanket, Irwin reached through the car window like a predatory dinosaur in the film *Jurassic Park*, snatching the fifteen-month-old and, in the process, bumping the child's head on the window frame. With the baby screaming in his arms from fear and pain, Irwin continued to defy Joan's mother, even with his friend pleading for the child's release. Finally, after almost an hour, he handed him over reluctantly.

Joan's father was the only one apparently undaunted by Irwin. Waiting one day with the three-year-old for Joan and the baby to join them in the car, he came face to face with Irwin leering through the front window. Hurling threats and obscenities, Irwin refused to leave, so Joan's father turned on the engine, preparing to drive off. In a flash Irwin threw himself onto the hood and, spread-eagle, refused to budge. Joan's father resolutely shifted into drive and began inching away from the curb. Irwin remained steadfast. The car picked up speed. Irwin continued to cling to the hood as Joan's father drove three blocks, stopped abruptly, and gave Irwin a last chance to move. At that point Irwin slid off and stormed away cursing. "What would you have done if Irwin had slipped off and been run over?" his wife asked later in horror.

"Gone to jail a happy man," was his self-satisfied answer.

The Effect of Isolation

Researchers have done thousands of studies on the effects of isolation, using subjects as far ranging as birds and pigs to primates and humans. All report that isolation and the loneliness that ensues seriously damage the psyche. Dr. Meyer Mendelson of Yeshiva University found it to be "a major and not enough recognized factor in psychosis" (*Contemporary Psychoanalysis*, April 1990). Drs. Stanley Brodsky and Forrest Scogin of the University of Alabama concluded that "individual isolation and restrictions have clear potential for negative psychological effects" (*Forensic Reports*, December 1988). Apparently social abusers know what they are doing.

Isolation is a powerful weapon under their control, wielded to create the desperation of abandonment and aloneness that makes a woman totally dependent on the only person left, her abuser. Over a period of time he forces her to retreat not only from the significant individuals in her life but also from the broader human community to which she once belonged.

When I worked as a counselor to inmates in a federal prison—forgers, drug dealers, illegal aliens, bomb throwers—I saw them as not so much locked inside prison as locked outside of life. When the thick metal door slid shut behind me as I entered, hope, love, belonging—feelings that belong to life—remained outside for me and for them. Upon leaving, as I once again stepped out into the city, its limitless sky framed by tall buildings, its streets defined by white headlights and red taillights of coming and going cars, I would look up at the prison windows. There, behind the bars that kept me and the sky and the lights out, would be a face looking, a hand waving to a peopled world they were forbidden to enter.

That is how women feel when isolated through social abuse—locked outside the home, the love, the belonging that once meant life, now deadened in their solitary confinement. That is how Irene felt, locked outside the life she and her husband could have had together on the far side of the prison door he erected. As often as I saw her, I never suspected. I knew she and Sam rarely went out or had guests in, but I accepted Irene's explanation that "Sam is such a loner," so skillfully did she disguise her pain. The poet Richard Lovelace wrote of isolation in two lines that have come down through the years:

> *Stone walls do not a prison make,*
> *Nor iron bars a cage.*

The poem closes with these less familiar lines:

> *If I have freedom in my love*
> *And in my soul am free,*
> *Angels alone that soar above*
> *Enjoy such liberty.*

While critics may not applaud the poem's literary merit, women whose love and soul are imprisoned by social abuse cannot fail to feel its painful truth.

We human beings are social creatures, like ants and bees, like fish and birds, like wild dogs and lions and baboons, with whom we share this earth. When abandoned, our untamed earthmates die. Social abuse abandons a woman, rips away the community in which she thrives, leaving her in a wasteland of isolation. "Aloneness is the worst," says the psychiatrist Virginia Bird. "It's like being abandoned in the universe."

Mira Rothenberg is a psychologist who for more than twenty-five years has tried to break through the walls with which autistic children seal themselves off from human contact. In an unforgettable book called *Children with Emerald Eyes* she conveys the utter aloneness of a child lost for two days in the woods: "A forever, a death, an abandonment . . . the scope is beyond me . . . No one to take care of you, no one to attend to you—lost . . . losing identity, losing self in the morass of many feelings."

That child, that feeling, that loss of self is the woman isolated in the forest of social abuse.

CHAPTER 4

"I never have a penny."

The Destitution of Economic Abuse

"I NEVER HAVE A PENNY." It is not surprising to hear a woman on welfare complain of having no money: with prices high, food stamps limited, and weekly checks small, we understand. However, when we hear the same complaint from a woman in a high economic bracket, we assume she is speaking metaphorically. How could she be penniless—with an executive husband, a Cadillac and a Jeep in the garage, a view of Lake Michigan from her lavish suburban home, and the children in private school? It makes no sense: "You've got to be kidding. Right?"

Wrong. It makes sense. What makes even more sense is the number of penniless women in similar affluence who are too embarrassed to admit it to anyone. Even to themselves. I feel I know those women intimately through Irene, who gave me the following detailed account:

"Before Sam and I married, he spent not extravagantly but freely; we went to dinner and the theater; he brought me flowers and surprise presents; he gave me a large dia-

67

mond engagement ring; and he took—alone as he always
had—extensive luxury cruises on his vacations. After we
were married, the honeymoon was literally over.

"We lived meagerly. I, making a pittance as a researcher,
assumed he made little more than I although I knew he was
director of a department in his company. He didn't tell me
how much money he made, and I was too timid to ask. Years
later, when I grew less timid and asked . . . and asked . . .
and asked, he still didn't tell me. As you know, we had three
children rather quickly, who rather quickly grew up. Because,
as you remember, the schools in our community were notoriously inadequate, you and I both determined to send our
kids to private schools. Only your husband paid for them,
and Sam refused. That's when I took a job teaching.
Although I earned only a skimpy three thousand dollars a
year, I got free tuition for the children, so I didn't mind for-
feiting the larger salary I could have gotten with my master's degree elsewhere.

"By this time Sam had changed jobs and become top
management in another company. Not only was I still too
embarrassed to ask about his salary, having been raised
with the admonition that you *never* discuss money matters, but I even refused to let myself imagine how large
it might be. All I knew was that I still lived as scantily
as before with an inexpensive car—and only one, despite
the fact that we lived miles from the railroad station from
which Sam commuted morning and night with me as his
chauffeur. I didn't even have part-time domestic help like
you, and when you went to Macy's or Bloomingdales to
shop, I made up excuses and got clothes at Sears or a
discount store. For years my spending money for the week
to feed and clothe all five of us, buy gas, drug items, etc.,
was twenty dollars, left in a single bill on Monday mornings on the kitchen windowsill. If Sam had held a low-level

job, I would have accepted all this willingly, but I later learned that he was earning well over a hundred thousand a year.

"When my dad saw the twenty-dollar bill on the windowsill one morning when he was visiting, he was aghast. 'Dear God,' he scolded, 'you let him act like it's a whorehouse.'

"What my father didn't know was how much money I borrowed from my mother and never paid back, how much of my own small salary, which I had earmarked for bank accounts for the children, I had to spend to make ends meet. He didn't know that I paid for every trip any of us ever took, that I never had a checkbook or a credit card, that when inflation hit the country Sam left forty dollars on the windowsill. He didn't know how many times at the checkout counter I had to return items to the shelves because I didn't have enough to pay for them. He didn't know—or maybe he did know—how I had to summon all my courage to ask Sam for extra money when I really needed it and how humiliated I felt when I did. What my father didn't know was that I didn't know—and never knew—how much money my own husband earned or had. All I knew was that it wasn't enough to pay the bills, because when I retired he took my social security each month. When he died, he left piles of money; even his accountant was surprised. He left only a small spendable sum to me, though. The bulk he left in trust, a final message of economic control.

"I blame myself as much as my husband for living with economic blinders on, because I could have demanded an accounting and refused to be put off with nonanswers. I didn't because I was raised to consider money a taboo subject like sex: too personal for discussion. 'You never ask anyone how much he makes,' I remember my mother telling me. I learned my lesson well.

"I should have known better. After all, I was a college graduate, earned a master's degree and a doctorate, for which I paid, needless to say. I was also privileged: I maintained a degree of independence by working and earning my own money. Although I could never have adequately supported myself and three children, I could supplement the necessities, treat us to extras, buy all the Christmas presents, and save small amounts in the bank for me and the children.

"The deprivation I felt was less a lack of money than a lack of respect. The five-dollar bill Sam handed me one morning when I explained I needed some money to buy socks and underwear sent a message so coldly abusive that I still feel its chill today. It is sad but true that money determines the value of a person in our culture—salary, cars, clothing labels, country clubs, home, neighborhood, etc. It is also sad but true that the five-dollar bill that day shouted Sam's contempt, and the fact that I held it in my hand sobbed my feelings of worthlessness."

Not every woman is as naive as Irene was; divorce courts are filled with wives fighting for large financial settlements. And not every woman is as lucky as Irene was; some with no education, no job, no mother to "borrow" from are fully dependent on an abusive husband or boyfriend.

The economic abuser typically doles out money in amounts so small that the woman is forced, like a child, to ask for more. If he grants it, his condescension humiliates her; if he refuses, his stinginess leaves her in need. In either case he leaves her helplessly in his control. Some men give their women no money at all. An emotionally battered Latvian mother came to court one day with her eight-year-old daughter to translate for her. Desperate for protection from her abusive husband, we went through the customary process, after which we gave her our card, asking her to phone if she needed further help or information. The little girl didn't bother to translate for her mother and answered on her own, "She can't call you. She has no money." No money—not even a few coins for a phone call.

Contrary to the principles of counseling, I have given money to women who come for help. I gave ten dollars for food to a woman with an infant in her arms who left a boyfriend because, although he had agreed to take care of her, he wouldn't give her money for the baby. I have given cab fare to women who fled abusive men to seek shelter in a safe house. I gave bus fare to an abused woman so she could get to her mother's. Although what I did was unprofessional, it took more than professionalism to assure those destitute women safety. Contrary to what Karl Marx said about money turning people into commodities, the money I gave those people had the possibility of turning them back into human beings.

In many countries today, as in the past, a woman is required to present gifts to her husband before marriage— a dowry—and the greater the gifts, the more desirable is the woman. An article in *The New York Times* (December 6, 1993) reported that when a recent bride came from India to join her lawyer husband in New York, he hurled abuse at her as she unpacked her suitcases. "He was expecting gold bracelets and pendants," she explained through tears.

An economic abuser follows in that old dowry tradition. If a wife enters marriage with her own savings, he has her turn it over to him with a verbal brushing aside: "I'll handle the money." If she has a job, he makes her deposit her salary in his account: "It's easier to keep track of our income this way." One woman who reported that she was penniless said that her husband put his seven-hundred-dollar weekly salary plus her two hundred into his bank account and listed their car and condominium in his name. "I think that's unfair," she said. I was nodding my head in agreement when she added, "What's worse, he has all the bills sent to me."

Economic dependence diminishes a woman, and a man may flex his economic muscle in many ways. First, while both appropriating his woman's money and depriving her of his, he may indulge himself lavishly. I knew a young woman, no more than a girl, struggling at home with a baby to buy enough food with the few dollars her husband gave her and to enlarge their small house by redoing the garage so they could use it as a living room. She cooked, cleaned, wallpapered, painted, laid linoleum—like Cinderella, a drudge. Her husband, meanwhile, bought suits that struck his fancy, ate with his friends in posh restaurants, and drove a Cadillac. I couldn't understand then why she stayed with him; I understand now that she couldn't save enough money to leave.

Some economic abusers do their lavish spending not on clothes and cars but on other women, intensifying their wife's hurt by doing so openly. I spoke with a woman whose husband sent flowers to his girlfriends over a period of time, charged them, and had his wife write the check when the bill came. I have spoken to more than one woman who in verifying credit card charges learned of dinners at restaurants to which she was never taken. These men thrust twice with their economic weapon—once to make their wife totally dependent on them for subsistence and again to further debase her through their lavish spending on other women.

Extravagant living at the expense of their wife or girl-friend is a lifestyle to which some economic abusers become quickly accustomed. Unlike social abusers, who forbid their wife to work, many economic abusers insist that their wife take a job to bring in extra money for their bank account; one woman took two jobs and came close to a physical collapse from exhaustion. Others won't let their wives quit jobs and, when circumstances force the issue, resort to even harsher methods.

Doris, for instance, was married to Ralph, a telephone repairman who made an adequate salary but only half as much as hers as a buyer for a retail store for women. Although the disparity of the two paychecks undermined Ralph's ego, he fortified it by banking his own income, squandering Doris's, and emotionally abusing her in the bargain. So stressful did the abuse become that Doris's health began to deteriorate, and on the verge of a complete breakdown she saw a doctor, who advised her to stop working. Ralph refused. Doris grew sicker. The doctor insisted. Ralph still refused. At last Doris collapsed and was forced to quit her job.

"You'd think he would have felt bad and taken care of me, wouldn't you?" Doris asked rhetorically. "He felt bad all right—bad because that money wasn't coming in each week—and the way he took care of me was to beat me black and blue and throw me down the stairs." Although he had never struck her before, he took the loss of her salary as a deliberate attempt to rein him in, resorting to physical battering to maintain control.

An economically abusive man often uses money as a threat. He doesn't control her through fear of losing her children or receiving a beating; he doesn't have to. Just letting her know that at any moment he can deprive her of a home and food and clothes keeps her in willing submission as an alternative to the streets. One woman was so stressed when her husband threatened to sell their house and abandon her that she had an asthma attack and had to be rushed to the hospital.

Another woman found herself in a dead-end situation. Destitute and homeless when her boyfriend walked out on her, she went on welfare. "Only temporarily," she was quick to explain. When I met her, she was in the process of finishing a GED program and was putting her life on track again when the boyfriend sweet-talked his way back into her home. Although his salary as a delivery man raised her economic status above the level of welfare eligibility, he pressured her to continue accepting the weekly checks illegally and depositing them in his account. Finally, her guilt outweighing her fear of him, she rebelled. As she prepared to terminate welfare against his orders, he threatened to report her to the authorities for the fraud she had committed for him.

Now, with eighty credits toward a college degree, which she is determined to earn so she can leave him and support herself and two children, she feels trapped: if she takes the legal choice and gives up welfare, he will report her past illegality; if she continues to collect welfare under false pretenses, he will constantly hold the threat over her head.

Money is a natural weapon for men to wield because, like a gun, it represents power, which according to psychologists, sociologists, psychiatrists, child developmentalists, and other explorers of the human mind, men live in fear of losing. Male vulnerability, it is thought, begins in infancy, where their virility is undermined through dependence upon the Strong Mother. As a result their subconscious plots revenge by gaining dominion in adulthood over all Strong Mothers and their sisters. The adult male, therefore, grows up leery of the adult female because, as Dorothy Dinnerstein writes in *The Mermaid and the Minotaur*, "If he lets her, she can shatter his adult sense of power and control."

To preclude any such possibility, a man takes preventive measures, of which Dinnerstein mentions two. First, he builds male groups within which he feels secure, not simply by clustering with his own kind but by undermining the other kind through exclusion. Male bonding finds greater solidification as an in group when it has an out group to demean; thus, the world sees military units and neighborhood bars and pool parlors and university clubs where a man and his buddies "stick together."

Second, according to Dinnerstein, men protect their vulnerability by keeping sexual relationships at a superficial level on the assumption that if they don't allow themselves to be engulfed as they were by their mother they won't be overpowered. Women may have power by virtue of childbirth and child rearing, men seem to say to themselves, but we call the shots when it comes to sex. As a result, they follow Hugh Hefner's *Playboy* approach, which downgrades love into sexual fun and games, enabling men to think they're in love when they are really only in lust.

A third way men protect and conceal their vulnerability, which Dinnerstein does not mention but which is commonly acknowledged, is by resorting to abuse. A man who feels unafraid of his vulnerability and secure in his power—not necessarily as a man but as a human being—can welcome women into his world and love a woman in an equal relationship. An insecure man, however, threatened by the closeness of a woman, needs continually to reassure himself, like Muhammad Ali, "I am the greatest."

Years ago a man named Leon Samson wrote in *The New Humanist* that "money is the power of impotence." The economic abuser, fearful, weak, threatened, asserts himself as history has paved the way for him. He forces his wife into dependence not only by undermining her self-worth, her sanity, or her social community, as the other types of abusers do, but also by holding over her head deprivation of the body's most basic needs—food and shelter.

Women are able to adapt to economic abuse more readily than to the other three kinds, probably because they have been financially dependent on men all through history—first on their father, then on their husband. As sisters they didn't expect education if there was funding for a brother only; as spinsters they expected to become the charity case in their brother's home; as widows they expected to remarry a "well-off" man; as mothers they sought a "good" marriage for their daughters. Economic abuse is therefore almost a genetic inheritance, but like hemophilia and Tay-Sachs, it destroys.

Some women, however, develop tricks for coping with it. Since the economic abuser treats his woman as if she were a child, she in turn may have to act like a child to survive. Children, much to their dismay, are forced by our culture to endure a long period of parental dependence during years of school and perhaps college and graduate work, having no means of self-support. For most, their after-school jobs do little more than buy CDs, movies, and, if they are lucky, eventually a secondhand car—a mere taste of the honey of independence.

Economically abusive husbands put their wives in a similar situation. When denied the privilege of earning and saving for themselves, these women must seek other—childish—means of coping. One woman admitted to cajoling her husband as she had her father when she was a little girl. "I'd fix a nice dinner, light candles, tell him how wonderful he was, agree to any kind of sex he wanted no matter how weird. Eventually I'd work up to needing another ten or twenty dollars. Sometimes it worked." However, sometimes it didn't, resulting only in greater abuse.

Other women, far less theatrical, use a direct approach: they steal. Many women have told me how they slip a bill from their husband's shirt or pants pocket when he's asleep, praying that he won't count what remains. If he does, the jig is up: he hides his money or sleeps with it under his pillow. Irene says she knows how they feel because she resorted to the same ignominious means, sliding a few bills from those clipped together in her husband's side trouser pocket, working deftly to avoid rattling the change. Irene felt—all of them feel—ashamed, belittled, self-hating. Never guilty.

On a Sally Jessy Raphael television show early in 1994, a man and his abused wife described their relationship with candor: she complained that he made her obey his every wish and gave her no money; he justified his behavior as his male right. So controlling was this husband that no one in the audience volunteered support for him. One angry man was compelled to remark, "Why don't you buy a dog instead? It'll do anything you want."

Many men and women in the audience were outraged, urging the wife to leave; one asked what the man would do if she did. With the assurance of an absolute ruler, as if bestowing the wisdom of imperial Caesar, he replied, "She has no choice but to stay with me."

Therein lies the tragedy of the economically abused woman: because she never has a penny, she never has a choice.

PART II

How Does Nonphysical Abuse Happen?

CHAPTER 5

"It's always been that way."

The Historical Acceptance of Abuse

Such duty as the subject owes the prince,
Even such a woman oweth to her husband.

SHAKESPEARE WROTE THAT in the late 1500s, putting in
Petruchio's mouth the conviction that every red-blooded
man of his time believed and that Tennyson echoed 250
years later: that "woman is the lesser man."

The history of woman's place in the world has been written in similar words and deeds from earliest times. Visiting
Lascaux or Les Eyzies, one can almost see the caveman dragging his woman to his lair, keeping her there to tend his
fires and whelp his babies while he joins the company of men
to bring home the woolly mammoth and paint his courage
for the ages on the wall.

Imagination plays games in creating that scenario, but
history need not play games. So consistent has it been in rel-
egating women to inferior status that it is on the same set

and with the same script that scenes of abuse are staged today.

In ancient Egypt, while spectacular feats of engineering built the pyramids, filling them with gold for the miraculously preserved bodies of kings, men were legally knocking out the teeth of wives with bricks if they dared to speak ill of them.

Centuries later in ancient Greece, even in the Golden Age at the height of civilization in the 400s B.C., men were regarded as so far superior to women that only they were credited with the ability to feel life's great passions. To experience love, for instance, a young man was attached not to a woman but to an older man. Later, though the young man would marry and have children, he would continue to love that man, fighting to the death alongside him on the battlefield. Marriage to a woman, according to the Greek playwright Menander, was "an evil, but a necessary evil."

When the Romans conquered Greece several hundred years later, they brought with them a justice system, their legacy to the development of much of the Western world, among which were laws regarding women. In those laws the Romans formalized the servile status of wives, packaging them as property. Like his house, his furnishings, his land, and his gold coins, a woman was owned by her husband; like his slaves, she owed him obedience.

The passing of time did not improve the status of women. In the Middle Ages they were still taken into marriage as property and treated with less care than their husband's armor and tapestries. It is not difficult to picture a group of thirteenth-century men nodding in agreement and laughing over this aphorism, which was popular at the time:

> *A spaniel, a woman, and a hickory tree,*
> *The more ye beat them, the better they be.*

In newly settled America, wives remained as dependent and insignificant as their children, especially their daughters, and were lawfully exposed to public stocks and dunking for crimes such as nagging their husband. As recently as the late nineteenth century they were still legally forbidden to declare ownership of property, money, and even their own children. While wives were granted no legal grounds for divorce, not even for adultery, which was considered a woman's shame, not a man's, their husbands had no difficulty in obtaining one. If, in lieu of the divorce a woman was denied, she ran away, her husband published public notices threatening to sue anyone who took her in.

Some women, of course, made the break, being forced afterward to spend a lifetime fighting the scorn of society while most men regarded them at best as fools and at worst as wantons. Some few men, however, applauded these early feminists. Sir James Barrie, that most proper knight of the realm, wrote a one-act play called *The Twelve Pound Look*, in which Kate, the former wife of Sir Harry Sims, another proper knight of the realm, appears at his home, now graced by a new wife, some years after their divorce. She enters, typewriter in hand, sent out by an agency in response to Sir Harry's request for a temporary secretary. Having been puzzled for all these years over why Kate was so foolish as to leave her good husband and good life, Sir Harry receives the following explanation: since he had treated her like a nonperson, she had rented a typewriter, taught herself to type, and, when she had saved enough money—twelve pounds to be exact—bought her own machine and set out, a free woman.

Lady Sims, who has heard all this from the doorway, asks her husband's permission to come in and watches with envy as Kate leaves, eyes a-sparkle. The play ends with Lady Sims reflecting as she asks her husband, "Are they very expensive?"

"Are what expensive?" Lord Sims asks gruffly with little interest.

"Those machines," she says, a faraway dream in her eye. And the audience silently cheers for a new woman in the making.

Across the water in Norway, Henrik Ibsen wrote an even more pointed play that ends with the slam of a door that has echoed for 125 years—*A Doll's House.* Explaining why she is leaving her husband, Nora tells him, "You arranged everything according to your own taste, and so I got the same tastes as you—or else I pretended to. . . . It seems to me as if I have been living here like a poor woman, just from hand to mouth. I have existed merely to perform tricks for you. . . . You have committed a great sin against me."

The world was shocked. So great was the outcry against Ibsen after his sympathetic portrayal of a woman who pinpointed every husband's "sin" against his wife and dared to seek independence, that he countered it by writing the opposite scenario in *Ghosts.* In this play he turned the tables by having a wife remain with her profligate husband, only to be ironically rewarded by her husband's contracting syphilis, her son's becoming blind, and her own suffering. Although Ibsen's feminist message rang thunderously in the hearts of women, it did little to alter their status. Even today American institutions mirror not Ibsen's but history's view of women. To give just a few examples:

Marriage

Until recently marriage was a legal way to subjugate a woman: "Love, honor, and obey" said it all. Even with *obey* stricken from the vow, tradition kept women duty-bound to please their men: Marabel Morgan devoted a whole best-selling book, *The Total Woman,* to step-by-step instruction in diverse imaginative techniques a woman could employ to keep her man happy enough to stay, and each month women's magazines reveal endless secrets on "How to Hold Your Man," "How to Make Sex Better for Your Man," "How to Prepare Erotic Dishes for Your Man," etc. Female subjugation apparently sells.

The very fact that a woman relinquishes her own family name for her husband's announces his ownership to the world. Those women who retain their maiden name or link it to their husband's are the Kates and Noras of today. They are also pragmatists, since tracing the whereabouts of a married woman is all but impossible unless you know whom she married . . . and where . . . and when. That too makes a statement.

Law

Statistics indicate that men frequently receive better treatment than women in our courts of law. Women have been hounded into lives of running and hiding with their children for refusing court-ordered visitation with a father who has sexually abused those children. A woman's underground, as efficient and courageous—as hazardous too—as the slave underground prior to the Civil War, exists to protect these women from capture and imprisonment.

Until less than ten years ago a man could rape his wife with impunity; if she put up a fight against his sexual use of her, the crime was hers, not his. Despite the law passed in the mid-1980s that made wife rape as criminal an offense as any other rape, many men believe that sex, consensual or forced, is a husband's right; as I write this, just this week a woman came to the court where I work seeking protection from her estranged husband, who kept crashing into her home to rape her as his husbandly claim.

Juries have been accused of leaning toward the old belief that if a man rapes a woman she asked for it. Capitalizing on this, defense lawyers in alleged rape cases work hard to switch the role of victim from the woman to the man by focusing on her checkered past and loose morals. William Kennedy Smith, who was charged with rape, was ultimately aquitted in part, many think, because the woman had picked him up at a neighborhood bar and voluntarily accompanied him to his uncle's beach house.

An Englishman named George Horace Hatherill expressed some years ago what many feel is America's legal position on women in America today when he jested, "There are about twenty murders a year in London, and not all are serious—some are just husbands killing their wives."

Human Sciences

A great deal of antifeminist thinking is attributed to Sigmund Freud, based on his presumption that women's emotional problems stem largely from penis envy. That men have something women lack and long for seems far more metaphorical than actual because it is not those few inches of flesh women want but the power and control its owners are afforded by the world.

Much of accepted psychological thinking relies not only on Freud's views of women but on other questionable sources as well. For instance, the late Dr. Lawrence Kohlberg of Harvard developed a theory of moral development that attributed higher levels of maturity to men than to women. However, his female co-worker, Carol Gilligan, realized after the study was acclaimed as a breakthrough that since Kohlberg had carried out his studies on only male subjects, he had produced male-slanted findings. She challenged Kohlberg. In her subsequent book, *In a Different Voice*, Gilligan set the record straight, supporting the belief that because women's moral values differ from men's—are neither better nor worse, just different—Kohlberg could not draw unisex conclusions based on the male population of his study.

The social sciences are famous for creating indexes on which to measure society's problems and progress. While for a hundred years and more they have studied and tabulated statistics on a broad range of events from homicides to births, levels of poverty to limits of education, and marriages to divorces, not until 1970 did they consider the need for measuring spouse abuse; it simply did not exist.

Politics

A look at American government does not convince one that the promise of sexual equality has been fulfilled. Women outnumber men in the country's population, yet not until 1994 did the one hundred members of the U.S. Senate include enough women to count on one and a half hands— 7 percent—nor did the House of Representatives with 435 members have enough women to count on eight six-packs of soda—11 percent. Legislators have refused to pass an equal rights amendment on the grounds that it is superfluous, the Constitution having granted Americans equality more than 200 years ago; yet despite constitutional equality, it took 150 years for women to be granted an equal right to vote. A scan of history further reveals that legislators are far more reluctant to pass financial bills to help women than munitions bills to help men, as welfare, child care, low-cost housing, and abortion indicate.

Presidents too have expressed their antiwoman sentiments. In 1945 when a group of women met Harry Truman with well-researched arguments for an equal rights amendment, he dismissed them, according to David McCullough in *Truman*, with the comment to his aides, "What a lot of hooey!" More recently, in 1981, Ronald Reagan, righteous proponent of the American family, expressed his sentiments by shutting down the Office of Domestic Violence, an agency set up to protect women. As Randy Shilts asked in *Conduct Unbecoming*, "Was he saying a program to stop wife-beating was anti-family?" Or, as I ask, was he simply saying, "If a man batters his wife, don't interfere"?

The Arts

While the names of even dubious male artists are familiar, the average person can name only a few, if any, women artists. Yet from the earliest Native American weaving and leather painting through colonial quilting, nineteenth-century portrait painting, and more recent pop art and feminist painting, women have produced memorable works of art. But it hasn't been easy. They have had to contend with what Charlotte S. Rubenstein in her book *American Women Artists* calls "piety, purity, submissiveness, and domesticity," finding little time to focus on painting and little support for it when they did.

Mary Cassatt, according to the author, was a dedicated artist; yet when she announced to her father that she was going to study at art centers abroad, as her male counterparts regularly did, he proclaimed that he would rather see her dead. When she came back to the United States some years later, highly acclaimed throughout Europe, the *Philadelphia Ledger* announced her return with the following short notice:

"Mary Cassatt, sister of Mr. Cassatt, President of the Pennsylvania Railroad, returned from Europe yesterday. She has been studying painting in France and owns the smallest Pekingese dog in the world."

In 1898 a woman artist's corporate executive brother and her unique dog were more noteworthy than her art.

Almost a hundred years later another American artist, Helen Frankenthaler, whose work has been shown extensively and praised by critics and the public alike, received a review from a critic who echoes the attitudes of the *Philadelphia Ledger*. The reviewer for the *Washington Post*, after her last show there, felt that her work was much overrated, pointing out her flaws and failings in detail. To have a fact-based opinion is his right and his obligation as an art critic. However, this critic continued, not with a valid opinion but with oft-heard macho reasoning, to attribute her success to factors other than talent: first, that she was a woman and an attractive one at that; and second, that she was married to the artist Robert Motherwell. Though separated by almost a century, the two journalists dismissed the talents of Mary Cassatt and Helen Frankenthaler not on the merit of their work but also on their alleged achievement through the merit of the men in their lives.

Women writers and actresses have shared a somewhat similar history. The former for years were forced to use male noms de plume to be published. I have shocked many a college student in my class by breaking the news that George Eliot was really Mary Ann Evans, and I myself am shocked to read current book reviews more than a hundred years later that refer to a "woman novelist" while never reading one about a "man novelist."

As for actresses, women were not even allowed on a stage until long after theater had become a major art form. While Italy allowed women to perform in Commedia dell'Arte in the sixteenth century, England and France continued to have boys take women's roles in plays for another hundred years. Now, although women are welcomed into the theater—for who would pay to see a man as Juliet or Blanche DuBois?—their common complaint is the paucity of good parts. Man is the hero whom the playwright and screen-writer deem worthy to explore; man is the hero the public pays to watch. Since the wives and lovers of heroes are mere women and therefore less riveting, few Candidas, St. Joans, and Madwomen of Chaillot are given birth.

The Military

So obvious is the military degradation of women that it hardly bears discussion. War is a macho endeavor, which by its very nature solidifies male bonding by dehumanizing the enemy—sometimes the "Huns," sometimes the "Japs," sometimes the "geeks," always the women. Women were the spoils of war in primitive tribes, in so-called civilized third-century Rome, and still are in our American wars, where soldiers purchase women with as little as a chocolate bar or a pair of nylons in the countries they occupy. The opera *Madama Butterfly*, the play *Miss Saigon*, and the movie *Platoon* turn military exploitation into art forms. The Vietnam War turned it into tens of thousands of Vietnamese-American children, abandoned, ejected, living in the streets.

The military exercises the macho, antifeminist attitude toward women in times of peace as well. I interviewed marines who with only minor embarrassment chanted for me a name to which they drilled in rhythm every morning—Susie Rottencrotch. For years navy men sexually abused women at their Tailhook convention; "We were just having fun," they explained. When one navy woman dared spoil the fun by blowing the whistle, the whole navy rose in defense, even the top brass. Only when scapegoats were found and the case tried did the navy take responsibility, not for assault or harassment, which were the actual crimes but not the ones with which the navy could cope. The navy charged the men with what the navy considered the only real crime—conduct unbecoming an officer.

President Clinton's effort to end discrimination against homosexuals in the military aroused strong resistance on the grounds that gays and lesbians pose imminent danger. Gays threaten them: in the words of many soldiers, "I couldn't take a shower or walk around like I do with them there." It is ironic—and tragic—that they attribute to gays the same predatory feelings for men that they themselves deny having for women, despite statistics that report a far higher rate of sexual crimes among heterosexual than among homosexual men, especially in the military.

Lesbians threaten military men too. As Randy Shilts points out in *Conduct Unbecoming,* sailors make frequent passes at their female shipmates. If a woman rejects their sexual advances, men defend their wounded ego by labeling her a lesbian; why else would she not succumb to their charm? Why else, indeed? This might be as funny as Aesop's fable of the fox and the grapes, which he labeled sour when he couldn't reach them, except for the fact that many women have been forced out of the navy with less than honorable discharges because of the false accusation. The hierarchy obviously protects the navy by supporting the pride of one of its men over the reputation and the job of one of its women.

Medicine

A famous word puzzle went like this: after an automobile accident a man is rushed into emergency surgery, where the surgeon pales upon seeing him and cries, "This is my son!" However, the surgeon is not the man's father. How can this be?

Today it is obvious—or almost obvious—that the surgeon is the injured man's mother. Twenty years ago, when I first confronted the puzzle, it was far less obvious because mind-set had established that surgeons were men. Even now with our acknowledgment that women doctors exist—although we still hear "I wouldn't go to one"—we think last of women surgeons, despite evidence, I am told, that their smaller fingers equip them better for work such as brain and open-heart surgery and angioplasty.

A great deal has been written lately about the abandon with which doctors perform hysterectomies and mastectomies. Some statistics as high as one in twenty claim the operations are unnecessary since other, less deforming methods are available with equal rates of success. I myself underwent three breast biopsies, which my surgeon said were warranted, to remove calcifications indicated on a mammogram. Although in the three processes he cut away half of my left breast, he never found the calcifications, nor have I had any trouble in the ensuing eight years. The radiologist who assisted him, a "woman doctor," told me afterward that she believed I didn't need the biopsies in the first place and would never have recommended them.

A report by Paul Hoffman on the March 8, 1994, "MacNeil/Lehrer NewsHour" revealed some shocking statistics. In the same way that Lawrence Kohlberg applied to women his findings from male studies, many medical researchers broaden their findings from men to encourage treatments for women as well. Results in some cases have been tragic: Hoffman gave examples of thalidomide, which damaged thousands of babies because it had not been tested adequately on women; of aspirin, which has been prescribed to fight heart attacks in men but not in women, although the rate of heart attacks is about the same; most recently of painkillers, which have not been developed specifically for women, whose brains react differently to pain from men's. "Scientists cling to the male body as the norm," Hoffman claims, impeding development of treatments that could save the lives of women.

Medicine's male focus bears directly on abuse. In an article entitled "Medical Therapy as Repression: The Case of the Battered Woman" quoted by the Center for Women Policy Studies in Washington, D.C., Evan Stark and Ann Flitcraft report that doctors appear reluctant to attribute women's injuries to battering. While they, particularly doctors in hospital emergency rooms, dress the wounds and set the bones of thousands of battered women, they identify only one out of twenty-five cases as abuse. The other twenty-four are either dismissed summarily or categorized as problem women because they appear so often—"Oh, *her* again!" In either case doctors, in a strategic position to treat the cause of injury as well as the injury itself, do nothing, and the abuse continues.

Religion

God became a male when the great pagan earth goddess became a threat to men. When Father Abraham established the first monotheistic religion about seven thousand years ago, he mirrored God in his own male image just as God had created Abraham in His image. Down through the ages the Judeo-Christian tradition has reaffirmed sexual inequality throughout its teachings and practices. In the beginning the "evil" with which the Greek poet Menander associated wives manifested itself in Eve, the seductress who lured Adam into the fall of man. From that time on—in women like Lot's wife, Delilah, Jezebel, and Salome—Eve's seduction and Adam's fall have been reenacted in the Bible. What of the good women of the Bible? What of Sarah, the patient wife of Abraham? And Queen Esther, who risked her life to save the Jews? And Judith, who killed Holofernes? What of the three Marys in the New Testament—Virgin Mary, the maternal; Mary the mother of James, the faithful; Mary Magdalene, the redeemed? Had the goodness of these women been allowed to offset the general evil men attributed to women, for all time men might have judged women as they judge themselves, with ambivalence, saying, "We are the same in goodness and evil. We are the same human mixture. We are equal."

However, it didn't work that way. Man's psyche faced a dilemma: to deny that *all* women were basically sinful meant acknowledging them as equals, thereby relinquishing male dominion; to deny that *some* women were basically virtuous meant grouping all of them together in a circle of sirens, depriving men of acceptable wives. Neither alternative being acceptable, they created the ideal solution deep within their subconscious, where sexuality plays. While they were still unable to merge two conflicting aspects in any single woman, they split womankind down the middle into the whore and the madonna. The whore woman bears the evil of sexuality; the madonna woman bears the fragile purity men protect on a pedestal. The result, psychohistorians like Dr. David Beisel of Rockland County Community College claim, has shaped the role of women throughout history and established man's supremacy forever.

Employment

History is the long, long story of the male workplace—a throne or a boardroom, an assembly line or bank, a battlefield or the Oval Office, a science lab or an art gallery. Wherever man has worked, history has happened; and wherever it has happened, men have recorded it. The story of women's workplace is short—in the kitchen, the broom closet, the delivery room, and the nursery.

While men have received pay for their work in either money or glory and sometimes in both, women, unsung volunteers, have for the most part received neither. Several years ago a woman suing for "back pay" in a divorce case listed the jobs she had performed for her husband, for which he owed her money: cook, chauffeur, laundress, cleaning woman, governess, teacher, hostess, bartender, secretary, buffer against the world, and mistress. As she pointed out, if she had been a hired employee, she would have earned hundreds of thousands of dollars of marriage time.

Not only are women deprived of an income as housewives, until fairly recently they have been deprived even of a chance to work outside their home. During World War I they were propagandized with patriotic words to replace their men in factories, to become teammates making the clothing and arms their men needed to "fight the Hun." After the war, however, their men needed them back home, so off they went away from the work world, out of overalls into aprons. World War II recalled them again to man the assembly lines and desks and construction sites their men had marched away from, but as soon as they marched home again, Rosie the Riveter lost her job to woman the kitchen.

Statistics indicate that today more women work than stay home, which sounds encouraging until you realize that they have lower-level jobs than men and that they are paid on a far lower scale. Few top corporate executives are women, few financiers, few utilities owners; fewer control the stock market and international trade. Even in education, the second-oldest profession for women, they are disproportionately kept out of top positions. Elementary schools couldn't exist without them as teachers; middle and high schools might find themselves understaffed; but at the college level fewer than half the faculty are women, and fewer than a third attain administrative positions.

Church bureaucracies are notoriously antiwoman. The Catholic Church stands staunchly against women becoming priests; Protestant Churches and Jewish synagogues have only slightly more than 8 percent women leading congregations; and *The New York Times* reported in early 1994 that despite 70 percent female membership in black churches, no women are granted the power to preach.

The Continuation of Historical Abuse

Men have used their political and economic power not only to keep women in their inferior place but also to humiliate and brutalize them. For more than a thousand years Western law exonerated men who beat their wives, although civilization imposed some restrictions: for instance, in the Middle Ages a man had to follow the rule of thumb when beating his wife, which meant using a stick no thicker than his thumb. While the early Puritan settlers in the New World meted out public punishment to errant wives, men in the new America of 1800 adopted the harsher English law of wife beating. While it was revoked on the books seven years later, according to Emerson and Russell Dobash in *Violence Against Wives*, "the law winked at wife beating."

It seems times have not changed. Lenore Walker in *The Battered Woman* reports on a test in which the reactions of passersby to two people fighting on the street were observed; while many tried to stop a fight between two men, far fewer interfered when the fight was between a man and a woman. The attitude appears to have come down through the years that "when a man beats his wife, he probably has a good reason that doesn't involve the law or me."

Some men look at wife beating as a joke. Dallas Green, manager of the rock-bottom Mets baseball team in 1993, when asked how he copes with his failure, was reported in *The New York Times* as saying, "I just beat the hell out of Sylvia [his wife] and kick the dog and whatever else I've got to do to get it out . . . and then come back to the park and try to smile a little bit and get after it again." No one asked whether Sylvia was laughing at her husband's attempt at humor. And the millions of wives whose husbands and boyfriends do exactly what Dallas Green quipped about don't have to be asked.

Although statistics indicate that the United States has the highest rate of wife abuse today, they ignore those countries in which the law either condones it or looks the other way. For instance, the Chinese government, which supports forced sterilization and abortion to maintain the one-baby law, ignores the thousands of girl babies put to death in infancy because boys are considered more valuable. Sudan and Somalia still demand clitoral mutilation. In Burma and Thailand girls are forced into prostitution, and it took a full half century for the Japanese to acknowledge the Korean women they turned over as playthings for their soldiers in World War II. In Saudi Arabia the law allows a maid to be beaten. In the Congo adultery is illegal for women only, not for men. In Zaire two-thirds more girls are forced to abandon their education than boys (*The New York Times*, February 3, 1994).

I have winced over photographs of the Central African Sara tribe's mutilation of Ubangi women: the pierced lower lip stretched with hard wooden disks from birth. I have learned that suttee, though illegal now in India, is still forced on many women by the families of their dead husbands. And I have seen firsthand in the Long Neck hill tribes of Thailand young girls, their necks elongated by metal rings circled one on another, and their mothers whose necks have stretched even longer with more rings over more years.

History and custom have set the stage for men to batter their women, to create lawful sexism, and to empower a privileged male minority. Without a sense of wrongdoing. Without guilt. With self-righteousness. "What a piece of work is a man!" exclaims Hamlet for all men.

In *The Mermaid and the Minotaur,* which explores the sexual inequality of men and women, Dorothy Dinnerstein proposes that men acquire the right to batter women at birth. "Men's feeling that we are not really human originates in their infancy," she writes. "Our own reactive feeling— that it is men who are not really human, 'not all there'— comes late." Too late in history. Too late in the lives of battered women.

CHAPTER 6

"I didn't even know
what it was."

The Subtle Patterns of Abuse

IT WAS 1943. American boys were sailing to France and Italy
for World War II, American girls were knitting Red Cross
socks, and American parents were believing in patriotism.
Terry was nineteen, a junior in college and as caught up in
the motions and emotions of war as everyone else. From her
dormitory window she watched Waves who were training on
campus march briskly to their classes and men in navy dress
whites and army khakis stroll between buildings with their
dates.

John and she would be one of those couples tonight.
Having graduated from Tufts two days before, he was driving down to ask her to marry him before he left for Officers' Candidate School in New Jersey. *Ask* was the wrong
word, she knew, because John never asked for anything;
demand was more his style.

Terry had begun dating John when they were in high school together—only occasionally, though, since she didn't want to go steady. Yet she would spy him following her like a private investigator when she dated someone else and find him waiting at her door when she came home. He had vowed never to let her go and had persisted so relentlessly in his demands that she had finally acquiesced and accepted his class ring. Now, she wondered whether, under his relentless pressure, she could stave off a wedding ring.

He would arrive later in the day with flowers, handsome in his uniform, an engagement ring in his shirt pocket. Terry felt trapped. On one hand she was flattered; on the other, suffocated. He had been steamrollering her for years, it seemed, and she was worn down. He loved her; she was sure of that. As she stood at the window waiting, she guessed she loved him, and the war was on, and he would go overseas and maybe get killed, and everyone was getting married, and how could she be so cruel? Terry married John.

In 1993, at a party arranged by their three children to celebrate their golden wedding anniversary, amid the toasts and hugs and kisses, Terry whispered to me, "What a joke! These fifty years have been a journey into hell." She climbed aboard for that journey the first night she invited John into the house for coffee when she found him at her doorstep after her date with Whatshisname; the journey continues still because John is an abuser.

No woman enters marriage saying "This man will abuse me, but I don't care; I'll marry him anyway." Most enter never knowing; some, like Terry, may subconsciously suspect but rationalize away their doubts; and a few marry fully aware that he is an abuser but convinced that with the "right woman" he will change. The second wife of a man I met falls into this last category. Although his first wife obtained a divorce on the grounds of mental cruelty, of which the second wife was aware, she convinced herself that the other wife had been half crazy and that all he needed was a good woman to put his life back on track. She, like all abused wives, accompanied Terry on her journey into hell.

Terry's journey began with a surprise outburst of name-calling when her train arrived late at John's ocs camp one weekend; blaming her instead of the Pennsylvania Railroad, he yelled, "You are so damn dumb. Couldn't you have caught an earlier train?" Although staggered, Terry found a way to understand—the war and all—and John apologized so profusely and made love so urgently that she soon forgot.

Until next time, when they were living in a rented apartment in Monroe, Louisiana, and he told her to get out and go back home to her mother since she wrote her so many letters. And next time, when he made her give away the stray cat she adopted. And next time . . . and next time . . . and next time, yelling at her, blaming her, cutting her off from friends, making her feel like a nonentity. Terry explained John's outbursts as fits of bad temper, usually deserved, and worked ever harder to please him to make life smooth.

What Terry and most women do not know is that wife battering, whether physical or nonphysical, is not a lone instance of bad temper or two or three instances. A man doesn't commit a single abusive act in anger, apologize, and then in another fit of pique strike out again sometime later. That's an outburst of temper, of which most of us are occasionally guilty. Abuse is different: rather than a series of unrelated events in which a man lashes out randomly, abuse is systematic behavior following a specific pattern that is designed to gain, secure, and exercise control. What shape that pattern takes depends on the way different professionals interpret it.

The Escalator of Abuse

John's abuse of Terry followed the pattern of an escalator; it kept going up and up and up. As a high school sweetheart he pursued her with phone calls, followed her home, guarded her jealously at social events. As a husband, by playing sick or demanding her help on an undertaking, he manipulated situations so that she felt compelled to stay home with him, or else he injected himself into her outside activities by joining her book club and standing by as an extra when she played bridge. He wouldn't even let her go to college reunions without him.

When, having come slowly to the realization that he was taking over her life, she defied him, her situation worsened because what had been coercion became commands. Although she usually obeyed to avoid the fury of his name-calling and threats, he took no chances but began monitoring her phone calls and followed her when she did errands in town. When she applied for a secretarial job as an escape hatch, he canceled her application and later made her drop the volunteer work she had signed up for at the hospital. "I just couldn't fight him," Terry explains. "It was less painful to give in." She had given in to his ring with marriage, to his manipulation with pliability, to his orders with obedience, and at last to his rules with submission.

Women caught on the escalator of abuse claim they can't remember when it dawned on them that it was abuse. It happens so steadily, so inexorably that there's no time out to gain perspective. They can't cite one lone traumatic moment that identifies their partner's behavior as abusive—not "the day he said I couldn't go to my mother's," nor "the time he called me a stupid bitch," nor "the morning he hid the car keys." No, the escalator pattern of abuse creates a lifestyle of whole cloth from which the woman can no more pull individual threads than the so-called rich and famous can point to their swimming pool or designer gown as a singular evidence of their status.

Women cope with this escalator of abuse in one of two ways: they either fight it or submit to it in the way of a cornered animal that either bares its teeth and attacks its captor or falls on its back in submission. Those like Terry who choose the latter route try to meet every demand their husband imposes, catering to his every pleasure, making his displeasures go away, humbly acknowledging his power. For the sake of peace they accept isolation and blame and low self-esteem, and though they end up having no support system, no one to call friend—not even themselves—they consider their survival worth the pain.

Despite their willingness to pay whatever price is exacted, their husband cheats them, for as soon as they meet his demands, his demands increase. No longer is he satisfied that they cut off relationships with their friends; now they must stop contacting their family as well. No longer does he tell them what to wear; now he also shops for them. What they had learned he wanted of them before they have to unlearn; and what he now wants they must learn anew. No matter how submissively they defer to his control, be it with the fear of Simon Legree's slaves, he requires constant new shows of power.

If, on the other hand, a wife takes the alternate course, to fight his abuse, she is even worse off. Each challenge she throws at him becomes a threat to his control. She won't recook his dinner; she won't stop visiting her mother; she won't have sex on demand. She won't? She *will.* Like a parent withholding candy from a recalcitrant child, he punishes her in ways designed to hurt the most: he locks her in the house, twists her mind, abuses her children. Because she has dared defiance, his demands become greater and his punishments harsher. And so the abuse escalates.

According to most professionals, abuse takes place on a continuum on which there is a point—a specific instance perhaps—at which the woman says, "No more." I have seen women in court who have lived with escalating abuse for as long as forty years and then suddenly refused to take any more. Luckier women—or stronger or more desperate or more resourceful or more supported or suddenly freer women—reach this point sooner. Some leave their men. Some kill them. One cut off his penis. Some women, like Terry, haven't yet reached that point on the continuum. They are still there.

The Never-Ending Cycle

A second pattern that has been identified by professionals who work with abused women shapes itself into a cycle. They see not the steady upward climb of an escalator but the continuation of a circle that, like a wallpaper design, repeats itself again and again. Even though many professionals interpret abuse as a repeating cycle, they identify different events as the thrust from which the cycle gains momentum.

From Stress to Abuse

Lenore Walker in *The Battered Woman* describes a cycle of violence in which many abused women see themselves trapped. It begins with the normal stresses with which all relationships have to cope, stresses brought on by children, jobs, financial concerns, irritating habits, and mere differences of opinion. In nonabusive relationships people cope with such stresses by either ignoring them or talking them out, with the result that tensions abate and the couple goes on as before. Unable to do that, they end up in either an unhappy marriage or a divorce court.

In abusive relationships, however, which may continue for years, the tension does not abate. It increases. Lacking coping skills, the man grows angrier as his nerves become more frayed. The woman becomes frightened, and he, like a jaguar singling out a weak gazelle, pounces for the kill. Battering takes place. While Walker deals primarily with physical battering, nonphysical battering follows the same pattern. Instead of slapping or punching, the man screams, calls her names, locks her up, threatens, hits the children, throws things, cuts up her clothes, maybe for days and weeks. Fear, humiliation, and a sense of worthlessness overwhelm the woman in both cases. In physical abuse, however, a woman bandages her wounds; in nonphysical abuse she can't reach them.

The next point on the cycle, according to Walker, is a time of contrition, during which he says he is sorry, brings flowers, cries, promises it will never happen again. She begins to feel better. He explains that he didn't mean what he said and wouldn't have acted that way if she hadn't brought it on. She agrees and promises to be more careful in the future. Now ensues a period of calm, a honeymoon. He is friendly, even affectionate. They talk, see friends, make love, and get along like any nonabusive couple. As the seductiveness of this truce sets in, she allows herself to hope, even to believe that the trouble in their relationship is over and things will be better from now on.

However, the everyday stresses of life know no truce: irritations and frustrations and failures inevitably arise. While he may cope with them adequately for a week or a month, they begin to stretch his nerves taut once again. Tension builds. Battering erupts. Apologies pour forth. Calm ensues. Hope springs anew . . . and there are life's stresses again.

This stop-and-go process of abuse is difficult to deal with because in addition to the pain brought on by the abuse itself is the pain brought on by never knowing when it will erupt. We have all experienced the heightened pleasure that anticipation adds to a happy occasion like a vacation; women caught in the cycle of abuse experience the heightened anguish that anticipation—call it foreboding—adds to their already anguished lives. One woman described it as living on the edge of a volcano. "I rebuild my home after it's been damaged by the lava flow, only to have it totally destroyed by the next eruption. Then I rebuild again."

We see cyclically abused women in Family Court frequently. They come in after a bout of battering has pushed them over the brink applying for orders of protection, which they get on a temporary basis the same day with a date to return to court in three or four weeks to make the order permanent. A good many of these women don't return because their abuser has pulled back, allowing hope to reemerge. As a result, the court invalidates the temporary order, and the women are back where they were before the battering incident that brought them to court in the first place.

A few months or a year or so later, we recognize the face or the name as the woman reapplies for an order of protection. We dig out the old file and ask why she didn't follow through last time. "Things seemed to get better," she explains. "I thought he had changed." He hadn't changed, and things got better only for a short time. The cycle continued, and we who are trying to help her pray to ourselves that the next time she will understand the overall pattern of which she is a part and will follow through to end it.

From Resentment to Despotism

Ernest Andrews in *The Emotionally Disturbed Family* describes the cycle of abuse somewhat differently. He sees it beginning in resentment that both the man and his wife feel. Although he does not detail what gives rise to the resentment, a hundred abused women can give a hundred different sources of their resentment: his air of superiority, his lack of communication, his friends, his discipline with the children, his insistence on having his way, his refusal to help, his disapproval of her cooking, his sexual demands, etc. A hundred abusive men can also give a hundred different sources of their resentment: her stupidity, her arguments, her childishness, her demands for money, her friends, her disobedience, her dependence on her parents, her overuse of the telephone, etc. And each man and each woman can give at least ninety-two additional wellsprings of resentment.

As a woman's resentment builds, it shows in her face and tone of voice and general response to a man, all of which add fire to his smoldering resentment. This drives the relationship into the second phase of the cycle, which in Andrews's words is "despotism," in our words abuse. Worn out from perhaps years of previous rotations of this cycle and having learned that fighting back only makes matters worse, the woman responds with what Andrews calls "compliance with passivity." As a result, both slide into the fourth and final phase in which she is frustrated by her inability to stand up to his abusive behavior and he is frustrated by her increased helplessness and his own lack of control. Now, with the cycle complete, the old resentments reestablish themselves on a scale made even larger by the new ones that have accumulated.

When Irene tries to shape her own marriage into a pattern, it is the Andrews pattern it most closely fits. She can remember entering marriage with nothing but love and a belief in forever. Her husband grew resentful of her pleas for affection and her efforts at closeness, so foreign to his understanding that he interpreted them as childishness. She in turn grew resentful of his hardness and coldness and of his meanness with money, all of which she interpreted as hatred.

His "despotism" took the form of emotionally withdrawing, isolating her, undermining her self-confidence, forcing economic dependence on her. She used to have a recurring dream in which she saw a fragile crystal ball in the palm of a hand, and the hand would unremittingly close on the ball, slowly crushing it. Then, turning upside down, the hand would let the thousand broken bits of glass fall away and reveal itself unbleeding and uncut. In time she knew she was the crystal ball shattered in her husband's uninjured hand.

In response to her husband's "despotism," her "compliance with passivity" took the form of avoiding him as much as possible by absorbing herself in the children and in her work, asking nothing of him and eventually giving little. Each of them, unable to fulfill the other's needs, grew frustrated and angry. Her response turned inward into desperation: what could she do to make him love her? His response turned outward into rage: what could he do to control her? Since the questions were asked with increasing intensity and never answered, the result was deeper resentments, stronger abusive behavior from him, greater submissiveness from her, and a playing-out of the cycle again . . . and again . . . and again.

The Wheel of Abuse

The Domestic Abuse Intervention Project in Duluth, Minnesota, sees abuse taking a different shape—a wheel. At the hub is the single unit of Power and Control. On the outer rim is violence. Each of the eight spokes leading from Power and Control to ultimate Violence is a different form of non-physical abuse:

1. *Economic abuse*, as discussed in Chapter 4.

2. *Coercion and threats.* One husband used this when he threatened to commit suicide if his wife left him. Joan's husband used it when he said he would kidnap the children. The husband who threatened to sell the house and abandon his wife used it; so did the man who held illegal welfare over his partner's head.

3. *Intimidation.* The husband who kicked his wife's dog, the officer who played with his gun in front of his wife, Ellie's husband, who gave away her favorite dress, the many men who raise fists and knock down doors—all these men use intimidation. Their actions warn her, "Watch it. You could be next."

4. *Emotional abuse,* as discussed earlier. The Domestic Abuse Intervention Project includes psychological abuse in this category as well.

5. *Isolation,* as discussed in Chapter 3 under the name of Social Abuse.

6. *Minimizing, denying, and blaming.* Men who tell their wives "Oh, all men do that" use this form of abuse. So do men who deny their actions: "I never called you a slut." And men who pass the buck with "You started it." A husband used it in court to exonerate himself when in the process of raping his wife he had told her to shut up because women weren't supposed to enjoy sex. And thirteen years after their divorce Joan's former husband used it when he told the policeman arresting him for a

violation of a court order, "It's all her father's fault." Her father had been dead for three years.

7. *Using children as weapons.* The tens of thousands of men who harass their estranged wives over visitation use this—keeping children past the court-appointed return time, disappointing the children by not showing up, taking the women to court for withholding a visit when a child is sick. The man in court who tried to sneak his children out of the country used this. Irene's husband, who called their children daily to report on her failings, used this. The judge who accused a father of using the children as weapons against his wife understood this form of abuse.

8. *Using male privilege.* I have never met an abuser who doesn't use this—keeping his woman barefoot and pregnant as the saying went in more innocent days. He watches the ball game while she cleans and cooks and chauffeurs the children and markets and takes out the garbage and gets him a beer and has sex when he's ready and paints the kitchen and mows the lawn and finds him the misplaced hammer to lend his neighbor. How does a man help with the housework? a recent joke asks. Answer: He lifts his feet so she can vacuum under the chair. Women laugh at male privilege to keep from crying. Men laugh because it works.

Coercive Control

Along with others involved in abuse, Diana Russell, author of *Rape in Marriage,* and Ginny NiCarthy, author of *Getting Free,* believe that emotional abuse of wives, under which they include social and psychological abuse also, parallels the coercive techniques used to brainwash political prisoners.

As I listen to hundreds of women detail what their husbands have done to them and how they feel about it, I agree with Russell and NiCarthy. Although I discussed brainwashing briefly in Chapter 2, it is worthwhile, I believe, to look more closely at coercive control as still another pattern that abuse may take.

Biderman's Chart of Coercion, published by Amnesty International, pinpoints a pattern of eight specific actions that a controller imposes for the purpose of obtaining submission from another person:

1. *Isolation.* This, according to Ginny NiCarthy, is "the most effective way to set the stage for brainwashing since it removes a woman's support system, forcing her dependence on her husband."

2. *Monopolization of perception.* This eliminates outside stimuli such as phone calls, club activities, even television shows, all of which would provide the woman with a reality check by letting her compare what happens in the real world with what happens in hers.

3. *Induced debility.* Overwork and undersleep wear down her resistance.

4. *Threats.* These keep her in continual fear for her safety, as well as for that of her children, family, and friends. As NiCarthy says, "Emotionally abusive people . . . can be just as frightening to their partners as are physically violent partners."

5. *Occasional indulgences.* These throw a woman off guard by playing with her feelings of hope and despair like a yo-yo and are particularly effective in strengthening a man's control, since she submits to all his demands to keep the yo-yo on an upswing.

6. *Demonstrating omnipotence.* He reminds her of her help-lessness with such acts as hiding the car keys, locking her in her room, refusing food she prepares, etc.

7. *Degradation.* By drumming into her that she is fat, stupid, ugly, talentless, etc., he lowers her self-esteem to the point where she feels unworthy of better treatment.

8. *Enforcing trivial demands.* By making her adhere to relatively insignificant requirements such as dressing as he wishes, eating promptly at a specified time, or watching the TV shows he selects, he conditions her to obey weightier demands.

At the end of her poem "Patterns," Amy Lowell cries out in pain and rage at the death of her lover in the war, "Christ! What are patterns for?" While an abuser and his abused woman may be unable to articulate an answer to the question, the systematic pattern an abusive man follows speaks for them: patterns are for gaining control. The pattern in Amy Lowell's garden controlled her grief; a dress pattern controls the fit of a garment; the pattern of a spider's web controls an entrapped insect. The pattern of abuse controls a woman's life.

CHAPTER 7

"Why does he treat me like this?"

Profile of an Abuser

ARTHUR IS AN ELECTRICAL ENGINEER in Wilmington, Delaware, with one of the nation's Big Ten corporations, a Yale graduate earning $200,000 a year plus bonus. Tom is a shoe salesman earning $36,000 plus commission, living in a modest home in Kansas City. Jefferson and the woman he lives with are on welfare in a walk-up apartment on the South Side of Chicago. Drew is a Fort Worth construction worker; Maurice is a dentist in Gainesville, Georgia; Howard is a student at a New York community college who works two shifts at Burger King; Bennett is collecting unemployment insurance in Wisconsin; Charles works in a small library in Newton, Massachusetts; Vince is a policeman in Seattle. A disparate group, yet all are nonphysical woman abusers.

Despite the dissimilarities among these nine men and among the hundreds of thousands of other abusers, the general public sees the abuser as a stereotype: ignorant, low-class, rough and tough in looks and actions—Charles Bronson, not Kevin Costner.

The public is shocked when a member of the establishment is found to be an abuser. Many of us remember pictures of the bruised and beaten face of Hedda Nussbaum after we learned that Joel Steinberg had systematically battered both her and their daughter, finally killing the latter. How could he? He was a lawyer, educated, well-to-do. The stereotypical picture of an abuser exists only in the minds of those who want to remove themselves from the possibility that an abuser can be just like them.

There is no single profile for an abuser of women. He can be anyone. The common denominators researchers look for, therefore, are not demographic but personal, social, psychological. The noted psychiatrist Karen Horney in her essay "The Dread of Woman," quoted by Maggie Scarf in *Unfinished Business*, attributed men's emotional abuse of women to their "psychic reactions to certain given biological facts," a genetic root.

Most psychiatrists, however, do not hold with this theory. Some of the more recent studies, according to Joan Zorza of the National Battered Women's Law Project, indicate that abusers have what psychiatrists call *psychopathologies* and what we of the lay public call *mental illness*. In an effort to understand and eventually eliminate the phenomenon of battering, researchers in the field of abuse have drawn a variety of profiles of abusive men after years of working closely with them.

Jeffrey Edleson and Richard Tolman in *Intervention for Men Who Batter: an Ecological Approach* describe three kinds of men whose different psychopathologies may lead to abuse:

1. This man, considered to have a borderline personality disorder, is "asocial, withdrawn, moody, and hypersen-

sitive to interpersonal slights." He overreacts, has sudden outbursts of anger, and may have an alcohol problem.

2. This man, narcissistic and anti-social, is self-focused, taking from others and giving only when it is to his advantage.

3. This man, a dependent compulsive personality, is inflexible, has low self-esteem, and requires continual support from his wife or girlfriend.

Zorza also refers to the studies of Renata Vaselle-Augenstein and Annette Ehrlich in "Male Batterers: Evidence of Psychopathology" (published in *Intimate Violence: Interdisciplinary Perspectives*, edited by Emilio Viano). These researchers identify eight groups of batterers:

1. Men unable to control their impulses, who change swiftly in a Dr. Jekyll–Mr. Hyde pattern

2. Men who demand strict adherence to rules and, with no emotion, mete out punishment to those who break them

3. Men who are "rebellious, hostile, dependent, and low in self-esteem"

4. Men who are aggressive and antisocial

5. Men who exhibit great and inexplicable mood swings

6. Men who are outwardly pleasant but unable to handle rejection and aggressive when they feel their wife or girlfriend has let them down

7. Men who are excessively dependent, anxious, and depressed

8. Men who show only minor signs of the other seven characteristics and have, the authors feel, no psychopathology

This last classification is the one with which most workers in the field agree, attributing the underlying causes of battering to social rather than to psychological circumstances. Although it is true that childhood trauma often results in psychopathology such as schizophrenia (Who can forget the incredible case presented in *Sybil?*), it is believed that the majority of abusers do not act out of mental illness but instead from the socially developed use of immature or neurotic defense mechanisms to satisfy—or seek to satisfy—the emotional needs that may have been unfulfilled in childhood.

Defense Mechanisms Gone Awry

Defense mechanisms are methods by which people cope with the conflicts in their lives. We all use them but use different ones depending on our personalities and the circumstances that have shaped our lives. For instance, one person handles the emotional impact of failure by attributing its cause to someone else; another laughs his way through it; another strikes out in rage; still another denies its existence. Each finds the defense that works for him.

The defense mechanisms people use are not the same as the everyday decisions they make, because while the latter are choices they make consciously, the former are unconscious processes. For example, a person faced with a business failure may opt for any of a wide selection of possible ways to go, like filing for bankruptcy, seeking advice, taking a business course, looking for a job. He lines up his options, analyzes the pros and cons, and makes a selection, fully aware of what he is doing and why.

On the other hand, a person who uses a defense mechanism may deny the failure, get drunk to escape it, see it as someone else's failure, beat his son to rid himself of it, or tell a joke about it. In each case, though aware of *what* he was doing, he would be unaware *why*, knowing only that it helped make him feel better.

In his book *Adaptation to Life*, George Vaillant reported on the Grant Study, which followed thirty-eight potentially successful and healthy men over a period of forty years with the purpose of identifying the defense mechanisms they used and relating them to their personal and professional successes and failures. He classified them into three levels of maturity:

Immature Defenses

Fantasy
Projection
Passive aggression
Hypochondriasis
Acting out

Neurotic Defenses

Intellectualization
Repression
Reaction formation
Displacement
Dissociation

Mature Defenses

Altruism
Suppression
Humor
Anticipation
Sublimation

As I look at abusive men—those I know personally, those I have studied or read about, those whose women I counsel in court—I find three defense mechanisms that most of them use; one qualifies as neurotic, two as immature.

Repression

The first is the neurotic defense of repression. This is the defense through which men have forbidden themselves the expression of feelings that would pose a risk to their vulnerability, probably since childhood, and have buried them deep down in the vault of their subconscious. There the feelings lie, unacknowledged under a pile of succeeding feelings that they dare not admit into their consciousness either. Years later, no longer able to hold in the accumulation of unexpressed hurts and anger, the men spew them forth like a volcanic eruption in the physical or nonphysical battering that brings them relief at last. But not for long: the volcano must systematically erupt, over and over and over.

The German psychiatrist Alice Miller attributes Nazi brutality to the pent-up rage of young German boys, including Adolf Hitler, under the Prussian authoritarianism of their fathers. Beaten and belittled, she explains, they repressed the rage they dared not express for fear of worse retaliation and grew up waiting for an opportunity to vent it. In Nazi anti-Semitism they found it (*For Your Own Good: Hidden Cruelty in Child-Rearing and the Roots of Violence*).

Of those who repress fear and rage, Miller writes, "Common to them all is the sense of strength that it gives the adult to face the weak and helpless child's fear and to have the possibility of controlling fear in another person. . . . *Contempt for those who are smaller and weaker thus is the best defense against a breakthrough of one's own feelings of helplessness*" (my italics). Long before psychiatry's explanations, Seneca, the Roman writer of bloody tragedies, understood what Alice Walker was to explain two thousand years later: "Cruelty," he wrote with nontechnical directness, "springs from weakness."

Statistics indicate that a large percentage of abusive men were themselves abused as children. That they as adults, as a means of relieving the rage packed years earlier into their subconscious for survival's sake, disgorge it on their women follows logically. What weaker person can they find? Who more helpless than the woman dependent on them for their survival as they once depended on their father? Obviously the children of a wife abuser are equally dependent on him, yet he abuses them less frequently: first, because society is more watchful of child abuse than of wife abuse; and second, because it is to his advantage to use his children not as an object of abuse but rather as a weapon of abuse against his wife.

Anna Freud, psychiatrist daughter of the famous Sigmund, added an interesting facet to the analysis of repression. Abused children, she felt, repressing in their helplessness the hurt, fear, and rage they dare not feel, undergo a process called *identification* with the aggressor. All children, she explained, cling to a positive image of their parents, defending them against the world and against their own inadmissible realization of wrongdoing. Since parents are the one base of security children have to rely on, they forbid themselves any possibility of undermining it. Even abused children will lie to defend their parents, deny abuse, feign excuses, take any step to keep a sure footing.

This being so, according to Anna Freud, they convince themselves that they deserve the ill treatment meted out to them; they, not their parents, become the villains of the scenario. As they grow, then, they identify more and more with the "good guys," their abusive parents who are justifiably punishing the "bad guys," themselves, arriving finally at the point of becoming their own aggressors. At the end, therefore, they take on a new role and do unto others as their parents did unto them. Many abuse their children. Many more abuse their wives or girlfriends. Some abuse both. As

the old saying goes, parents drive the devil out of their garden only to find him again in the garden of their children.
The garden of these parents grows abuse.

Acting Out

A second defense mechanism evident in the behavior of
woman abusers is the immature defense of acting out. Anyone who has either raised a child or taught kindergarten is
well acquainted with this mechanism. The sweet little boy
whose mother returns from the hospital with a new baby suddenly begins hitting, kicking, and knocking down his classmates' block towers. The overindulged little girl who wants
an extra cookie snatches it from her neighbor's plate at juice
time. The child not chosen to be leader bangs his head
against the wall. These children are acting out.

Men who scream at their wives, cut up their clothes,
break their car windows, spit at them, throw dishes and food
are also acting out. They *do* so as not to *feel.* In other words,
they act out their anger in place of experiencing it because
the tension created by their feelings is too much to bear.
Haven't all of us kicked a chair or banged our fist against a
wall when we couldn't stand the anger or frustration we were
feeling a minute longer?

Different kinds of parenting can result in an adult's
acting out:

Overindulging. Children who have never been afforded
an opportunity to handle a parental "no" are unable to
develop mature coping skills for adversity. When parents
promise and provide their children a rose garden, they send
them through the gate into the adult world ill equipped to
deal with it maturely. The mother of an abuser I know
proudly told me, "I never even let my son get his own glass
of water when he was a child." No surprise. He grew up as
the little prince, demanding the same indulgence from his

wife as from his mother. When she didn't oblige, he threw temper tantrums of abusive behavior.

Inconsistency. If a parent says no but relents and takes the easy way out in the face of screams and kicking, the child resorts to screams and kicking the rest of his life. The man who nonphysically abuses his wife has never outgrown that little child determined to have his way. On the other hand, if one parent says no, and the child turns to the other parent, who says yes, the child learns the fine art of manipulation. The man who controls his wife through implied threats and other brainwashinglike techniques remains the successful child manipulator.

Abuse. As discussed earlier, the abused child who represses his rage may vent it explosively as an adult without consciously understanding why. Another child, however, through therapy may come to acknowledge the anger he feared to express in childhood. In the safety of adulthood then he may hurl at his wife the rage he dared not hurl at his parents. The husband who burned his wife's guitar because she was "a bitch just like my mother" was acting out his childhood anger and knew it.

Projection

A third defense mechanism commonly used by abusive men is also categorized as immature—projection. This enables a person to maintain an unblemished image of himself by attributing his faults and failings to others. Oscar Wilde's novel *The Picture of Dorian Gray* is a concrete representation of projection. The hero, who lives a life of debauchery, shows no marks of the libertine, his face ever young and unblemished. Meanwhile, high in the attic hangs a portrait of him with a face once as beautiful as he and now year by year, evil by evil, growing twisted, fleshy, and diseased.

Children often use projection, especially those who can

distinguish right from wrong. A child in the preschool where I was director is a classic example of projection. He returned home each day relating to his mother tales about Craig, a naughty boy in his class who punched children, grabbed their toys, tore down the houses they had built of blocks. Concerned that a disruptive child such as Craig might be limiting her child's learning experiences, she spoke to the teacher about him. The teacher's reply stunned her: "We have no Craig in the class. I hate to tell you, but it's your son, Alan, who does all those things."

Adult projection is not so obvious as Alan's and Dorian Gray's. The abusive man attributes to his wife his own feelings of weakness that he won't acknowledge and is therefore able to rage at her instead of at himself. Inadequate, he rails at her stupidity; unlovable, he accuses her of infidelity; insecure, he undermines her strength; out of control, he punishes her disobedience; guilty, he heaps her with blame.

Projection grants the abuser self-righteousness because on the conscious level he sees himself as the perfect husband, and the defense mechanism works to obliterate what seethes in his unconscious. On the conscious level his wife becomes a helpless failure, his responsibility to keep in line and make over, and the defense mechanism works to render him blameless. As a result he feels no more guilt over his treatment of her than the schoolmaster who raps the knuckles of the spitball-throwing student or the slave owner who rapes his wife's housemaid.

One day in court an ex-convict husband accused of abusing his wife gave the judge the excuse that "she always starts it." When the judge sought details on exactly how she started it, the man explained, "She won't do what I tell her." He had become the law that he himself had broken: that is projection. From what Irene has told me, I believe that her husband used projection too, for in repeatedly calling her childish for seeking intimacy in their marriage he was ridding himself of his own stunted emotional growth in being unable to provide it.

The Abuser in Person

Still we return to the question "Who is the batterer?" We recognize his defense mechanisms, his motives, the social and psychological roots of his abusive behavior, but we still ask, "Who is he? What does he look like?" V. D. Boyd and K. Klingbeil in *Behavioral Characteristics of Domestic Violence* have drawn up a list of characteristics that distinguish him. More extensive than other lists, theirs presents an overall picture, given below in summary:

- Poor impulse control

- Stress disorders, often masked successfully

- Emotional dependency

- Need for instant gratification

- Insatiable ego needs

- Low self-esteem

- Frequent promises to change

- Closeness only to wife/girlfriend and family

- Jealousy

- Close surveillance of wife/girlfriend

- No awareness of intrusive behavior

- Sense of acting in the woman's best interests

- Guilt-free

- History of abuse in his family as a child

- Participating in scapegoating

- Use of sex to punish

- Increased abuse when wife/girlfriend is pregnant

- Controlling through threats of murder or suicide

While many professionals like Boyd and Klingbeil who study and work with abusive men make no mention of drugs and alcohol, a connection exists. The idea that drugs or alcohol are responsible for a man's abuse of his wife is a myth; yet like many myths, it is a comfortable one, since it shifts responsibility. Clinging to the myth allows society, the wife, and the man himself to view the abuser as a victim instead of as the perpetrator he is. The myth provides society and the man with an excuse for battering that exonerates him and provides the woman with a reason to forgive it and go on living with it.

Still, drugs and alcohol are not completely guiltless. As anyone who has ever drunk one nip too many or been the victim of a crack-crazed assault knows, both drugs and alcohol release inhibitions. Therefore, the abuser who may have done no more than scream at his wife or refuse to give her money or keep her away from her family may under the influence of drink or drugs lash out more violently. That's when he may run off with the children, break the furniture, flash a knife, hide the car keys, and, of course, in many cases attack her physically.

Judges frequently give a protective order to a wife or girlfriend with the stipulation that the abuser cannot drink or take drugs in the house, nor can he imbibe outside and then return home under the influence. "He's bad enough when he's sober," a wife told me, "but when he's drinking I can't stand it." "Bad enough" it turned out was the usual onslaught of nonphysical abuse, including the phone yanked from the wall, three flat tires, and jealous phone calls to her boss; "can't stand it" was a broken nose.

However, neither the courts nor abuse professionals and certainly not abused women themselves should lean on drugs or alcohol as an excuse for any kind of battering. Granted, they provide a quick and easy explanation for abhorrent behavior, but in so doing they block the path to real understanding that could lead to prevention. Drugs do not create wife abusers—let all involved know it.

At the end of 1993 an international group of social scientists met to discuss their research on the relationship between alcohol and aggression, chiefly verbal aggression, the kind we see in nonphysical abuse. At the close of the conference they issued the following statement: "There is no support for the idea that alcohol causes aggression (*The Brown University Child and Adolescent Behavior Letter*, February 1994). Let us look for more valid and useful explanations.

To sum up the many viewpoints held and many studies conducted in efforts to understand why a man abuses the woman he says he loves, the woman he marries or forms a relationship with, a few conclusions emerge:

1. A large number of abusive men were themselves abused as children.

2. Abusive men operate on the stereotypes built and supported by society at large, regarding men as dominant and women as submissive.

3. Abusive men are low in self-esteem.

4. They seek to reinforce their self-image through macho power plays.

5. They are narcissistic, recognizing only their own needs, no one else's.

6. They are immature, unable to be accountable for their actions or to resolve interpersonal problems.

A New Jersey teenager, member of a group who routinely harass girls by calling them obscene names, pawing, and putting them down, explained his behavior this way: "If you dis a girl, you get respect. . . . It's the male nature in a way. If they [the other group members] are caught treating a girl well, they lose the approval of their friends" (*The New York Times,* July 11, 1993). If you line these young boys up against the profile of abusive men presented here, the outlines look similar. Both hold on to sex role stereotypes. Both need to reinforce their self-esteem. Both display macho power. Both are narcissistic. Both have never grown up. Both, perhaps, were abused as small children.

The prognosis is frightening. Are the boys in this group and in hundreds of other groups across the country the woman abusers of the future? Are the girls they are harassing today the battered women of tomorrow? Or will we learn in time the secret—from lists and profiles and psychiatric studies—that will save them both?

CHAPTER 8

"Why doesn't she just leave?"

The Reasons a Woman Stays with an Abuser

VALERIE THOUGHT ABOUT SUING her husband for divorce after eighteen years of nonphysical abuse that left her feeling "as stupid as my father said I was because I couldn't get chemistry through my head." She gave up the idea, though, ten years ago. Laura came to court for an order of protection against the man she'd been living with for eight years "because he scares me." Although he had been socially and emotionally abusing her throughout their entire relationship, what finally made her seek protection was that he threatened to leave if she didn't quit her job and she feared being alone. My good friend Irene stayed with her husband for more than forty years although she says she cried herself to sleep almost every single night for half of those years. Another friend of mine is still with her husband after fifty years of "doing what he wants to keep the peace." The most obvious question for all of them is Why? Why do they continue to stay?

When people hear the details of life with an abuser, whether physical or nonphysical, their common response is "Why don't you just leave?" They are appalled that a woman will put up with the pain and degradation of abuse when all she has to do is grab her coat and her children and walk away. It seems so easy. "I have no patience with all your concern for abused women," the husband of a friend said to me. "They don't have to stay. They're not being held by force." His response is typical of the lack of knowledge and self-delusion of many men and women.

Common Misconceptions

Why women remain in an abusive relationship is so complex and so misunderstood that few of them can articulate the reason themselves. Irene says she couldn't leave because she didn't know that she should. She's not even sure she knows now that she could have—should have—left. She only knows she stayed. Three explanations that have been given—and previously believed because there was no other explanation—will probably sound familiar to many readers because they themselves have believed them:

The Woman Wants to Be Abused

Masochism is a popular explanation, since it shifts the blame from the abuser to the abused, one more instance of blaming the victim, which, according to Brent Staples in *The New York Times* (February 13, 1994), "has become a celebrated state—and a license." The basis for determining that women are abused because they want abuse lies in good measure with Sigmund Freud, who propounded the idea that women were predisposed to want pain. People are ready, therefore, to assess the abusive man as an instrument of a woman's need for fulfillment, believing in fact that she may have selected him as her mate because of his ability to do just that. As a man in the audience of the Sally Jessy Raphael talk show on abuse put it in the nonpsychological terms of his and the audience's understanding, "No one can walk over you unless you want him to."

There is a big difference between submitting to abuse and wanting it. Of the hundred or so women I have interviewed and the hundred or so more on whom I have read reports, not one asked for it, liked it, or wanted it. Each one of them tried to stop the abuse with efforts that lined up on a continuum from pacification to homicide. And all of them give the lie to Dr. Freud.

In *Women, Violence, and Social Change*, Emerson and Russell Dobash attack the therapeutic approach to abuse that labels women as masochists and treats them as such. Because this theory throws the onus of an abusive relationship on a woman, they state, it gives the appearance of support and encouragement for a man to abuse. The musical play *Carousel*, an adaptation of Molnár's *Liliom*, presents the anti-hero Billy Bigelow, who beats his wife out of his own sense of inferiority. "Is it possible for someone to hit you and it doesn't hurt?" Billy's daughter asks her mother near the final curtain.

With the audience in tears, the mother answers, remembering Billy's beatings, "Yes." This is beautiful theater and totally false life. It *does* hurt, and no woman wants it.

Those therapists who attribute a woman's remaining in an abusive situation to masochism—sexual gratification to the point of orgasm—not only present a far too simplistic explanation, but more dangerous, they reinforce a man's right, almost his duty, to abuse. "Nonsense," says Joan Zorza of the National Center on Women and Family Law in response to those therapists and the approach they use.

"The only thing that determines whether a woman will be battered is whether she is in a relationship with a batterer." And the only thing that determines whether she will stay in the relationship is whether she can leave.

The Woman Has Developed a Pattern of Learned Helplessness

In 1904 the psychologist Ivan Pavlov won a Nobel Prize for the findings from his study with dogs. Ringing a bell just before feeding them over a period of time, he found that dogs, having learned that dinner was on the way, began to salivate as soon as they heard the ring. At that point Pavlov altered the procedure, still ringing the bell but not offering food, and he discovered that the dogs continued to salivate. Thus was the theory of conditioned reflex born.

In 1967 Dr. Martin Seligman of the University of Pennsylvania took Pavlov's theory of conditioning a step further. Also working with dogs, he enclosed them in cages, where he delivered intermittent shocks whenever they pushed against the doors, making their attempts at escape both painful and frustrating. Although the dogs tried hard at first, after a while, realizing there was no way out without an electric shock, they stopped trying and accepted their imprisonment. Like Pavlov's dogs, Seligman's dogs behaved with a conditioned response.

Dr. Seligman, however, did not stop there. Next he eliminated the electric shocks and opened the doors to the cages so the dogs could escape freely. The dogs looked. They saw the open doors but made no attempt to leave, remaining inside, resigned as they had been before. Observing this behavior, Dr. Seligman developed the theory of learned helplessness: that intermittent maltreatment over a period of time leaves the subject unable to assert self-will and, as a result, compliant to the will of the controller.

Lenore Walker applied the theory of learned helplessness to battered women with the publication of her book *The Battered Woman* in 1979. She believed that a woman caught in a pattern of abuse over time becomes passive and, like Seligman's dogs, seeing no way out, gives up. Although she may at first have tried to control her husband's abuse by placating him, blaming herself, changing her behavior, and avoiding explosive situations—just as the dogs tried to control their imprisonment by attempting to open the cage door—she eventually came to realize that nothing she did would alter their relationship or free her. Resigned to her fate, she gave up trying and submitted to his control.

While learned helplessness seemed to explain the previously inexplicable reason for abused women's remaining with their abusers, people began to realize that, like the masochist theory, it was too simplistic. It was easy to cluster all abused women under this one umbrella and ignore the root causes such as the failings of a society that allowed abuse to happen. As Joan Zorza told me, the helplessness is ours, not the abused woman's. Edward Gondolf in *Battered Women as Survivors* agrees. Abused women, he says, unlike Seligman's dogs, do try to escape; "their effort to survive transcends even fearsome danger, depression or guilt, and economic constraints." Even Lenore Walker herself, making a 180-degree change of mind, came to a similar conclusion years after her original study reported in *The Battered Woman Syndrome*. It is generally understood now that there is far more to an abused woman's submission to abuse than learned helplessness.

The Woman Deserves Abuse

I heard the following conversation in court as a woman's boyfriend, the respondent in an abuse charge, stood before the judge:

Judge: You locked her out of her own house. You drove off her car and hid it. You threatened to take her children to Colombia—and they're not even yours. Why did you do all that?

Respondent: Well, you see, your honor, she goes out a lot, and I don't know where she is, and I don't even believe what she tells me. She's a liar. Ask her, judge.

Judge: That's no reason to harass and threaten her.

Respondent: What else can I do to make her obey? You tell me, your honor.

With complete self-righteousness the man tried to enlist the judge's support. His honor did not explain how to make the woman obey, but he clearly made the man obey by ordering him to vacate the woman's apartment and stay away or face arrest.

This man's brazenness was unusual. However, in so bluntly attempting to justify his actions to the judge, he spoke unwittingly for many others who believe as he does— that a man abuses a woman because she deserves it and that she knows she deserves it. Dog owners can recognize the skulking look of guilt on their pet's face when it has torn open the garbage and the righteous resignation with which it accepts its punishment without snarls or bites. Parents can recognize the conscience-stricken child who confesses to having eaten the forbidden chocolates or broken a sister's doll and accepts shameful exile to his room without tears.

Casting himself in a similar role as trainer and teacher, an abusive man enacts the same scenario, disciplining his discipline-deserving woman. Like pet owner and parent, he punishes her when she is naughty and disobeys; like pet and child, she acknowledges her misconduct, accepting the punishment he has long since convinced her she deserves. She sees no way out because only he, she believes, can keep her "badness" in control.

One day I heard a sermon preached to a congregation who, pained by the world agony surrounding them—war and disease, earthquakes, floods, and fire—sought an explanation. "Why does God allow so much suffering?" they asked.

"God is the Head of our world household," the minister began. "He brings us pain out of love, to teach us to abandon our evil ways and live as He wants us to live." You could almost hear a sigh of relief breathe through the pews as the men and women of the congregation nodded in understanding. Like the respondent before the judge, they accepted the fact that whatever power metes out punishment—be it God or a human male—does so justly, and whatever underling receives it deserves it.

People who work with abused women repudiate that thinking, as do most ministers in their efforts to understand human suffering. Nothing a woman does warrants abuse. Nothing. And no woman stays with an abuser because she deserves abuse. No woman. The abuser chooses to abuse; the abused woman stays because she sees no way out. The world must not be allowed to write off wife abuse by blaming the victim, which is unacceptable and untrue, but must understand instead that abuse stems from men's "inability to accept reasonable responsibility for their . . . actions" (*Crossing the Postmodern Divide* by Albert Borgmann).

The Logic of Staying

Society grasps the easiest explanation because its members cannot wend their way through the maze of an abused woman's feelings. Often neither can she. Yet explanations exist, whether conscious or unconscious, that to her justify submission to continued abuse.

Trade-Offs

First, she may make trade-offs. A woman often remains in an abusive relationship because she gets something she wants from it, not masochistic pleasure but something far more tangible. Although she pays dearly—too dearly, others may feel—she makes a conscious choice by balancing the pros and cons as most of us do every day in one way or another. The choice: to buy or not to buy those kidskin gloves. The pro argument: they're elegant, and good leather lasts. The con argument: they cost a lot more than wool and won't provide as much warmth. We make our choice one way or the other by determining what is worth most to us—the money, the looks, the durability, or the comfort.

One of the trade-offs a woman in an abusive relationship makes is a matter of money, and she goes through a similar process. Her choice is to stay or to leave. If she stays, she will continue to enjoy whatever material benefits she has had, but she will have to suffer continued humiliation and dependence. If she leaves, she will be free, with a new sense of pride and identity, but she may be on the streets or in a homeless shelter. The choice is not easy because, having suffered through abuse, she is well aware that her husband will use money as a weapon of vengeance. Lawyers tell me that "even nice guys get mean when it comes to money in divorce."

Older women are more apt to stay with abusive husbands than young ones because they have put more time and effort into their marriage and because they are more hesitant to tackle a less comfortable lifestyle. However, this is not always the case. A woman in her twenties comes to the Family Court where I work every year when her protective order runs out because her husband begins gearing up for renewed abuse. "Have you considered leaving him so you don't have to go through this again?" I asked her.

"No, I can't," she answered without hesitation. "I'd have no money to live on."

On the other hand, I know a middle-aged woman who rather than remaining in a high-income, high-status abusive marriage, set out on her own with three daughters, no job, and no money. Although she would have preferred to continue her skiing vacations and biking trips, she found a job—several jobs in fact—and built a good life for all of them. Statistics on the rising middle-age and senior-citizen divorce rate indicate that my friend is not unique.

Many older women, however, are not so brave. Women in their sixties and seventies whom I interview may describe their nonphysically abusive marriages as intolerable, yet they choose to stay rather than leave because they feel that giving up a comfortable life would be worse. As one of them said, "I may not draw a salary, but I'm sure not about to give up the perks."

It is easier for young women to break free because youth gives them greater flexibility; they haven't yet dug themselves into a rut. In addition, they may have no children and therefore less to worry about; and in today's culture, they may not even be married, so they have no legal ties to disentangle. My own daughter with two small children left an abusive husband, who is still angry about her professional and financial success. "I'll put you on welfare," he had screamed at her when she left. He continues to wreak vengeance on her for dodging what he considered his strongest weapon, poverty.

A second trade-off that a woman may make when she stays in an abusive relationship is avoidance of being alone. Nora, a highly respected university professor, has been struggling for seventeen years to leave her emotionally abusive husband. Having a good income and no small children to support, she knows she won't have to relinquish the afflu-

ent lifestyle she enjoys with her husband. What she fears
raises a terror far worse than poverty: the dread of aloneness.

So terrifying is the thought of life without the closeness
of another body, another voice, that, like a fortress wall, for
thousands of women it blocks the way to fulfilling new lives.
And so terrifying is the reality of it that women who summon their courage to leave their abusers for life on their
own often renege, returning to them as many as five times
before daring to make the final break. Some women feel that
leaving their abusive partner is like standing on a high diving board looking down at the water below, afraid to jump.
They back off, pluck up their courage, and venture to the
edge again. Once. Twice. As many times as it takes. Some
finally jump. Some stay on the diving board.

One way to evaluate the wholeness or mental health of
a person, says the psychiatrist Virginia Bird, is her ability to
be alone—her inner resources, her self-enjoyment. So many
abused women have been deliberately deprived of inner
resources by their abusers that there is no "inner" left of
them. So many have been humiliated and degraded systematically day after day that if there is any self left it can
only be loathed, not enjoyed.

In paying the price for not being alone, women endure
what seem unendurable indignities to keep their man. I see
women who stand by and watch him bring other women into
the house or consent to a sexual performance with his
friends or not consent and be forced. I see women who beg
their husband for sex, and after he turns away, beg again.
These women don't want a divorce; they don't want him to
go away with the other women. They want to keep him, not
out of love, but out of fear of the alternative: being abused
is better than being alone.

A third trade-off abused women who remain in the relationship often make is for the welfare of their children. I
shall never forget a scene I witnessed in Africa—a mother

warthog running back and forth and around a tree in front of a panther that was stalking its young. Clumsy and certainly not fleet of foot, it braved the claws of a lethal hunter to protect its offspring. Whether it would have succeeded or not, I never discovered because, much to the dismay of my party's guide, we scared the panther away and cheered as the warthog family escaped.

I have seen a blue jay dive-bomb a cat that crept too near its nest, a mother bear in a Russian zoo claw the air at spectators who rapped the cage bars near her cub, and I received from a mother lemur nursing her baby the dirtiest look ever given when I reached out to offer a peanut. I have even seen sunfish in a pond circling the nests they had scooped out of mud to ward off predator turtles that could quickly snap up the cluster of eggs that would hatch into babies. When I got measles as a child, I remember my mother saying, "I wish it were me." I couldn't imagine why anyone would want measles. Now I know: because that's what mothers do—protect their young.

Society has long instilled the idea that unless children are raised by two parents (one of each sex, please), they will grow up somehow warped; as a result mothers often suffer prolonged abuse for what they explain as "the good of my children." Children need their father. That's what the court says when it turns them over for visits to the man who sexually abused them. That's what fathers say to frighten their wives. That's what social workers say as they keep at-risk children in their at-risk homes. That's what studies say in reporting the percentage of drug abuse among children from one-parent homes. That's what abused women hear, so that's what they say too. They live with their abuser because, like the warthog, the bird, the bear, the lemur, the fish, and the mother of a child with measles, they protect their children.

The truth is that it is far better to have no father than to have a destructive one, because as psychiatrists have found, one nurturing parent is sufficient to foster a child's healthy development. A child who grows up hearing his father's constant put-downs of his mother, who absorbs his father's manipulative skills like osmosis through his pores, who models his father's macho domination and watches his mother submit in fear—this child cannot grow up whole. He will instead grow up twisted by the dread he felt, guilty over his inability to protect his mother, and angry that, too small and helpless, he couldn't cry out.

So damaging is the chronic exposure of children to their father's abuse of their mother that therapy and counseling programs throughout the country have sprung up to help them. Typical is the STEPS program developed in Harlem and run by the Sisters of Notre Dame. Coordinator of the program, Sister Andrea Dixon, explains, "It's very hard for children to make a distinction between a father who could love them and yet abuse their mothers" (*Daily News*, April 5, 1994).

Unaware of her child's stressful ambivalence, an earnest mother may work hard to sustain her child's relationship with the father, keeping his image shining even in the face of abuse—all "for the good of the children." Yet this doesn't always work, as the divorced woman who left her abusive husband with her three daughters learned. For years she followed a counselor's advice, never speaking a negative word about their father to the girls. Though he continued to harass her with obscene phone calls and threats, she held her tongue. Their father was upset, she explained; be nice to him; he has outside problems; he's really a nice guy, etc. Unable to identify any "nice guy" qualities, the girls doubted their own perceptions and became more troubled than ever. Finally, after a particularly abusive incident, their mother sat them down and in total calm said, "Forget it. Your father's an out-and-out shit, and you can stop pretending he isn't." Relieved, the girls began to heal.

All women want what they say is "the best for their children," which may mean a college education, a nice home, health, and happiness as defined by the American dream. Abused women are no different, and sticking it out with their abusers may be the only way they see to achieve that dream. Staying rather than leaving may mean the difference between Yale and night school, between an available mom and a mom too exhausted from her job to play, between meat and fresh vegetables and a diet of pasta.

At My Sister's Place, assistant director Thea DuBow says they have many women who seek shelter with their children for a few days, until the abusive situation cools down, then return home because "they think the children's father can give them what they need." What the women aren't ready to understand is that he also gives them what they don't need— a negative role model. For instance, the infamous Gary Gilmore came from an abusive home. A more recently publicized example was the May 15, 1994, unprovoked shooting of a woman by a young boy of fourteen and a ten-year-old child, who, according to *The New York Times*, had both witnessed their fathers abusing their mothers. The Menendez brothers pleaded innocent of murdering their parents on the grounds of their father's repeated abuse, a trial watched by millions on Court TV. What doesn't make the news are the tens of thousands of nonphysical abusers who model the emotional, psychological, social, and economic abuse of their fathers, raising in their homes future hundreds of thousands of abusers who model their behavior.

When women remain in abusive relationships for the sake of their children, not only don't they provide "the best for their children," but they often subject them to abuse as well. It is generally known that nonphysically abusive men who abuse their wives hurl their verbal battering on their children as well, but *Today's Woman* (Westchester County, New York) reported in 1992 that half of all wife abusers, physical and nonphysical, actually beat their children severely three or four times a year.

Lack of Resources for Survival

The second reason a woman stays with her abuser is that she may realize how ill equipped she is to be on her own. While some women may have the option of giving up a comfortable life for hardship in order to escape abuse, others are less fortunate—they simply have no options. They stay because they have to. I think back to some of the women I know who walked out on abusive relationships: one lived with her parents until she found a job; the mother of another moved in with her while she studied for a master's degree; another lived with her new boyfriend. They felt secure in making the decision to leave because they *were* secure. I also think back to some who wanted to walk out and couldn't: a pregnant sixteen-year-old whose abusive boyfriend didn't want the baby and whose parents wouldn't talk to her; a woman married for forty years who had never worked and had never even taken a vacation without her husband; a woman with six small children; an asthmatic. They saw abuse as payment for survival.

One winter in Murfreesboro, Tennessee, where I was sent to observe the state Teacher of the Year in action, two inches of snow fell. Schools closed; businesses ran half-staffed; buses cut their schedules; people stayed home. The city had an emergency. A few weeks later I flew into Minneapolis in a blinding blizzard with my heart in my throat and a prayer on my lips. Nothing special: schools were open; cars traveled the roads; stores bustled with customers. Life went on as usual in snowbound Minneapolis.

The difference between Murfreesboro and Minneapolis was a matter of preparedness: the former, unused to more than a powdering of snow, lacked equipment to handle two inches, while Minneapolis, snow-wrapped for half the year, was always ready to drive out the plows, trucks, and tractors. Preparedness may also be the deciding factor in the stay-or-leave choice of a woman in the storm of an abusive relationship. With the proper equipment she can plow her way out; without it, she remains snowed in. What does she need?

Somewhere to Go

First she needs a place to go. While she may be able to find refuge in a safe shelter on a temporary basis, even that is not certain. There is still such a shortage of shelters in the country that fewer than one in four women can find room, and, according to Jane Brody (*The New York Times,* March 18, 1992), if she has a child, 95 percent of the shelters will turn her away. At court the other day we had to send a woman and her baby to a shelter for the homeless because with no family or friends and no available space in shelters within seventy miles, she had nowhere else to go.

Even the shelter that accepts a woman won't keep her for more than a month or so, since shelters are not set up as permanent lodging, so she will still have to find a home. The husband who finds her gone won't be in the mood to vacate their living quarters for her comfort and convenience, nor in many cases will the court order him out of the home they have shared until she reaches a settlement through divorce. Few friends or siblings are in a position to invite her in as a new family member, and she is loath to forfeit her independence by returning to live with her parents even if they have the room and the inclination to have her. She is, therefore, stuck.

Homelessness turns out to be for some the only and a dangerous alternative, especially for a mother with children. I worked with a family of four living in one room of a homeless shelter that had once been a Howard Johnson motel; a week earlier a woman had been murdered in a room two doors down; drugs were sold openly in the hallways; rapes were almost commonplace. I have seen women on the streets of New York pushing babies and plastic bags of their few possessions in carriages, living on grates and in doorways, hiding from the police rather than go to homeless shelters. Living with an abuser may not seem like such a bad alternative.

Money

Second, she needs an income. Many abused women have no jobs, often through the imposed decision of their husband, as discussed earlier in the book. The majority of those who do work, like the majority of all women in the country, earn considerably less than the men with whom they live, although economics does not determine abuse. In fact, a large number of abused women earn high salaries as professionals and business executives. However, the income of the average abused woman alone would put her in such financial straits that she has little choice, especially when children are involved. Her options, therefore, limit her to staying in the abusive relationship or leaving with the hope of getting a low-paying job or living on public assistance—food stamps and welfare checks. Despite the accepted belief that welfare recipients relish a so-called free-lunch lifestyle, most of the women to whom I speak shun it. "I'd be too ashamed," they tell me, putting aside for a minute the shame they already feel. Like pelicans dive-bombing their ocean prey, abusive men—Joan's husband, for instance—may zoom in on public assistance in anticipation of a retaliatory feast. "You and the kids will have fun picking up your welfare check every week, won't you?" I heard one husband say with a smirk.

To cling to remaining shreds of pride is important to the women I see. One attractive young woman, embarrassed to stand before the judge in worn-out blue jeans but unable to buy new ones, expressed horror at the suggestion of the thrift shop down the street. Another on a snowy winter day turned down a pair of boots left in our office with a "Thanks anyway, but I haven't reached the point of charity yet."

Women who have no means of self-support must have at least skills that offer the possibility of it. A school dropout or an immigrant who can't speak English obviously lacks job skills to sustain her if she leaves her abuser, so she stays. A high school or college graduate has a better chance of earning a living when she sets out on her own—unless she is caught in a recession, so she stays. A middle-aged woman never having worked outside her home can offer experience and skills only in cooking, cleaning, and caring for children, so she too stays.

Some women plan an independent future around promises of job training and education—to become nurses, computer operators, medical technicians—only to find they lack money to complete the course or can't find a job when they graduate. They are back at Start, faced with their original abuse and no options. What do they do? They stay with their abusive mate.

Child Care

Third, if a woman has children, she needs child care. Since the United States is one of the few developed countries without generous child-care services through either the government or private business, the abused woman has to struggle through this all-important problem in addition to finding a job if she wants to set out on her own. The "good old days" of extended families are gone—moved to Florida retirement homes—so few single mothers can rely on parents to take care of their children while they work. While some find day-care programs, they are too few and far between to handle the demand. Unlicensed private homes in which many mothers leave their children are rife with fire and health hazards, and even licensed ones, headlined in cases of sexual abuse, can be dangerous.

I spoke last month to a group of women who work in the financial world, many of them single mothers, all of them financially secure. Asked to identify their single greatest problem, almost all of them agreed it was child care. Some had live-in nannies; some sent their children to expensive nursery schools; some used part-time baby-sitters. Yet a large majority were dissatisfied with the care they were getting. If women in this socioeconomic group, the top 1 or 2 percent of all working women, could not find adequate child care, how then can less financially secure, less skilled, and far more stressed mothers be expected to leave home, even if it is a place of abuse, without someone out there whom they trust to care for their children?

Help from Society

Fourth, if a woman is to leave an abusive relationship, she needs help. As Thea DuBow, assistant director of My Sister's Place, repeats endlessly to anyone who will listen, learned helplessness is not the abused woman's syndrome; it is society's. She knows, not only from touching the desperation of women at the shelter, but from suffering through her own. By herself. Society has a habit of shutting its eyes to problems that make it cringe. We openly confront issues like dishonest politicians, street crime, drugs, etc., with outrage, annually renewing our determination to eliminate them. We feel secure to discuss and debate these issues because although they loom large, they don't belong to us individually. They belong to society.

Yet society is us. We have learned that lesson slowly and only spasmodically throughout history, and what we learn we seem to forget quickly. How long it took us to open our eyes to the fact that black men and women are born as free as white; when we eliminated slavery, we forgot to provide for equal education and housing and justice in the courts of law. How long it took us to open our eyes to the fact that women Americans were constitutional citizens as well as men; when we gave them the vote, we forgot to equalize pay and job opportunity. The result has been rage and revolution against the undeniably white male power structure whose memory by choice remains short and loose so as to maintain its control.

At least we are beginning to confront the political issues of women and minorities; we argue about them in terms of political correctness and pass laws for change. However, nonpolitical issues that touch chords of guilt we keep locked in the dark within us, and nonphysically battered women lie deepest in the darkest places. Who can face them? Not men, who fear discovering their own control needs there. Not women, ashamed of their powerlessness. While society today sees the blood of a physically battered woman's broken nose, bruises across her chest, and her body dead by gun or knife or lamp cord, it remains blind to the nonphysically battered woman's wounds because she has nothing to show at all.

In its protective blindness, society offers little help to the battered woman who, without a home, a job, and child care, cannot escape. As Edward Gondolf writes in *Battered Women as Survivors*, "What they need are the resources and social support that would enable them to become more independent and leave the batterers." Existing resources and social supports are too meager to rescue more than a small percentage of women who need them. The majority remain trapped—in abuse if they stay, in deprivation if they leave.

What we as society have to do is acknowledge our responsibility to these women. First, we have to clear our vision of the defenses that blind us and recognize that hundreds of thousands of women—some of the wives and girlfriends we may know—live in silent abuse. Next we have to determine what kinds of resources and support they require to rebuild their lives. Finally, we have to allocate money to meet those requirements. Since America pays for what it considers important—hundreds of billions for flights into space and weapons of war—our country must underscore the importance of social services. Surely a good life on earth warrants as much as a search for life elsewhere; a peaceful life on earth warrants more than death in a foreign war. In the same way an abusive man strips a woman of freedom, so society strips those women of deliverance, and both must change.

The Underlying Fear

A fourth reason a woman remains in an abusive relationship is her fear of increased abuse if she leaves. Since an abused woman spends most of her days anticipating her husband's next move, she is alert to the dangers her leaving would impose. The first possibility she weighs is whether he will harm her or the children. While this will be discussed more fully in Chapter 14, it is important here to acknowledge this fear as one of a woman's chief reasons for subjecting herself to continuing abuse. The threats an abuser holds over her head while she lives with him loom still more ominous if she should leave.

Some men spell out their threats directly without mincing words. They can't be more direct when they warn, "If you leave me, I'll kill you." Others sound even more menacing, like the man whose wife came to court for protection when he told her, "I'd follow you wherever you went, and someday you'd be walking down the street and find a knife in your back."

A woman named Beryl said that although her boyfriend had never laid a hand on her, he "tortured" her in other ways until she could no longer stand it. In her words: "I packed a bag one day when he was out and went to my girl-friend's. She had been trying to get me to leave for a long time because she saw what he was doing to me. Well, to make a long story short, he came there. We wouldn't answer the door, so he kicked it in and found us in the kitchen. Boy, was that the wrong room to be in. He took a long knife from the drawer and waved it in front of us. 'You're coming home with me,' he screamed, 'and if you ever try this again, you see this knife? Well, just remember what it looks like.' I went home with him, and I stayed too." She is still there, too frightened to leave, but she calls the director of a safe house once in a while and may eventually make a break.

An altogether different kind of threat keeps some women chained to their abusers: "If you leave, I'll kill myself." Not you, myself. That works with the guilt-ridden, but if Beryl's boyfriend had made such a threat, she probably would have handed him a gun. He knew his woman, however, and used a fear tactic designed for her. Abusers are clever in manipulating fear. For instance, the corporate exec-utive husband of a friend of mine threatened not to kill her or commit suicide but to go to Mexico and become a cab-driver if she left him. "I was so afraid he'd do it," she told me, "that I decided to stay. Poor Jim; he can't even drive in Boston." Jim didn't have to brush up on his Spanish; he knew he had scared her enough to stay.

Another kind of fear a woman harbors that often makes the abusive status quo look safer than the alternative is dread of a court procedure. Whether she is filing for a protective order or testifying in a criminal case against him or suing for divorce, she has to stand before a judge, a situation that can be as scary as the accounting on Judgment Day. In black robe on the raised bench, a judge can make the innocent feel guilty and the petitioner wish she could drop the charges. Often before going into Family Court with a woman, I have her write down what she has already told

me—details of the abuse she has suffered along with the specific protection she wants from the court—so she can refer
to them when fear ties her tongue. I have sat with women
so intimidated by the judge that they dared not even look
at the notes they took.

The unknown is as frightening as the judge—papers to
fill out, questions to answer, personal details to confide,
secrets to reveal. Never having been through a court procedure, many women feel too unsure to tackle it, and even
after a court appearance, many drop the whole thing and
return to their abusive relationship. Lawyers offer little support. If they are court-appointed, they often don't even see
their client until the court appearance; and even private
lawyers, energized as they are by a courtroom, may have little empathy for the unsure women they represent.

For women who want to flee abuse, the greatest fear is
the fear of losing their children through the court. Headline instances of the court's granting custody to fathers, even
sexually abusive fathers, have made many women ready to
endure abuse in the home where they know they will have
their children. I heard of a situation in a large midwestern
city where a woman brought her husband up on charges of
sexually abusing their children and made him vacate their
home. While the Child Protective Service, which investi-
gates and takes action on reported abuse, was looking into
the charges, corroborated by medical examination, the husband brought unfounded countercharges against his wife.
As a result she was forced to turn the child over to CPS custody and a foster home. Hers was a fear come true.

Even if the court doesn't grant custody to an abusive
father, women may harbor the persistent fear that he will
take the children and run. If he takes them out of the country, there is little the mother can do to regain them. I have
seen instances where fathers either take the children or ship
them off to grandparents, often in Central America, and the

news media has reported on children abducted to the Middle East. In either case the mother has little chance of reclaiming them and may put herself in imminent danger by trying, as reported firsthand by Betty Mahmoody in *Not Without My Daughter.*

A less obvious fear that keeps some women from breaking away from abusive husbands is the age-old impact of "What will people say?" While one in three marriages in America ends in divorce, the statistics give only an overall national picture. They don't separate the religions that forbid divorce or the ethnic groups that frown on it or regions of the country where divorce is not an acceptable option. In these cases women stay with their abusive husbands because it is expected, and what would people say? People would say that the woman failed her duty: a wife should serve her husband. They would say she couldn't hold a man: she probably drove him off. They would say she's no good: the Bible considers divorce a sin. They would say she forgot her place: a woman belongs with her husband. They would say she has shamed her family and community, and she would know they are right.

Some may laugh at this attitude as belonging to Jane Austen's eighteenth-century *Pride and Prejudice* world, in which Mrs. Bennet advises her daughters to "smile and hold your tongue," as she has done while married to Mr. Bennet. After hearing Irene's story, I don't laugh at Mrs. Bennet for the simple reason that she claims her mother pounded the same lesson into her: "It doesn't matter what you feel. Just put a smile on your face." Irene did, and many women of her generation did too—for a long forty years or fifty.

Women have been putting up with nonphysical abuse rather than fall short of expectations that, like a hair shirt, they wear in pain. One young woman told me that her husband began belittling her while they were still on their honeymoon, which is not uncommon, since the trap has been sprung. "I should have left then and there, and I seriously thought about it," she said, "but I hadn't even written all the thank-you letters for our presents yet. How could I?"

An older woman explained that her grown children threatened to cut off all contact with her if she left their father. "They knew how he treated me, but they didn't care as long as it looked good from the outside," she said with hesitation.

Other Emotional Factors

The fifth reason holding a woman back from escaping abuse is a variety of emotional factors. If there is one sure truth I have gleaned during a lifetime in counseling and education, it is that people learn only when they believe they can learn. Most children, unfortunately, are subjected to a school system predicated on the contrary belief that low marks and discipline will scare and humiliate them into learning. Education statistics have long proved the theory wrong: self-esteem, not failure, is the foundation of learning.

A woman in an abusive relationship is rather like a child in school. Her controller, like the school system, uses fear of retribution and the humiliation of failure to force her compliance; and, like the student, she sees herself as what I heard both a child and a woman call "a no-good person." She, like the child, accepts the problems as hers—not the abuser's, not the teacher's. As a result both child and woman, drained of self-esteem, perpetuate their failing situations.

In *Unfinished Business: Pressure Points in the Lives of Women*, Maggie Scarf speaks of the drought a woman experiences when her emotional life runs dry of love and support. She becomes "far more critical in her assessments of herself, in her feeling worthless, useless, helpless about her particular circumstances, helpless about her capacity to change them." This surely is the abused woman struggling through the drought each day, parched for the drops of affection that never fall.

An abused woman who remains in the relationship isn't staying because she wants to, but because she feels incapable of leaving. As she looks in the mirror her abuser holds before her, she can't see herself; all she can see is the "no-good person" he has painted there. Dr. Lois Veronen, the psychologist on the January 27, 1994, Sally Jessy Raphael television show, explained that an abuser paints that picture by repeatedly telling her what she thinks and feels until there is none of her own honest thinking and feeling left. Although longing to escape—to build on the life she had begun maybe years ago before entering this relationship, to be independent, to have friends, to find a man who would love her—she knows she is not good enough or smart enough or strong enough to do it. So she stays.

In "The Battered Woman Syndrome" (*Domestic Violence on Trial*, edited by Daniel Jay Sonkin), Mary Ann Douglas pinpoints the way in which low self-esteem holds a woman back. The abused woman, she writes, believes her acceptance of abuse "proves her to be worthless as a wife and mother, worth neither the time nor attention required by others to help her create a safe environment." Her abuser has trapped her, not so much through fear and shame as through the conviction of her own worthlessness.

Three other emotional factors may also play a role. One is guilt. If her man has been successful, he has manipulated her into accepting responsibility for the abuse he heaps on her: she must be stupid, or he wouldn't say she was; she must be crazy, or she would remember where she left the keys; her friends and family must be as bad as she, or he would let her see them; she must be incapable of handling money, or he would give her some. Guilty, therefore, of the behavior that provokes his justifiable abuse, she must deserve what she gets and has no cause to leave. One woman had so completely accepted her guilt that she made excuses for her husband, saying, "You know, he doesn't want to treat me that way, but what else can he do with me?"

Hope is a second emotional factor that plays a part. The on-and-off pattern of abuse discussed in Chapter 6, women tell me, keeps hope eternally springing, with the result that they can't settle into a mind-set that convinces them life is intolerable and will remain so until they leave. Their life does change, sometimes from day to day. While a man may call his wife a bitch and lock her in the room on Monday because dinner was cold, on Wednesday he may apologize with a bunch of flowers in hand. On Thursday he may take her out to dinner and whisper words of love over candlelight and on Friday break her car window because she dared visit a friend. If she were able to step out of the scene and watch it objectively from afar, she would see it as the cyclic abuse it is. She can't do that, though, because she believes in the magic of hope, which is really only the make-believe of self-delusion.

The opposite of hope, emotional numbness, may also keep a woman clinging to the status quo of abuse: "It doesn't hurt so much anymore." The gazelle I saw caught by a jaguar in Africa struggled for a moment, then lay motionless in the jaguar's grip while the lifeblood drained from it. Hopelessness—for the gazelle had no chance of escape—made it stop fighting and accept its fate. That's what many women do, resign themselves to what they consider an inescapable life of abuse instead of fighting to get free.

Recently a young woman led a friend of hers into court for an order of protection. As the latter stood as pale and expressionless as a zombie, her friend explained that she needed protection from an agonizing marriage. "Does she want to leave?" I asked.

Her friend explained, "She says whatever he does doesn't hurt anymore, but she's afraid he may kill her." In the process of giving up the fight, whether it is a gazelle or a woman, feelings of pain subside. Most women who have given birth within the past twenty years or so have experienced this through natural childbirth. What used to be so body-wrenching that we reached for whiffs of twilight sleep or the gas mask on the delivery table has been transformed into manageable pain by going with the flow of labor. By not fighting the contraction as it rises and crests but relaxing and riding with it, a woman controls her pain.

There is the key to lessening pain—control. A physician explained to me that while certain wounds and diseases hurt, what increases the pain is not knowing how much more they will hurt in a minute or an hour or a day. He made it sound like being on a torture rack that you could endure at the present rate but could not control against possible greater pain. To lessen pain and anxiety today, many hospitals no longer make patients rely on a nurse but turn control over to the patients by letting them regulate their own dosage of painkillers through intravenous tubes. As a result the hospitals find that, being in control, the patients require far less medication than with the traditional method. With no need to fight pain, they feel less pain.

In the play *Three Hotels* the woman in a hurtful relationship makes the observation that "a particular brand of cruelty ceases to hurt." I think it would be more accurately stated that a particular brand of resignation makes cruelty cease to hurt. An abused woman who surrenders hope surrenders a large share of pain. Like the gazelle, she stops fighting; like the woman in labor, she relaxes with each pang; like the hospital patient, she doses herself with the painkiller of choice—resignation: "It doesn't hurt so much anymore." So she stays.

PART III

Reactions to Nonphysical Abuse

CHAPTER 9

"Just another domestic dispute."

The Police Response to Abuse

"TED WAS MY HERO," Carol said as she began the story of her marriage, which had been headlined in local newspapers and viewed on national television not because it was worse than many stories of abuse but because the abuser was a police officer. For ten years he had used every nonphysical means to batter her. Socially he isolated her from her family and forced her into his family, even living next door to them. Emotionally, she says, "I walked on eggs" to avoid confrontations. Psychologically, after battering her, he made her kneel down beside him and say the rosary with him until she didn't know whether she was praying to God or participating in a satanic rite. Economically, he insisted on high living—two boats, cars, expensive vacations, a $300,000 home—all on the money she earned as a district manager of a large firm.

"I was so busy being supermom," she explained, "that I didn't have time to notice the abuse. He made me do everything and do it right and do it on time—cook, clean, care

157

for the four kids—and all the time I had to travel a lot because of my job. Life was such a mad rush that he set up dinner and lovemaking by appointment." As a result, Carol had a breakdown and fell into a clinical depression so severe that her therapist felt the need to hospitalize her. Ted refused, insisting, "I need her at home."

Carol had to quit her job because of her poor health, and without her ample paycheck rolling in each month, Ted grew more abusive and she more depressed. "I wish I were dead," she sighed one day.

"You do?" Ted screamed. "I'll show you what dead's like," and he proceeded to beat her up and down the stairs for thirty minutes or more. When she ran for the phone, he threatened to kill her. Hearing her screams for help, his family rushed in and restrained him, making it clear that they did so not to save her but to keep him out of trouble. On their tenth wedding anniversary, with a big party under way and Carol cooking up gourmet dishes, Ted cornered Carol in the kitchen, yelling, "You know, I really hate you, hate you, hate you."

Stunned and enraged, Carol dared to yell back, "Fuck you," at which Ted assaulted her, pulling out handfuls of her hair and tearing her thumb from its socket; then he grabbed his gun and ran out. At that point with her nine-year-old son crying, "Mommy, can I help you?" she made up her mind to leave.

"Some women stick around because of their children," she said concluding her story. "I left because of mine. I only wish I'd done it before he began the physical stuff." The kind of abuse Carol had suffered for years when she was too busy and too naive to recognize it was a natural precursor to her beatings.

While the abuse Carol suffered was traumatic, as all abuse is, the reaction of the police from whom she sought protection was even worse. She received no help from the police during her ten abusive years with Ted, nor has she in the four years since she left him. They never arrested him, never removed him from their home, never even wrote up a report to send, along with a file number, to the local crime victims board. Carol couldn't accuse them of erasing it from the slate because they had not even put it on the slate. What they did was worse—acted as though it had never happened.

Outraged, she persisted in her demand for a police investigation of Ted's behavior, and although the police chief denied it repeatedly, in a final decision to quiet her he acquiesced. The investigation was perfunctory, ending with the expected finding that there was no substantiation for her charges. That, she felt, left her only two ways to go: a private investigation and the media. The police chief refused the former, so she took the latter into her own hands.

As Carol's story became news, she began receiving calls from wives of other police officers, who told similar horror stories of battering by police husbands and police systems. Nancy Moshe wrote in the local *Women's News* in June 1992, "The stories were legion about inequitable treatment and powerlessness; of women being patronized, told to seek counseling, and even ignored while police officers continued to lead normal lives, working and having enormous power. Cops in question are even allowed to keep their guns, it was reported." No longer alone in her hurt and frustration, Carol formed a group called Partners of Police Officers, whose mission, she states, was to enhance the quality of life in the police home. Though Carol's group is no longer in operation, similar groups exist in scattered parts of the country.

Why, people ask, do wives of policemen need to unite for self-help? Why not wives of bankers or physicists or accountants? Statistics answer with the finding that 64 percent of police officers have family violence; a woman police sergeant whose name I won't mention for fear of reprisals from her male counterparts concurs. "No wonder," she says. "Many of them get into the force for the power trip."

Carol offers this explanation: "Any man who has power over life and death expects full control." Certainly abuse is a matter of control, but there are other factors as well.

One factor may be what originally draws a man into police work. It is dangerous and potentially violent; it reinforces a strong male image; until recently it created a male world, proudly excluding women; it commanded respect through a uniform and power through a gun. While no studies linking the characteristics of police work to the characteristics of the men in it exist, it seems logical that it would draw a larger proportion of macho men than most other professions, with the exception of the military.

Some years ago I conducted a study of marines to discover whether any common characteristics emerged to a significant degree. They did—authoritarianism, antifeminism, and dominance. As an aside, it is interesting that Carol's husband Ted wanted to join the marines, as his father had, but was rejected because of a back problem. Carol concluded that the police was the closest he could get. This being the case, it might follow that the mixed elements of violence and domination are personal needs that many policemen seek to fulfill through their daily work by sublimation. Since violence and domination are also the personal needs abusers fulfill through their marriage, a link between the two seems plausible.

Another factor, it is suggested, that plays a role in the high percentage of policemen who are batterers may well be the undue amount of stress under which they work. While they are in a position to mete out death any second of their day, they are similarly in a position to have death meted out to them—around the next corner, from the next rooftop, across the next street, through the next window. When they stop a cruising car to check a license, the driver may shoot them; when they question a kid with drugs, he may knife them. Helpless and blaming themselves, policemen may see their partners gunned down before their eyes.

Stress leads a policeman to overreact on the street, seeing a gun where there is none, taking aim too quickly, restraining too forcefully. To scream at his wife, humiliate her, demand her obedience, threaten her, beat her, and even kill her may be a policeman's method of choice for relieving the buildup of stress. It is hard to avoid the conclusion that policemen's use of violence as a pressure valve for releasing stress is usually directed at those with less power, those over whom they fear losing control—the prisoner, the rebellious teen, the wife.

Policemen give their own explanations for the jaded view they take of wife abuse. Many of them point out that more police are injured in answering domestic violence calls than any other way. The husband and wife are "going at each other," they say, and she calls for help. When they arrive to separate them, the couple turns on the policemen, and they leave with a bloody nose. Others feel there's no point in arresting a man even when the woman wants it because there is so little follow-through from the justice system. Although they may keep him locked up during the night, the next morning the judge lets him go with a warning, or the woman drops the charges, and they go home together, until the next time. These officers, it seems, simply do not want to believe that an abused woman who calls the police may be in danger of being seriously injured or killed. If she later tells them everything is all right it's because she is afraid to tell them everything is all wrong. Whatever factors come into play, it is a fact that policemen are more prone to wife abuse than other men—certainly not all of them, not even a majority, but a large enough number to warrant concern and action. It is perhaps their individual perception of men's and women's sex roles and the abuse it leads to that colors their response to abused women when they are summoned. This being possible, it is also possible that as they learn more about abuse, their attitudes and behavior will change. Therein lies hope for their own wives and for wives of abusers across the country.

What seems to be a larger percentage is the number of police systems that, like Ted's, turn a deaf ear and a blind eye to the woman whose abuser is one of their own. Jeanine Pirro, the Westchester County (New York) district attorney who some years before her election established the county's domestic violence unit, recalls an incident that explains police deafness and blindness in the face of abuse. She was explaining to a group of forty-three police chiefs the sober realities of woman battering and the desperate need for the new unit. When she finished, one of the police chiefs felt no shame in making the following statement: "There isn't a guy in this room who doesn't think it's okay to beat your wife" (*Scarsdale Inquirer*, November 23, 1993).

Typical of that thinking is the police lieutenant with an officer married to a woman who appeared in Family Court for an order of protection. After years of threats, deprivation, degradation, and finally actual assault, she went to the lieutenant with charges that from a total stranger would have warranted an immediate investigation. But the charges were against one of the officers in his precinct, so the lieutenant, without even questioning her husband, much less investigating on a broader scale, shrugged off her accusations with "It's your word against his. Forget it."

In another case a woman emotionally and economically abused to the point of total dependence called the police because her policeman husband wouldn't give her medicine their child needed. Before the police arrived, fearful for her safety under her husband's threats, she locked herself in the bedroom. Her husband meanwhile waited downstairs at the door to greet his fellow police when they arrived and to give them his version of the story. With no further inquiry the police broke into the bedroom and ordered her out of the house, threatening to arrest her if she didn't comply.

One woman who called the police on three occasions of battering with the plea that they arrest her husband told me, "All my husband had to do was flash his police badge, and they would wink, give me a dressing-down, and leave with a warning—to me, not to him."

For many policemen the code of brotherhood under which they operate extends beyond their fellow officers to include all their fellow males. Family Court judge Adrienne Scancarelli hopes police will learn to take family abuse more seriously. "They answer a call and see a hysterical woman and often a calm man who manipulates them into thinking his wife imagined or exaggerated the whole thing," she explains. Then the police tell the woman to "go to your mother's and calm down," they leave, and the man continues to abuse his wife.

Women being the gentle sex the stereotype claims they are, one would expect female police officers to respond to abused women with greater empathy than their male counterparts do. According to Lisa Frisch of the New York State Office for the Prevention of Domestic Violence, however, this is not always the case. "Women police may be worse than men," she says. "They may try to distance themselves from the submissive stereotype in order not to feel powerless." She adds that most women have probably had negative experiences during training—harassment and social exclusion—in response to which they determine "to be men" as a means of self-defense.

Regardless of sex, police too often fail to provide protection to the abused woman who calls out to them for help. A middle-aged woman has come to court many times to report violations of her protective order, which stipulates that her husband is not to harass, assault, or threaten her and which he ignores. Although he had never touched her, he regularly beat her down by calling her stupid, by denying her money, by refusing her phone calls, by threatening to turn her into the street—by generally dehumanizing her. The several times she called the police, her husband convinced them she was crazy, and, shaking their head in sympathy over the burden he had to bear, they left. One day this woman came to us in court with a broken nose and bruised arms and torso. The police, having readily identified with her husband, never extended themselves to evaluate the situation from her side of the battering.

In another case, when the ex-husband of a woman who for six years had been nonphysically abused in the extreme was screaming and trying to kick down the door of her apartment, even urinating on it, she called the police to have him removed. "I just want to see her," he wept to the police when they arrived. "Poor guy, let him in," the police called through the door.

As Judge Scancarelli indicated from repeated experience, this man had used an abuser's favorite ploy and succeeded in manipulating the policemen into viewing him not as an abuser but as a loving husband who merely wanted to make amends with his former wife. Instead of dragging him away or locking him up for a violation of his wife's protective order or at least for disorderly conduct, the police lent their voice to his and urged her, "Open the door and let him in. He only wants to talk to you." She refused, because the last time she had let him in "to talk," he broke two chairs and threatened to beat her up.

Another woman whose husband had her on the verge of a breakdown from intense nonphysical battering finally called the police to have him removed from their home. The last straw had been a rage in which he trashed the house, threw boxes of frozen food from the refrigerator onto the sofa, emptied the cat box in her closet, and broke her favorite knickknacks. The police admitted the man had made a mess but refused to file a report because "it's only a family affair." The irony in all these cases is that, had the situation involved any man other than a husband, they would have arrested him immediately.

There are worse stories we hear in court, stories played out after the police have ignored and all but encouraged nonphysical abuse. For instance, as her husband was beating her, a woman escaped to the bedroom and called the police for the second time within a week. When they arrived, although bruises and bleeding cuts were apparent, they greeted her with "Oh, it's you again." Her husband had been arrested three times for rape, drugs, and assault, yet the police did not arrest the man or order him to leave. Instead they suggested that she leave until her husband calmed down. Sometimes, of course, they are more considerate and tell the man to walk around the block until the woman calms down!

One young woman who came to court was in such pain that she could barely move her arm and shoulder. The night before, her husband had punched her, thrown her against the wall, and, knowing she had kidney stones, beaten her on the lower back. He then held her while his girlfriend hit her. In a feeble effort to free herself, she clawed at him, leaving fingernail scratches, and was finally able to call the police. When they came and looked over the situation, they told her husband to go to the hospital to get medication for his scratches and left her there alone in her physical and emotional pain.

These are not isolated incidents. *The Ohio Report on Domestic Violence* (Ohio Attorney General, 1980) states that the police file few reports on family abuse and rarely make arrests. Of 15,000 calls in one city, they filed reports on only 700 men and arrested only 460. Although nonphysical abuse qualifies as a punishable offense in most states, almost no reports are filed or arrests made until the abuse is not only physical but severe. Even then, police officers tend to look the other way.

Sometimes an arrest is not made because the woman drops charges when the police threaten to arrest her as well as her husband. For instance, she may have grabbed a kitchen knife and stabbed him in self-defense as he beat her. When the police arrive, although they see her with a black eye, bloody nose, and purple arm and neck bruises, they also see the cut on his hand she made while trying to ward him off. The situation is not hypothetical: the other day a woman dropped charges when the policeman told her, "I'm putting you both in jail because I'm not going to sort this out."

Sometimes an arrest is not made because there is no one to arrest when they answer the woman's call for help. A man doesn't run if he has learned from previous experience that the police won't arrest him or if his rage is so out of control that he doesn't care or if he has torn the phone from the wall so the woman can't call for help in the first place. Otherwise he has sense enough to disappear before the police get there. Unfortunately, he doesn't always need a great deal of sense, like the batterer whose wife called the police at 6:40 P.M. amid an abusive scene, only to wait until 9:10 for them to arrive.

To assure greater justice, many communities have instituted arrest policies. The most effective is a mandatory arrest policy that requires police to make an arrest in all family abuse calls; similar to it is a pro-arrest policy that, while not requiring automatic arrest, urges it in most cases. However, regulations determining arrest often preclude the possibility in either case. For instance, although nonphysical abuse may completely debilitate a woman, unless it includes threats of bodily harm, there are no grounds for arrest. In addition, while in some communities police can arrest on evidence of battering, in others they have to witness the actual battering themselves. Since few men will pummel their wife while a policeman takes notes, there are still few arrests, but with statistics showing that incarceration cuts down further abuse up to 41 percent, for a period of time at any rate, many communities are making an effort to install policies that will ensure arrest.

Despite the triviality with which many policemen view wife abuse, a woman does have recourse to fight it. One is the Citizens Complaint Board to which she may appeal for disciplinary action against the police she feels treated her wrongly. Unfortunately, many communities have no complaint board; New York, for instance, abandoned its boards throughout the state several years ago. Another recourse is a woman's right to sue a municipality for liability when a police officer fails to protect her from her abuser.

This is Carol's hope, but she, along with many other women, discover the hopelessness of such action without what the court calls solid evidence; and by the time the court calendar schedules the case, the solid evidence has long since healed under its splints and bandages. Although the court admits photographic evidence of battering wounds, many women have no available camera or are too traumatized to use one in the aftermath of a beating, and there is no way to pose for the throbbing hurts of nonphysical battering.

The greatest hope for changing the attitudes of policemen toward family abuse is education, which is being instituted in police academies across the country and is required of police already on the job in many cities. Lisa Frisch of

the New York Office for the Prevention of Family Violence
runs a course to teach police why they can't just shrug off
family abuse. Sergeant Anne FitzSimmons of White Plains,
New York, says that even though she was sympathetic to wife
abuse before taking the course, it made her examine it from
an entirely different viewpoint. "I used to see abuse and
think, Why doesn't she just leave?" she explains. "The course
made me understand why."

Whether a majority of police react as positively as
FitzSimmons did is questionable. Some who take the course
become aware of their own liability, realizing that if they
fail to act on a battering charge and the woman is later
injured or killed—as all too often has been the case—they
will be held personally responsible. "It doesn't take a lot of
brains to know what to do after you hear that," an officer
told me. In that respect education works on behalf of the
battered woman, altering, if not police attitudes, at least
police responses.

Whether a day-long seminar or a two-day course can
change sexist attitudes remains unsure. The machismo that
makes men accept or at least look the other way in the face
of abuse of women is deeply rooted in prejudice that reinforces society's stereotypes of the dominant male and submissive female. According to Theodor Adorno, et al. in the
book *The Authoritarian Personality*, a definitive work on prejudice, "Individuals are most receptive to ideologies that are
most compatible with their over-all personality structures."
These individuals, the book goes on to say, are ready and
willing to obey a strong authority above them and release
their pent-up hostility against members of a weaker group
from whom they fear no reprisal.

Although prejudice is absorbed in early childhood
through parental teaching and role modeling, it is reinforced through interaction with members of one's own

group. Men call it *bonding*, which welds together men of a police precinct under the authority of their captain in the same way army basic training welds together privates in a platoon under their sergeant. Even though police are required to take courses, it is doubtful that the courses will be able to eliminate their prejudicial attitudes toward wife abuse because one of the chief characteristics of prejudice is its resistance to change. Any successful program must delve into the roots of the policeman's attitude as it grows from his environment and from his own individual personality. This might take years of therapy, certainly not a few days of lectures and films.

A small group of policemen whom I was interviewing one day referred constantly to "spouse abuse" in answering my questions about "wife abuse." I asked them why. "You have to be fair," one answered. "Women hit on their men too, you know." Yes, I know. I know that in fewer than 5 percent of physical abuse cases wives are the abusers, and a majority of those cases are in self-defense. I also know that in cases of nonphysical abuse, where wives may nag or belittle their husbands and dole out their paycheck in nickels and dimes, society neither condones nor reinforces their behavior. Certainly the police force doesn't.

Spouse abuse is a euphemism for skirting the truth that men abuse women. Until the police can admit *wife abuse* into their vocabulary and into their consciousness, they will continue to encourage it in their own lives and in the lives of the citizens—even female citizens—whom they have a sworn duty to protect. The media might lead the way by also naming abuse for what it is.

A gleam of light is beginning to illuminate murky misunderstandings held by police, however, the source of which is insistence by public officials and government agencies. Chapter 15 will discuss in detail two cities that have developed model "domestic violence" programs that are being adapted by other cities and entire states across the country. However, even cities still unready to install full-scale programs like these are enough alarmed by the increasing incidence of abuse to create their own programs to combat it. For instance, in April 1994 New York's mayor Rudolph Giuliani assigned a police officer and a detective in every police precinct to follow through on wife abuse cases and also instituted a course aimed at making police more aggressive in arresting abusive husbands. In response a woman who had been shouted down by the police after asking them to arrest her abusive lover told me bitterly, "I never suspected the police needed lessons in aggressiveness."

Whatever steps communities take to lead the police across the barriers of their stereotypes into understanding and action will surely save lives, some of the thousands of women lost to battering in America each year. What it will do in far greater numbers, however, is reinforce the hundreds of thousands of women who have no escape from the fear and humiliation of nonphysical abuse. Since women vote their concerns, perhaps the steps will be speedy ones. As *The New York Times*, on April 26, 1994, wrote, "Both the Council and the Mayor appeared to be vying to demonstrate which is more serious about tackling the problem of violence against women." Competition holds out promise.

CHAPTER 10

"Go home and behave yourselves."

The Court Response to Abuse

THAT MASTER OF LANGUAGE H. L. Mencken encapsulated the sometime lunacy of a courtroom in the following observation: "The penalty for laughing in a courtroom is six months in jail; if it were not for this penalty, the jury would never hear the evidence."

Women who appear before a judge seeking protection from their nonphysical abusers might agree with Mencken that what transpires in court is often so illogical as to be ludicrous. They might laugh if they weren't crying. As Lucy, who has been through the courts for ten years, said, "The justice system is a joke: all system but no justice." Her story is not atypical.

When Lucy and Joe married, they had the bakery write on their wedding cake, "For as long as possible." Instinctively they knew "forever" wasn't for them. Joe, who had done a good job of convincing Lucy of her incompetence during their two years of living together, considered wife abuse a male sport like football; Lucy let him play.

It wasn't long after their marriage, however, before the game got rough: in a back-to-nature surge, Joe quit his job, rented a farmhouse in the middle of the West Virginian nowhere, and sat back while Lucy fed and watered the two cows, four pigs, and a dozen chickens, raised and canned vegetables, and repainted their six rooms. He forbade her family to visit, and when her mother did anyway after the birth of their baby girl Cassie, he chased her away with an ax. Lucy protested, so he trashed the house and drove off in the car with the baby.

As his abuse increased, Lucy plotted ways to escape, but with Joe ever watchful and threatening, it took her two years. While he was napping one day, Lucy took the baby and slipped away on the long drive to her parents in New Jersey. The next day she hired a divorce lawyer and got a temporary order of protection. Thus began ten years during which she traveled through the court system maze in an effort to find her way from Harassment to Peace, running into dead ends that blocked her way. Feeling like a player in a board game, she repeatedly found herself back at Start:

- Because Joe followed her, she and Cassie registered under a false name in a Trenton hotel. When he found them there, they spent three weeks racing from motel to motel along the turnpike with him stalking. When she returned for her court date, the judge, amused by her jaunt, told Joe to behave himself.

- She rented an apartment, and Joe kicked her front door in when she wouldn't talk to him. Back in court, the judge reminded Joe to behave himself.

- Joe phoned her, shouting obscenities, twenty to thirty times a day, and when she got an unlisted number, he began calling her parents, who took him to court. The judge said no more phone calls. That day he called them 134 times.

- When Joe returned Cassie, now almost four, from court-ordered weekend visits, Lucy noticed redness and swelling around her genitals and called the Child Protective Service. They felt there was sex abuse, so Lucy went to court again. Joe said, "They can't prove I did anything. Maybe her mother's not keeping her clean," and the judge gave him another chance.

- When Lucy, devastated over what she knew was happening to her daughter, refused visits, Joe snatched her from the baby-sitter in the park one day. The judge scolded Joe and limited visits to Sundays.

- Joe sent Lucy obscene postcards, taught Cassie to French-kiss, and returned her hours late from visits. The judge ordered supervised visits.

- Joe dodged the supervisors.

- When Lucy and Cassie moved to the suburbs, he rented a room in a house next door and hung huge signs on telephone poles along the school bus route that read, "Cassie, I'm here." The child cried and wouldn't go to school. The judge had him remove the signs.

- When Cassie played softball in Little League, Joe stood behind her at third base, talking. Cassie dropped out of Little League.

- At school plays or music programs he sat in the front row, calling to Cassie to make sure she saw him. The judge wouldn't order him to stay away—"fathers' rights"—so Cassie developed a stomachache on program days and stayed home.

- Joe stopped paying the thirty-dollars-a-week child support ordered by the judge. The judge allowed him visits anyway.

- Cassie hid when her father came to get her for visits and had nightmares afterward. The judge continued visits.

- Joe harassed Lucy on the phone at work and filled Cassie with hate talk about her on visits. He spied on her from outside her home and once waited in the garage to grab her from the car when she drove in (a bad idea: the dog bit him on the nose).

Through all this abuse over all those years, no one paid much attention to Lucy's protective orders—not Joe, not the police, not the court, and eventually, not even Lucy herself. And judge after judge paid little attention to the violation of child support payments, to the unceasing harassment, even to the possibility of sexual molestation. Only now, ten years later, has one judge finally cut off visits and disallowed phone calls and appearances at school. Against the court order, Joe still telephones several times a day; neither Cassie nor Lucy talks to him. He still sneaks into school functions, once dressed as a woman, but the principal ushers him out. He still gets by without paying child support by working off the books.

Lucy entered the court maze naive and trustful of the system set up to protect the innocent. That meant her, she believed then. What she believes now, however, after a decade of roadblocks and false signposts, is that she will never reach her destination because the courts are as abusive as Joe. In many ways they mirror the nonphysical abuse that she fled.

Like the average American household, the courts are male-dominated, a fact that biases them against women and, in the words of Daniel J. Sonkin (*Domestic Violence on Trial*), "prevents women from receiving equal treatment with men."

A nonphysically abused woman in court has no more control over her life than a woman in an abusive relationship. While she pleads for her sanity and safety in Family Court, the judge weighs the issue of rights—the abuser's rights—often arriving at decisions so off target that she can only feel along with Dickens's Mr. Bumble that "the law is a ass." At one hearing, when Lucy asked that visits be no longer than three hours for the sake of Cassie, and Joe demanded eight, the judge compromised on five . . . until against all rules he allowed Joe to approach the bench alone. After a few whispered words, Joe left with eight-hour visitations, and Lucy with no recourse.

Court abuse parallels the four kinds of nonviolent abuse women suffer in relationships, discussed in Chapters 1–4:

Emotional Abuse

The court further shrinks a woman who comes to it already diminished in size. I hear judges, like abusive husbands, scold women, laugh at them, and in some instances actually call them stupid. I see women fight to hold back tears of humiliation and stumble from the courtroom in disbelief after a curt dismissal. To give judges the benefit of the doubt, most of them, I suppose, are unaware of the degradation they reinforce in the women who come before them; they too are men and women conditioned by history and by society's mores. If wife abuse is systematic, court abuse is usually unconscious.

But not always. In one instance a woman had a hearing not before a judge but before a magistrate, a lawyer acting in the capacity of judge to speed up the court calendar. She, her lawyer, and her ex-husband met in his office, which had an adjacent bathroom. From the start he expressed such hostility toward the woman and her lawyer, also a woman, that they suspected he must be replaying a difficult relationship of his own. Time after time he smiled knowingly at the abuser as if giving the sign of a secret society, while cutting off the woman's lawyer at every accusation and piece of evidence she attempted to present. At one point he walked from his office into the bathroom, where, without closing the door and in full sight of both women, he unzipped his trousers and urinated. The woman was mortified; the lawyer was outraged, yet neither dared speak up or leave because the stakes were too high. In a letter she subsequently wrote to the chief judge, the woman complained that the magistrate had made her feel as if she were back in her abusive marriage.

Psychological Abuse

As Kafka scathingly dramatized in his novel *The Trial,* a court procedure so reverses reality that right twists around into wrong, truth into lies, and logic into absurdity. For instance, Judy Kissell, who worked for six years at the Northern Westchester [New York] Shelter for Victims of Domestic Violence, tells of a woman who, with her child, fled an abusive marriage to the safety of the shelter. Although she was a careful and nurturing mother who put her child above all other concerns, her husband sued for custody. In the court hearing the law guardian argued that if the woman would learn to live with her husband more smoothly—the husband who battered her in front of her child—she would be a better mother for him. The judge, relying on this skewed reasoning, awarded custody to the father. The woman was left with no choice but to return to her abusive marriage to avoid losing her child.

The court has used diametrically opposite reasoning with other mothers, decreeing that by staying with men who batter them in front of their children—whether physically or nonphysically—they prove themselves unfit mothers. These women either remain in the relationship and lose their children or, unlike the woman above, are forced to leave before they are emotionally or economically ready so as to keep them. As Camille Murphy, director of the Office for Women in Westchester County, New York, says, "Such actions do not necessarily provide safety for the children or the mother." What they do provide for the woman is further evidence that the court plays mind games with her.

A single judge's decision on either side of the game board does not stand alone in the record book of decisions, nor is Lucy the only woman misused in court. The media report dozens of cases of sexually abused children returned to their abusers, of battered wives denied protection who wind up in jail for protecting themselves, and of frightened women whose pleas for help go unanswered until too late, when they are found murdered.

The court thrusts an abused woman into the insanity of a Catch-22 situation, which one woman described to the *Scarsdale Inquirer* this way: "No matter what I said was dangerous. If I said I'd fallen apart and kept going back to him, how could I take care of the kids? If I was strong, I was described as this angry, vicious, jealous wife and asked why did I let this happen?" What she was saying in her distress was that if she used weakness as an explanation for her return to her husband, the court damned her as an unfit mother; if, on the other hand, she presented herself as adequately strong to rear her children, the court labeled her as aggressive, blaming her for provoking the abuse in the first place. The abused woman can't win: the court uses a stacked deck.

Social Abuse

Before an abused woman enters the courtroom of Family
Court, she sits for hours in a crowded room of wooden
benches, sometimes with male respondents having to be
quieted or removed by police, always with children and
babies fretting. When her case is finally called and she is led
by a policeman into the courtroom, she stands alone. In front
of her on a raised platform behind a large table sits the judge
in black robe glancing over her petition; to the judge's left
is the court stenographer, staring into space as his or her
fingers fly; to the judge's right, the court clerk is busy with
papers; and somewhere near the wall stands a police officer, somber-faced, with pistol clearly visible. No one looks
at her. Often no one asks her to be seated, so she stands
throughout the hearing. Some courts allow a court assistant
to sit behind the woman for moral support—not to speak,
just to be there—although her presence rests at the judge's
discretion. I have seen a court assistant refused admittance
at a hearing simply because a woman's abuser didn't want
her there.

Just as a woman's abusive partner turned her into a nonperson, so the court continues to treat her. Although upon
demand she states her name for the court stenographer to
record, she stands there a docket number and not always
the right one. More than once I have seen judges read off
the accusations on the petition before them only to discover
from the court clerk's whisper that they have the wrong person. Often the judge rattles off his decision so routinely and
dismisses the woman so quickly that she leaves like a sleep-
walker, not sure what has happened. "I don't think he even
saw me," one woman said, looking back from the hall at the
closed door of the courtroom.

The situation just described is what I see when I am in
the court where I work. In other courts the petitioner may

not even see a judge but may file with a court clerk and for a hearing come before a magistrate or general master. Judges may sign decisions without ever seeing the woman or even reading the papers she filed. One judge avoided hearings by automatically giving a woman who filed for protection a routine HAT order—a rather weak one that says the abusive man may not harass, assault, or threaten her. However, since she was denied the opportunity of pleading her individual case before the judge, he may have put her in jeopardy by not addressing her need for a stronger order that would make him leave and stay away from her home and children.

For fact-finding hearings the judge may assign the woman a court-appointed lawyer if her income does not exceed a specified sum, usually around $20,000. Some lawyers contact their clients by phone, but many, too heavily booked, first speak to them on the day of their court appearance, when they are also representing other clients. Having no voice in the lawyer's selection, even if the woman petitioner doesn't feel confident in the lawyer, she cannot change.

Law guardians and Child Protective Service caseworkers may also be assigned to a woman's case when her child is involved in custody or abuse. Yet they too, under the burden of excessively heavy caseloads, are able to invest little personal care or individualized attention. One day a woman whose child's visitation with an abusive father depended on what the CPS worker had to say was unable to contact the worker to have her appear in court. Another time I heard a CPS worker tell a lawyer, "If her case isn't called next, I have to leave," and she did. While these people may be drawn to the profession through caring, the nature of their work depends more on their time than on their heart.

Lawyers tell me that the most difficult professionals to secure for a court appearance in behalf of their client are

psychiatrists or psychologists appointed by the court to ver-
ify accusations of abuse. Unfortunately, theirs is the very testimony that could decide a case in the woman's favor. "They
won't sit around court waiting for a couple of hours, though,"
a lawyer complained to me, "and the judge won't take their
report in writing." Since the expert witness has to appear in
person, and since most of the time he or she can't, the
abused woman once again stands alone.

Economic Abuse

Most women are penniless while in their abusive relationships, penniless when they enter the court system, and penniless when they leave. If a woman is indigent, she has a court
lawyer with little time for her; if she has what the judge
deems an adequate income (often not taking into account
how many children she has to support and how little financial help she receives from their father), she hires her own
lawyer. Since the lawyer is paid by the hour, she wants to
waste as little time with the lawyer as possible, especially sitting around in court waiting to be called, which can add up
to hundreds of dollars a day.

If a woman has to pay a lawyer, she may quickly deplete
her funds, with the result that she will become eligible for
a court-appointed lawyer. However, since some states disal-
low a court lawyer in Family Court, the woman may have to
appear *pro se*—represent herself in court. This, according
to Judge Owen S. Allbritton of the Clearwater, Florida, Family Court, "is a real mess." As long as the law allows a man
to bring charges, appeal, and file for a new hearing as often
as he wants—as is the case now—and as long as he is allowed
to violate orders that force the woman to bring charges, the
lawyer she pays will drain her funds rapidly. This eventual-
ity is the goal of many abusive husbands and ex-husbands.
Joe, Lucy's husband, for instance, told both Lucy and her

father, who was helping out with the bills, "I'll see to it that you spend every cent of your savings. Then what?" The "what" he envisioned was Lucy crawling back to him, impoverished and helpless, the perfect scenario for abuse.

When Jawaharlal Nehru accused the courts of being "too impersonal, distant, and too little aware of the consequences of the sentences they award," the wisdom of his words stretched far beyond India. American women who reach out to the justice system from the helpless isolation and degradation of their abusive relationships too often find themselves further manipulated and mind-bent by the courts. Their judges are not deliberately heartless, merely "too little aware" of the impact of their decision. To them the case is closed. While the judge scans the next papers on the docket, the last docket number, who in reality is a person, a woman, leaves the court for a fearsome unknown.

Laws to help battered women look a lot better on the books than they act out in the court. All states and Washington, D.C., have laws that aim to protect them, forty-three of which, according to Lerman and Livingston's "State Legislation on Domestic Violence" (from *Civil Protection Orders* by Peter Finn and Sarah Colson for the National Institute of Justice, March 1990), enable women to obtain protective orders without instituting either a divorce proceeding or a broader civil suit. At last count thirty-three states allow police to make arrests when called in incidents of abuse, some counties and/or cities and towns within states having mandatory arrest laws, others giving police support with a pro-arrest policy. While most states do not legislate wife battering as a separate criminal offense, eleven states have enacted such laws. The federal government, however, has no legislation covering abuse, although a Violence Against Women Act, which has passed in the House, is still lying low in the Senate.

Adults appear to be of greater concern to legislators than children: all fifty states issue protective orders for abuse to adults, while only thirty-three issue them for child abuse. Not surprisingly, legislators react more readily to physical abuse than to nonphysical: every state issues a protective order for physical abuse, while only forty-three states do so for the *threat* of physical abuse, a threat constituting nonphysical abuse. Three fewer states, only forty, consider an attempt at physical abuse dangerous enough to warrant a protective order.

The core of nonphysical abuse, as women who have been the target of it know all too well, reaches farther and deeper and with sharper claws than threats. The burst of "I'm going to kill you" creates fear, but the steady erosion of personhood, the shame of worthlessness, the disorientation in a world turned upside down are far worse, women tell me. "I kept wishing he would kill me," Danielle said. The courts, however, give little credence to the kinds of nonphysical abuse that make a woman's life a living hell. And often a dying hell as well, since all violent abuse begins with the controlling acts of nonphysical abuse that the world blindly accepts.

Many states make no provisions for nonphysically abusive acts other than threats of a physical act. New York State, where I live and work, among other states, lists the following acts under the jurisdiction of either the Family Court or Criminal Court: disorderly conduct, harassment, menacing in the third degree, reckless endangerment, assault in the first or second degree or attempted assault. According to Article 8 of the Family Court Act, " 'disorderly conduct' includes disorderly conduct not in a public place," in other words, in the home, where most abuse happens.

While assault in both degrees and attempted assault are clearly physically abusive behaviors and are always seen so by judges, the other four behaviors are clearly nonphysically abusive acts and are not always seen so by judges. "It depends on the judge and the day," Danielle says in the wisdom of her experience. However, if anyone other than an abusive husband committed these four acts and anyone but an abused wife reported them, they would surely warrant fines or arrests. They are acts of wife battering:

- *Disorderly conduct:* yelling, obscenity, name-calling, breaking windows, kicking in doors

- *Harassment:* following her, hiding keys, letting air from the tires of her car, not allowing visits with family or friends, making repeated telephone calls, breaking her favorite things, disparaging her, making unreasonable demands

- *Menacing in the third degree:* locking her in a closet, locking her out of the house, waving a weapon before her, hitting her pet, cutting up her clothes, pretending to punch her

- *Reckless endangerment:* driving the child without a seat belt, forcing her out of the house at night, not letting her take prescribed medicine, forcing her to drink or take drugs

All of these are acts of nonphysical abuse from which a woman deserves the court's protection. She never gets it in states that classify these acts as merely family spats, and sometimes she doesn't get it in states that do. As Danielle says, it depends on the judge—some have their own agenda; and it depends on the day: maybe breakfast didn't sit right that morning.

Criminal Court is also able to give protective orders, although the abusive acts have to be more damaging for the district attorney's office to undertake prosecution. Physical abuse is the most common. However, the criminal court can prosecute for nonphysical abuse under three accusations:

- Harassment in the second degree: an act committed with intent to annoy, harass, or alarm another person or a series of acts that alarm or seriously annoy and serve no other purpose. If found guilty, the abuser can be jailed for fifteen days and ordered into counseling.

- Harassment in the first degree: the act of stalking a person or putting a person in fear of her life. If guilty, the abuser can get ninety days in jail and one year of probation.

- Aggravated harassment: acts of harassment over the telephone or through the mail. If guilty, the abuser may receive one year in jail and three years on probation.

In White Plains, New York, the district attorney's domestic violence chief, Mary Ann Martriano, reports that judges rarely jail a first offender and may or may not jail repeat offenders and those who violate orders of protection. Most women to whom I have spoken feel the judges are far too lenient, giving their abusers carte blanche to continue abuse.

Both the Family Court and Criminal Court laws outlined here apply only to New York State. Some other states are similar; many others differ. Joan Zorza of the National Center on Women and Family Law, which monitors family abuse laws throughout the country, says that most states do not allow harassment as a basis for abuse and that most states require more damaging evidence of stalking than New York. She finds, in addition, much to the detriment of abused ex-wives and girlfriends, that although phone harassment is illegal in most states, many judges shrug their shoulders and ignore it, saying, "What harm!"

Oliver Wendell Holmes was quoted as saying that "judges are apt to be naive, simple-minded men." As one of America's outstanding judges, he voiced what many women echo in the aftermath of court appearances from which they walk away stunned by a decision. "How could he have done that?" they often ask me, and I have no answer. How could the Mad Hatter have dunked his pocket watch in tea to tell time? I have no answer to that either.

Judges have no special training in domestic violence but bring to the bench the same myths and misunderstandings all of us have; the rest they learn on the job. Many judges, having little knowledge of psychology, misinterpret a woman's responses to abuse. If she drops charges against her mate instead of following through, the judge may condemn and castigate her like a naughty child without understanding the guilt and fear that blocks her. If she hangs on to an abusive relationship for longer than the judge deems sensible, he or she may accuse the woman of stupidity, never recognizing the desperate hope that keeps her there. If she pleads for her husband to stay away from her, the judge may order family counseling to settle their problem, unaware that the problem is not hers but her husband's for abusing her and the judge's for not knowing it.

More than naive and simpleminded, some judges seem so conditioned by historical and societal thinking that male respondents have an edge over female petitioners. The most prevalent evidence of this is the reluctance of judges to order men to vacate the homes they share with the wives they batter. On many occasions, according to my personal observation and to reporting by the *Scarsdale Inquirer* in November of 1993, if the judge refuses to grant a woman's plea to have her abusive husband removed from the home, the woman herself often leaves, possibly with several children and none of her belongings because she fears for her safety. In other words, when the judge won't protect her with justice, she settles for injustice and tries to protect herself.

Harriet is an example. Her husband literally forced her from their home, which was in her name, not his, taking also her money and other property she owned and threatening to kill her if she returned. When she came to court to plead her case and have her husband vacated, the judge denied her petition, explaining that both she and her husband had rights. Although he urged her to return home with him, fearing for her life, she refused. Now she is homeless, living with friends, who counsel her to move away and forget the whole incident. When she applied for an order of protection, the judge refused because there had been no incident on which to base the need.

Audrey is another example. My introduction to her was with these words: "I've been married forty years, thirty of them in hell." She is an educated woman and used to hold a job that earned her close to fifty thousand dollars a year, all of which her husband banked in his own account, giving her twenty dollars a week to run the house. He flaunts his girlfriends in front of her, lives with one woman part-time, and threatens to beat Audrey up if she dares to leave. The judge whom Audrey petitioned to have her husband removed so she could go on with a relatively peaceful life refused on the grounds that he hadn't beaten her yet. With that *yet* her future became clear: when he finally drew blood, she could get him out of the house . . . unless, of course, he killed her.

The Gannett newspapers in Westchester County, New York, ran a series of articles on Anne Scripps Douglas, a wealthy Westchester heiress who was beaten to death in her home on New Year's Eve. The apparent murderer was her husband, who fled the scene and committed suicide by jumping off a bridge. Two days earlier the victim had gone to court for an order of protection and an order for her husband to vacate the premises, but the judge was on vacation, and no one advised her to go to another nearby court. Earlier in December she had gone to court too, and although the judge was there, she showed no signs of knowing Ms. Douglas was living on the edge of danger: her husband remained in the home, despite the fact that earlier he had tried to push her from a moving car. Since the court repeatedly failed to protect her by turning down her pleas to remove her husband, she relied on their judgment and failed to protect herself. "The judge didn't take the case seriously and didn't look at it thoroughly," Ms. Douglas's first husband was quoted as saying.

In all fairness, we have to admit that judges in family violence cases don't have an easy time of it. First of all, the courts are inhumanly overcrowded. Often seating in pre-hearing waiting rooms is inadequate for the numbers who appear, and the judges' calendars are filled minute by minute, giving them little time to review a case before they see the petitioner.

Second, while many petitioners speak little or no English, often there is no interpreter in court to help the judge understand. I, with my few Berlitz phrases of Spanish, have even had to attempt translating for a Hispanic petitioner when the judge and others in court knew even less Spanish than I did. Third, the law itself often bogs judges down. Until recently and still in many states, a woman filing for a violation of the protective order she had received earlier wouldn't even see a judge but would fill out papers with the court clerk. Although the process saved court time, it frequently resulted in problems for which the judge had to bear responsibility.

In addition, the law that allows a petitioner to file for a protective order also allows the respondent to become a petitioner and counterfile for his own order. In simpler terms, when a woman applies for an order of protection against her mate, the man can legally file for one of his own against her. It is not unusual to see a man in court the next day, determined to "get even" with the woman who dared report him as an abuser. As a result the case becomes muddied, and the judges' time is further burdened.

Because they sit in such an exalted position of power, we expect Solomon's wisdom and God's justice from judges. We get neither because they are human and, like the rest of us, make mistakes. Our mistakes cost money and friendships and jobs. Their mistakes too often cost lives.

CHAPTER 11

"That's what marriage is."

The Views of Women on Abuse

WHEN I BEGAN WORK as a court assistant in Family Court, I was more deeply moved by the desperation of battered women than by any other group I had previously counseled, which included prison inmates, parents and teachers of at-risk children, and at-risk children themselves. So palpable were the pain and fear of women coming to court for orders of protection against their men—husbands, ex-husbands, live-in lovers, boyfriends that had been sent off and maybe replaced—that I felt only with the counseling and support our program provided could these needy women complete the process and achieve what we hoped was safety.

Since the court assistance program was understaffed, I urged a friend of mine to consider similar work. She listened sympathetically as I replayed the fear and pain of the women I faced each day, until I said, "The worst part is that since many of them have never been hurt physically, no one cares." She was appalled, not that no one cared, but that a woman whose man had not bruised and bloodied her was consid-

189

ered abused. That he had systematically used the weapons of nonphysical abuse to keep her imprisoned within walls of fear, degradation, and deprivation touched her not at all.

"For crying out loud," she blurted out, "no husband is perfect. What's all the fuss about?" I quickly changed my tack, suggesting she enter another line of work. Fortunately she did.

Although some women caught in abusive relationships fight as Lorena Bobbitt did, and some flee as women in safe shelters do, and some attempt to protect themselves through the courts, and some, as discussed in Chapter 8, make conscious accommodations, many merely shrug their shoulders as my friend did, believing "that's what marriage is." They allow themselves to feel no indignation over having to love, honor, and obey a man who demands control over their mind, their body, and their very soul, lowering them to the rank of servant or slave . . . to feel no shame at bending to his will so as to survive . . . to feel no hurt at being used rather than loved. Men are like that, they tell themselves; they knew what they were getting into. Because the world has imprinted its lesson indelibly on the tablet of their expectations, they do what even royal wives have done through the years—walk willingly behind their king.

Women on the outside of abuse look in on it differently. Some become haters of men, all men, unable to distinguish one from another. An example is a woman I met fifteen years ago who had been in what she called a so-so marriage for ten years, not abusive but not particularly happy either. However, media reports of battering and rapes and murders, along with outpourings from her friends about their abusive husbands, had begun to make her feel, as she put it, that "men are born brutes." So with her eight-year-old son she left her husband and took another partner, a woman.

That was fifteen years ago. In the ensuing years it has not been uncommon for women, both married and single, to reject male relationships and find companionship and love with other women. "There is more give-and-take when two women live together," a social worker explained to me. "Instead of competing for control, they are more apt to meet each other's needs on an equal basis."

Other women on the outside of abuse, like Sabine Reichel writing in the *Los Angeles Times,* react to the phenomenon of abuse with a 180-degree difference. They are just as hostile, but not toward men; they vent their anger on women for what Reichel calls "the female under-dog fairy tales." Women have no cause to complain, she rages, because they are responsible for whom they marry. They can "pick whom they want, be what they want, do what they want when and how they want it." If they wind up with an abuser, she rails on, "it's because that's what they chose; it's their own fault." With such vituperation, Reichel batters women as viciously as the men with whom they live.

She is not alone; multitudes of women throughout the country, instead of fighting like armies in support of their less fortunate sisters, join male forces to attack them. And with such uninformed illogic!

Can women really "pick whom they want"? First of all, a woman's choice is limited by the confines of her world, which may be a world of sex role stereotypes. By chance she is born there, to join the community there, to select a mate there. Second, it is limited by her expectations based on the role models available to her—her parents' marriage, her peers' values, the movie and television heroes she looks up to. She doesn't pick the man she wants; she picks the man fate lines up for her.

Can women really "be what they want"? It is difficult to believe anyone could make that statement today—today with millions of Americans living in poverty, more on the edge of it, hundreds of thousands homeless, numberless in such despair that they drop out of school, live in a stupor of drugs, and often die in it. Educationless, opportunityless, hopeless, these are not women able to be what they want; their aim is just to be at all.

Can women really "do what they want when and how they want it"? Even the most fortunate of women find it impossible to step outside the demands of society and act as detached individuals. They have children to consider, parents who may become their responsibility; duties to the communities that have fostered them. Less fortunate women are relegated to doing what they *don't* want, when and how they *don't* want it because society has stepped outside not their demands, which they have long since stopped making, but their needs. Few nonabused women, were they to search their souls, do what they actually want; all abused women do what they have to do.

Is abuse really "what they chose"? The man a woman marries is not always the man she lives with in years to come. Psychologists tell us that while a man, even one with emotional problems, may appear to handle a relationship maturely before marriage, in many cases after he marries he reverts back to the needy little boy he was. Only now it is his wife, not his mother, who must meet his demands. Those demands can turn into abuse. Even in nonabusive marriages the bride and groom in their twenties may mature and develop along paths so different as to be unrecognizable in their thirties or forties and later—not only to others but to themselves as well.

When Sabine Reichel writes that abuse "is their own fault," she is unfurling the time-worn flag men have waved in the face of battered women for years—blame the victim. Only this flag waver is a woman, joining the male legions, being one of the boys, which many other female wavers of the same flag discover has distinctive advantages. As part of the inner circle she dons men's feelings of superiority and arrogantly allies herself with the male scorn and mockery of women who "cry abuse."

They are free to leave, she lashes out: "These wives are the mentally lazy, disinterested women who are trapped and bored and angry, not because they are victims but because they prefer having a man around to living at their own risk." How little she understands human psychology! How little she acknowledges the shortcomings of society! And what damage she wreaks in charges against women trapped in situations unlike her own. What *is* her situation, one wonders? Married? Single? Divorced? Whichever, her voice calls out with smugness, "I made the right choice: I was smart enough to marry the right man . . . or strong enough to leave the wrong man . . . or careful enough not to marry at all."

This attitude flies in the face of facts. The truth is that the majority of women who continue in abusive relationships do so for valid reasons, their decisions consciously arrived at, as discussed in Chapter 8. The question then is not why abused women stay but why other women join the male attack against them.

One reason is out-and-out ignorance: they simply do not know what underlies the woman's decision to remain in her abusive relationship. They have no facts, nor have they sought to obtain any, but keep falling back instead on the meaningless repetition of "She could leave if she wanted to." Not knowing and not probing to find out, they interpret the abused woman's reasons for allowing abuse to continue on what they think their reasons would be in a similar situation, reasons stated with uninformed self-satisfaction by Sabine Reichel.

Projecting one's own reasoning into someone else's decision is always risky and almost always wrong, leading to many of the major interpersonal conflicts that complicate everyday life. For instance, parents who accuse a child of laziness for not doing his homework may understand their own laziness in shirking a job but not the fear of failure that paralyzes their child. Similarly, the wife who complains that her husband doesn't love her because he isn't affectionate attributes what lack of affection means to her to a man who may simply be undemonstrative. Even in the workplace, an employee who interprets her boss's imperiousness as conceit may miss the underlying cause, which could be insecurity.

Women who have not been in an abusive situation have no way of knowing what it feels like or how they would respond, no way of fearing and despairing and hoping as battered women do. No way without being told. No way to judge. A group of women I know were discussing Hedda Nussbaum one day after seeing her battered face in a newspaper. Their comments sounded like those of Sabine Reichel: "How could she? . . . Why didn't she take the child and leave? . . . She must have been sick to stay."

One woman, to illustrate her point, offered an analogy. "If I were in a room with a raging lion, I'd get out as fast as I could. Wouldn't you?" she asked. They all agreed. So did I. However, I pointed out, an abused woman isn't faced with the choice of letting a lion tear her apart or running to safety. That's no choice at all but instinctive survival. A battered woman, I pointed out, has to deal with ambivalent feelings and the needs of her children and the fear of her husband's retaliation and the alternatives that await her outside. I explained in detail.

The women listened as I spoke and were quiet when I finished. "I never thought of that," one of them said after a while. I believed her, and I believed the others who nodded in agreement because little has been written for their enlightenment and because they are not women of ill will. I also believe they won't blame the victim again.

A second reason that a woman may further verbally abuse abused women is her effort to escape discrimination.

Indignant over the social imbalance of men over women, a woman may devise a way to free herself from it by identifying with the male power structure, a behavior pattern that Dr. Joanna Landau, director of training and research at Four Winds Hospital in Cross River, New York, calls the Queen Bee Syndrome. The fashion industry has both accommodated to this trend and reinforced it by popularizing crossover designs such as pants suits, tuxedos, fedora hats, shirts, and ties. While designers speak of unisex fashions, they really mean male clothes adapted to female sizes since men are not about to wear traditional feminine styles.

By assuming male attitudes as well as male styles, women are able to identify even further with the male establishment, thereby taking on some of their power and prestige as their own. Having experienced discrimination in the male-controlled world—either openly in job opportunities or more subtly in sexual innuendos—a woman finds a way to deliver herself from it for all time by denigrating other women, especially the easily scapegoated abused woman. As Alice Miller puts it in *The Drama of the Gifted Child*, "Contempt is the weapon of the weak and a defense against one's own despised and unwanted feelings," and it is with contempt that a woman may cut out a path to equality: if you can't beat them, join them. What she won't admit, however, is that no woman ever really joins them, but only skirts the edge of the inner circle. Although she may win in the short run by mouthing men's patriarchal views of women, working at their jobs and even wearing their suits and ties, she never enters their network. That remains restricted to the "old boys."

A third reason for a woman's attacks on her abused sisters may be to dissociate herself from characteristics stereotypically attributed to women. Since the male world views women in general and abused women in particular as weak, she will prove herself strong; since it views them as submissive, she will prove herself assertive. It is not unusual for members of a minority group to seek acceptance in the mainstream in this way, reproaching their own people for characteristics with which they want no association: the Jew who becomes anti-Semitic, the African-American who stands against quota hiring, the congressman who condemns Congress. By lining up with the forces that attack abused women, other women follow a similar pattern, striving to shed feminine stereotypes that shackle them for masculine stereotypes that will set them free.

According to psychiatrists, these women are using the defense mechanism of projection. Since it hurts to be cast by society in an inferior role, they unload the powerlessness they feel onto abused women to avoid feeling it themselves. Few of us have not used projection at some time—or many times—to eliminate disquieting feelings: we have condemned others for making the same mistakes we make and hate others for qualities we hate in ourselves.

A fourth reason for women's disparagement of battered women may be scapegoating. The inequalities and injustices a woman confronts in the course of her daily male-dominated life can easily provoke bitterness. Some women acknowledge the unfairness, refuse to fight it, and get on with their lives. Strident feminists lash out against men openly with invective that incites male name-calling and female backlash. Other women, however, though as angry and resentful as their feminist sisters, suppress their feelings to avoid confrontation.

While externally calm and content, these women build up an internal volcano. Unless they want that volcano to erupt publicly, they must find an outlet for their pent-up anger, and what safer outlet than the vulnerable group of battered women? Onto them they spew forth the resentment they feel against men, not only without recrimination but actually with reinforcement from the male world.

   While the anger and disparagement of women like
Sabine Reichel arise from what they perceive as an abused
woman's weakness, accusations of other women arise from
her attempts at strength. According to them, the abused
woman should be less like the predatory jaguar and more
like the acquiescent gazelle. "If she'd just give him his way,
she'd have a decent life," the mother of an eighteen-year-
old girl in court whispered to me one day. Her daughter had
previously detailed for me horrors of nonphysical abuse
increasing over the eighteen months of her marriage that
she now refused to put up with any longer. Her mother did
not understand; she couldn't, because she herself had
learned long before to give her husband his way—with the
result that she had what she considered a "decent life." The
girl knew better.

   Many women like her accept submission not with bitter
resignation but with acceptance of the price paid for the
privileges it brings. The woman who relies on her feminine
helplessness doesn't have to make decisions or earn money
or solve problems; all she has to do is agree. While that may
build the kind of marriage certain women and their husbands want, it doesn't work with an abuser because his wife
can never agree enough. She can never "give him his way"
enough because he will change his way to tighten the grip
of control. Aware that her marriage relationship had arrived
at a state of peace through her submission, the mother of
the eighteen-year-old in court didn't realize that a similar
state would always elude her daughter's abusive relationship.
That is what all women who put the blame for abuse not on
the man for abusing but on the woman for resisting also do
not realize.

   Nonabused women seem to divide into two groups: those
who rage against the abuser and those who rage against the
abused. The former group write books and articles and tele-

vision programs to educate the public; they become social
workers who counsel victims; they pressure legislators to
enact protective laws; they write letters to newspapers and
carry signs in protest of judges soft on abusers; and they
shout, "I told you so" when an abuser kills his wife.

The latter group display their hatred of abused women
in less visible circles: no books or television shows, though
sometimes a sign or two in support of O.J. or Mike Tyson
or Daryl Strawberry; a politically incorrect whisper of "She
asked for it" or "She deserved it"; the smugness of knowing
it would never happen to them. Then when it *does* happen
to them or to their sister or to their best friend, what can
they say? That disparity, of course, is exactly what an abused
woman lives with, and that anathema is exactly what a large
segment of women cannot admit into their own lives.

Dorothy Dinnerstein in *The Mermaid and the Minotaur*
says that women fear female power as much as men do, both
stemming from the woman's power to create life and dominate the shaping of it in infancy and childhood. "The cru-
cial psychological fact is that all of us, female as well as male,
fear the will of woman. . . . Female will is embedded in
female power, which is under present conditions the earliest and profoundest prototype of absolute power." Men, she
explains, subjugate women for fear of being pulled back
into the state of powerlessness with which they began under
the absolute rule of their mothers. Women accept subjugation for fear of reverting to this unharnessed, godlike power
that they, in the role of their mothers, would have to wield.

"Most men," Dinnerstein writes, "—even most men who
believe in principle that this right is unfounded—cling hard
to their right to rule the world. And most women—including many who are ashamed of the feeling—feel deep down
a certain willingness to let them go on ruling it. People balk,
brazenly or sheepishly, candidly or with fancy rationaliza-

tions, at any concrete step that is taken to break the male monopoly of formal, overt power."

If Dinnerstein is right—and since she wrote the definitive book on male-female relationships, we conclude she is—she solves the puzzle of abuse: why men abuse and, more enigmatically, why women let them.

PART IV

Can You Make It Stop?

CHAPTER 12

"I'll try, but it's not easy."

A Woman's Pain in Acknowledging Abuse

THE POET GOETHE WROTE, "None are more helplessly enslaved than those who falsely believe they are free." Though he may have been referring to Dr. Faustus in his bondage to the devil, his words apply equally well to many women in bondage to their abusers. While Faust lives a full and happy life, forgetful of the price his bargain will exact upon his death, the abused woman lives restricted, rationalizing her pain each day while she lives.

Hospital emergency rooms are accustomed to treating women who claim accidental injury instead of battering: their bleeding cuts are due to broken glass, their body bruises to falling downstairs, their broken noses to running into a door. I used to see a woman on my block, who appeared regularly with a black eye, which she attributed to her two-year-old's having kicked her while she changed his clothes. She stuck to her story until her husband was arrested for murdering a young woman in a drug trafficking deal, at which time she admitted to the police that she had suffered years of abuse.

If it takes a catastrophe for a woman with black eyes or cuts and bruises to face up to the fact of abuse, imagine how much more difficult it is for women with invisible wounds to admit abuse even to themselves. There is no one to validate the nonphysical battering they take in the form of words and manipulation and covert actions, no one to say, "Oh, you poor thing. Why do you stand it?"

The nonphysically abused woman most often doesn't put a label on what her man does to her. She knows how dumb and helpless and hopeless he makes her feel, but instead of recognizing her mistreatment as abuse, she questions herself, not him. As Dr. Joanna Landau puts it, "If the man doesn't drink, hit her, or fool around with women, and if he provides, she figures he must be a bargain." The woman, therefore, arrives at one of two conclusions.

On one hand she may convince herself that her expectations are unreasonable in thinking he should treat her with more respect, grant her equal rights, share the finances, or let her be with her friends and family more. She comes to the conclusion that she wants too much, that she doesn't understand marriage. She thinks she will learn. On the other hand, she may simply refuse to see what her husband does to her. Most of us are accustomed to using denial in painful situations—to avoid accepting a negative prognosis when a loved one is seriously ill, to refuse to believe a child is into drugs, to brush aside fear when a task cannot be avoided. So a woman finds it less difficult to deny her husband's abuse than to acknowledge it and deal with it.

Turning Away from the Truth

Several factors aid and abet a woman in her refusal to face the fact of abuse:

The Woman's Role as Peacemaker

First is a woman's basic instinct to make things right. Underneath the stereotype of compliance that has been drawn of women lies the nature of her role as caregiver; since the best care can be given only in peaceful surroundings, she has long backed away from conflict. Even the lioness that has made the kill for her family's meal gives no challenge to her mate as he stalks in for first pickings but stands back and waits until he has had his fill. Men are fighters; women, appeasers. How often we have heard people say, "If women ran the world, we wouldn't have any more wars." Perhaps it is true that women wouldn't send their sons and husbands to be killed as Churchill and Roosevelt did, and maybe it is true that like Neville Chamberlain, disparagingly called "the old lady," they would acquiesce to keep peace.

Given her pacifying nature, therefore, the battered woman exerts great energy to fulfill her role. She may do it with a conscious effort to avoid confrontation by acceding to her husband's demands or with unconscious rationalizations to shift the problem away from him onto herself or with the mechanism of denial by subconsciously looking the other way. Whichever device she uses works—at least for a while. For one woman it may work for eighteen months; for another, fifteen years; for Irene it worked for forty-two years; and for a friend of mine it is still working after fifty-one.

Other People's Opinions

A second factor in the difficulty of facing abuse is the opinions of other people.

Since an abuser is a master at manipulation and decep-
tion, he is well able to convince the outside world that he is
what one judge who was wise enough to see through his act
in a divorce case sarcastically called "Mr. Perfect." While battering his wife at home, he can turn on the charm for other
women with flattery and can outshine other men with his
wit and consideration. Mr. Perfect creates a persona that
fools them all.

Therefore, other men and women, instead of validating
the abused woman's feelings, help her deny them. When
they repeatedly tell her what a wonderful man her husband
is and what fun and how thoughtful, she begins to doubt
herself, wondering whether she is inventing her hurts and
fears. Eventually she erases the picture she has painted of
her husband as an abuser, replacing it with the image everyone else tells her exists. He must be a pretty good husband
after all, she decides.

One woman hadn't reached that point when in desperation she told her friend, "You know, you're all crazy. Andy
is an out-and-out son of a bitch. He may not beat me, but
he controls every move I make and treats me like his slave,
his imbecile slave at that." Her friend looked stunned as she
concluded, "I'm miserable and don't know what to do."

"You want to know what to do?" her friend answered,
trying to hide her impatience. "Forget it. He's a nice guy,
and you're lucky to have him. Go home and stop being
crazy." The woman did go home, and she convinced herself
for three years that she wasn't crazy . . . until she was.

Irene found herself in the same kind of situation with
Sam. His secretaries, she says, raved about him at office parties because he never ordered but asked them to do things;
the lower-echelon executives who reported to him and his
other business associates treated him like a father figure; and
the CEO told her more than once that Sam was the smartest

man in the company and the most honest because he didn't cheat on expense accounts.

How could such an exemplary person be mistreating me? Irene wondered. Sam is a great guy. Everyone says so. Amid this positive feedback, Irene came to the conclusion that she was imagining Sam's oppressive behavior, that she couldn't possibly be right because she didn't know then what she has since discovered: that it is possible for a man like Sam, who is gentle and considerate in the work world, to have problems and needs that make him a tyrannical controller in the home world. Robert Louis Stevenson didn't create Dr. Jekyll and Mr. Hyde from thin air.

When Irene and I discuss Sam and her marriage now, when she relived it for me over a period of weeks as I listened, taping her words, she often wept. "I don't think I'll ever stop being sad over learning this lesson too late to help him and help me and help us," she sighed.

The Need for Denial

A third factor contributing to the difficulty of facing abuse is probably the most common of all: the woman doesn't want to face it. A person who determines to deny reality can find a wide assortment of ways to do it, most of which we see— and use—every day. For instance, despite conclusive evidence that smoking causes disease, smokers deny statistics and continue to light up; despite the fact that no mortal escapes the sagging, wrinkling, and graying of old age, men and women pour millions into cosmetics, face-lifts, and hair dyes to convince themselves otherwise; despite warnings that pollution will be our earth's undoing, we say, "That doesn't mean me" and go on emitting toxic waste.

All women want a good marriage. Those who have one feel safe in picking at insignificant nuisances because the basic relationship is sound enough to weather them. However, a woman whose marriage is abusive may consider the pains and problems of a confrontation too risky, feeling the whole relationship would blow apart as if with a car bomb, leaving them with nothing but wounds to bind up and nurse. These women want to be in a good marriage, and by changing their perception of reality they can put themselves in the marriage they want. The human mind is frequently a magic wand.

A woman in the middle of a second divorce after seven years with a nonphysically abusive husband attributed her refusal to acknowledge abuse years earlier to the hope of avoiding the devastation she had felt after a divorce from her previous husband. "Once was a failure, but two divorces! Then I'd really be a loser," she exclaimed and stayed on for five more years of abuse.

Even one failed marriage poses questions that shake a woman's self-confidence about her judgment and wifely skills, and especially in the midst of abuse does she lay blame on herself rather than on her mate. Therefore, to hang on to self-confidence and let go of blame, she looks at her marriage through glasses that are not only rose-colored but also so fogged over as to dim its outlines altogether.

The surest way to clear her vision is to provide information that will break through the fog of her wishful thinking and light her relationship with the glare of reality. Although books, movies, and newspaper headlines are making it more and more difficult to ignore physical abuse with its photogenic injuries, nonphysical abuse tends to remain as invisible as the wounds it inflicts. Even women caught in abusive relationships for years—ten, thirty, or fifty—can't identify them as abusive.

In the Introduction to this book I reprinted a list of nineteen behaviors used by abusive men, compiled by the Battered Women's Task Force of the New York State Coalition

Against Domestic Violence. I think it is worthwhile to present the list again to let women—and men—see specifically what actions are abusive and to know that these actions are offenses not only against women but also against the law and warrant court-ordered protection. Again, note that only one of them is physical. Just the other day I saw a judge—a woman judge—lean across her desk in court, look in the eye a man who had threatened and harassed his wife until she was afraid to enter their home, and ask him, "Are you aware that I can put you in jail if you do this again?"

"Yes, your honor," the man answered, somewhat chastened.

"Don't forget it," warned the judge.

Although I am encouraged by the seriousness with which this judge and others I have seen take some cases of abuse, I am less than encouraged by their lack of follow-through: in all my time at the Family Court, I have never seen a judge send a man to jail for nonphysically abusing a woman.

Men's behavior may be considered nonphysically abusive if they do one or more of the following:

1. Hit, punch, slap, shove, or bite you

2. Threaten to hurt you or your children

3. Threaten to hurt friends or family members

4. Have sudden outbursts of anger or rage

5. Behave in an overprotective manner

6. Become jealous without reason

7. Prevent you from seeing family or friends

8. Prevent you from going where you want, when you want, without repercussions

9. Prevent you from working or attending school

10. Destroy personal property or sentimental items

11. Deny you access to family assets such as bank accounts, credit cards, or the car

12. Control all finances and force you to account for what you spend

13. Force you to have sex against your will

14. Force you to engage in sexual acts you do not enjoy

15. Insult you or call you derogatory names

16. Use intimidation or manipulation to control you or your children

17. Humiliate you in front of your children

18. Turn minor incidents into major arguments

19. Abuse or threaten to abuse pets

There is one more characteristic of nonphysically abusive behavior that is included in most other lists and causes great grief to women:

20. Withdrawing emotional, verbal, or sexual contact

I regularly speak with women who detail the horrors of their marriage in a state of uncertainty, wondering whether they are foolish in coming to court and should just drop the subject and go home. The greatest reassurance I can offer is the preceding list, which tells them more clearly than any words I can utter, "What he is doing is wrong." By identifying the actions of nonphysical battering, women validate themselves so they can believe without doubt, "What I am doing is right."

Until they are able to look abuse in the eye, however, women excuse the outrage of a man's actions by blaming, if not themselves, their abuser's bad temper. "He just can't control himself when he's frustrated," women tell me repeatedly. Yet studies indicate that a large majority of abusive men control themselves very well when it is to their advantage—with their buddies, for instance, or at work in front of their boss—and selectively explode only when it serves their purpose. In other words, while an abusive outburst may appear to arise from lack of control, it most assuredly is used selectively to exert control.

Facing Facts and Moving Ahead

Determining what constitutes nonphysically abusive behavior is therefore the first step in being able to face it. Three other points of information will help a woman go forward from there.

1. Calling It What It Is

The world glosses over the abuse of women with euphemisms like *domestic violence* and *spouse abuse,* which deny gender inequality. It's not domestic violence; it is a man's violence against a woman. It's not spouse abuse; it is a husband's abuse of his wife. It is inequality that traps women in abusive situations in the first place, and euphemisms not only permit society to avoid recognizing this as a uniquely female tragedy but also actually reinforce society's apathy toward abused women by implying that men are equally abused. They are not. *Social Work* states unequivocally in its September 1991 issue, "Women and men are not equally victimized by their partners;" 95 percent of "spouse abuse" is male against female.

When an abused woman understands this, she can more readily face the reality, not of being a player in "domestic violence" but of being a battered woman. And she can do something about it.

2. Recognizing the Shape of Abuse

A woman came to court one day for a protective order against her husband, then changed her mind and dropped the charges. She told me that after all, he had broken her car windows only once and usually only screamed and threatened to do it. I asked her, "You don't think he'll do it again?"

"I hope not," she answered feebly.

Hope is not enough to keep a battered woman safe. The pattern that abuse takes inevitably leads from lesser to more severe actions with respites and reconciliations in between. Yet, before reaching the point of acknowledgment, women too often look at abuse as individual incidents happening erratically now and again. *The New York Times* reported on April 4, 1994, that a man shot and killed the woman who had earlier broken off their relationship. Although he had been phoning her, bothering her at work, and forcing his way into her apartment under false pretenses, she sought no order of protection through the courts, thinking (probably as most women do) that harassment is not abuse. This woman's misunderstanding cost her her life. Other women can avoid continuing abuse and perhaps a similar fate by recognizing not only the specific behaviors of abuse but also the cyclical pattern in which it escalates, as explained in Chapter 6.

3. Admitting She Can't Change Him

Despite the time-frazzled adage that love conquers all, it is beyond the powers of even the most loving woman to change a man who abuses her. No more than love can stop an alcoholic from drinking or an addict from taking drugs can it stop an abuser from using his woman as an object of control. So entrenched are abusers' power needs that even therapists who work with them hold out a dim prognosis for cure.

What a woman really wants when she clings to the belief that she can change her abusive mate is to keep the good part and get rid of the bad. She remembers warmly the man who wooed her, and although he has all but vanished, he does make infrequent, cyclic reappearances that fuel her determination to banish forever the abuser who took his place. Just as the male psyche reconciles the madonna-whore components of womanhood by splitting them into two separate beings, so a woman hopes for change by making the hurtful part of her husband go away while retaining the part she loves.

It won't work. He is one man whom she cannot change, and until she accepts the truth of that she will continue to subject herself to increasing abuse. However, the change she is unable to bring about in him she can successfully make in herself when she is able to face the fact of abuse.

Taking the First Step

The first step a woman can take in that direction is to look at herself and see what is happening to her. Tied to a batterer, a woman is subject to trauma, which according to battered women is far more intense when inflicted by nonphysical than by physical abuse (see Chapter 1). Judith Herman in *Trauma and Recovery* quotes the psychiatric definition of trauma as "intense fear, helplessness, loss of control, and threat of annihilation," states with which an abused woman is all too familiar. If the woman is able to recognize these symptoms in herself, she is in a better position to confront the reality of her relationship—to admit that her husband isn't just occasionally angry, but is an abuser—and seek ways to terminate it.

If, however, her defenses are layered so thickly as to prevent the penetration of even a glimmer of reality, she will
add a second abuse to her husband's—abuse of herself.
Since the intensity of a trauma depends on the intensity of
the events that produced it, a woman must realize that the
longer she allows the escalation of battering, the more debil-
itated she will become. As a result, she will be less able to
cope with her situation and more apt to fall victim to it
because, as Dr. Herman writes, "Trauma tears apart a complex system of self-protection that normally functions in an
integrated fashion."

Pulitzer Prize–winning author Lewis Puller, a former
Vietnam marine who lost his legs and fingers, committed suicide on May 11, 1994. The war had so traumatized him that
for years afterward he had been unable to cope, escaping
into the darkness of alcoholism and depression. Although
eventually he was able to control the former, he continued
to suffer through black moods of despair and had to settle
eventually for the only deliverance he could see—death.
The madness of abuse deals the same kind of blow to a
woman that the madness of war dealt to Lewis Puller, of
which he said, "None of the lessons I learned as a kid seemed
to fit" (*MacNeil/Lehrer NewsHour* replay of an earlier interview, May 12, 1994).

The jungle war in Vietnam offered soldiers no way out;
an abusive marriage offers no way out unless the woman is
able to see it for what it is. While not every woman is in a
position to walk out of an abusive relationship, even the
woman whom social factors force to remain in it can help
herself by facing what is happening to her. Like the alcoholic who must hear himself say, "I am an alcoholic," so the
abused woman must shed denial and rationalization to don
the protective armor of courage, strength, and self-respect
necessary to defend herself. Only then will she be able to

pressure the police and the courts and the media and whatever social services exist to retain control of her mind and
eventually regain control of her body.

Men who abuse their wives subject their children
to abuse as well. A large percentage of them actually batter their children, either physically or nonphysically, but
even more men subject them to the secondhand abuse of
seeing their mothers abused. Following the natural course
of childhood in the face of tragedy, the children assume
guilt. If I weren't bad, this wouldn't happen, the children
think. Children who see their mother abused live in fear not
so much that it may happen to them also but that it undermines the only foundation of their life, which is their parents. And children who see their mother abused absorb role
modeling for later life—frequently to become the father-
figure abuser.

Women who delude themselves by denying their abuse
are doing their children emotional damage. When instead
they face the fact of abuse, even though they may not be
able to shield their children from it until they leave, they
can help them cope with it. By encouraging children to
share their feelings of guilt and clarifying for them that the
responsibility is not theirs; by easing their fear with assurances of their mother's ability to keep them safe, she will
help maintain the children's emotional balance. Above all,
by establishing herself as a role model who, instead of pretending, has the courage to face the awful truth and deal
with it within existing possibilities, she offers her children
a healthier future. Danger grows greatest when it lurks in
the dark. A woman therefore minimizes the emotional dis-
turbances that beset her children in her abusive relationship
by bringing them into the light.

While it may be true that a little knowledge is a dangerous thing, as many pundits have advised us, it appears

to this nonpundit that no knowledge can be equally dangerous. Ignorant of abuse, a woman remains a victim of her abusive mate, endangering both herself and her children; with even a modicum of understanding, she discovers possibilities for protection, for coping, and eventually for escape.

CHAPTER 13

"I guess I have a choice."

A Woman's Options

COMMENTING ON THE Communist occupation of East Berlin, the *Berliner Illustrirte* referred to the last freedom wrenched from millions of Germans trapped behind the infamous wall as "the freedom to flee." I saw some of those people years ago, before the wall came tumbling down, and shall never shake from my memory their faces as they stood by Checkpoint Charlie, straining to see across the wall to life as they once had known it. I recall in detail a drab young woman holding a little boy high above her head so she could pass on to him the only glimpse of a free world he might ever know.

Many women feel similarly trapped behind the wall of an abusive relationship, deprived of the freedom to return to a life without fear and degradation and constraint. Their faces haunt my memory as well, tear-stained and drained of hope. "Why do you stay on?" someone asks them.

"I have no choice," they say.

Despite the lack of support from society, they are wrong.

217

Every abused woman has options; the very act of staying in the relationship indicates a choice she has made of one of her options, influenced undoubtedly by circumstances, but still ultimately hers. While she has no control over the behavior of her abuser—and that she has to admit before she can take the next step—she has a degree of control over her own behavior. Exerting this control begins with an analysis of her options and a decision to take the one that holds the greatest promise of working for her.

The major choice she has to make is between staying and leaving, and she may not be able to come to that decision until she knows what options exist for her within each choice.

If She Stays

If a woman stays in an abusive relationship, she can either resign herself to her abuser's inevitable domination, like a small dog lying submissively before a larger dog to forestall further attack, or she can try to change her behavior in the hope of minimizing his. In either case, she may have to seek protection from the justice system, a process that will be discussed in detail in Chapter 14. Since humans operate on a less ritualized code of ethics than dogs and other animals, a woman gets no guarantee that either her submissive surrender or her changed behavior will lessen her mate's abuse.

She may begin by determining to meet his every demand in the hope of warding off his physical or nonphysical blows, only to find that his demands come faster and are more furious. She may try to avoid contact with him as much as possible by changing her work hours if she has a job or by devising other reasons for being out of the house more often, although he may respond to this with stricter rules to keep her home. Women have told me they have moved from the bedroom they shared with their husband to a room of their own, where they retreat and lock the door to find peace; but even this doesn't work, since he will have no compunction against kicking the door down in a worse rage than before.

For abusers, as indicated throughout the book, there can be no appeasement because bullies that they are, they need the power trip, as a junkie needs his drug high, to feel good. Therefore, the woman who decides to stay with her abuser will find only disappointment and further hurt if she builds her hope for change in him on a change in her. She needs to look elsewhere to ease her situation.

One possibility is counseling—not for him, which we will discuss in Chapter 16, but for her. Counseling centers for victims of abuse exist in most areas of the country, some attached to hospitals, some in conjunction with shelters, and others operated independently. A look in the yellow pages of the local phone book may help a woman find counseling. If not, a phone call to the domestic violence unit in her state or city or to the National Organization for Women will lead her to a counseling center for help. Although New York is the only state at this time that has an Office for the Prevention of Domestic Violence at the top level enacted by the legislature, many states have a governor's commission on domestic violence or have a unit within social services or the justice department. Even though they have less top-level clout than New York's legislatively ordered office, they all have the information and support an abused woman needs.

Counseling provides a battered woman with what might be the first person she has dared confide in. Like most women, she has kept her silence on the subject, not sharing with her family to spare them upset and not sharing with her friends to spare herself embarrassment. Finally with a counseler's empathetic ear and professional advice, she will find relief and comfort. She will have a chance to identify personal strengths to which she has been blinded and discover ways to use them in searching for a solution to what had previously seemed insoluble. From her counseling sessions she will begin to rebuild her self-esteem, eventually recognizing the person she once was and will one day become again.

In addition to individual counseling, peer group counseling is a viable option, and the two can be done simultaneously. While the former goes far in restoring personal worth, the latter leads the woman out of the isolation created by her abuser into a world of women just like her. With them she is no longer ashamed, no longer guilty, no longer "stupid" for having allowed abuse to happen; she realizes finally that she didn't bring abuse on herself but that, like them, she is a victim. A woman told me that at her first two peer group sessions she did nothing but cry uncontrollably, feeling as though a suppurated boil had been lanced to let the poison pour out. Another told me she felt like the Ugly Duckling, who had just discovered she wasn't a duck at all but a beautiful swan. Both expressed the relief a peer group brings in purging the self-blame that for so long has said "There's something wrong with me" and replacing it with "I'm just like everyone else."

Some women who undergo individual and peer group counseling uncover all-but-lost strengths within themselves that enable them to return to their abusive mates with new coping skills. Many who were on the verge of suicide report restored will to see them through, and one woman confided that without counseling she thinks she would have killed her husband. It should be pointed out, however, that women whom abuse has benumbed into a true clinical depression require more intensive help than counseling can provide;

the hope is that a counselor will be aware of this and rec-
ommend those women to therapy.

Lisa Frisch of the New York State Office for the Prevention of Domestic Violence details four specific objectives
that her office advises counselors to follow:

1. Identification of abuse. Many women, unaware of what
   constitutes abuse, think that if he hasn't hit her he hasn't
   abused her. Clarification of this common misunderstanding is an important first step.

2. *Validation of the woman's experience.* This entails listening
   to her, acknowledging the abusive behavior she reports,
   and supporting the feelings it has engendered. The
   counselor enables the woman to change "This *couldn't*
   be happening to me" into "It *is* happening to me," an
   all-important step in dealing with it.

3. *Advocacy for her safety and expanding options.* Counselors
   seek ways to ensure the woman's safety and work constantly through legislative pressure and fund-raising to
   ensure that further options will continue to open up.

4. Follow-up support. The counseling center is available to
   the woman for as long as she needs it, never passing
   judgment on the woman for her decision to stay in the
   abusive relationship and never urging her to leave.

Many women put the newfound strengths the counselor
has helped them discover to another use: on their own they
find a way to leave.

If She Leaves

If—and I would rather say *when*—a woman is finally able to
escape from an abusive mate, she has even more options. If

married, she can get a divorce on the grounds of cruelty,
but her first thought should be for a short-term rather than
a long-term plan. The immediate question is where she will
go: To parents? Friends? A sister or brother? A safe house?
A shelter? A place of her own?

Her decision has to be made by considering the vital
question of safety. Statistics, studies, and the experiences of
women with whom I work all support the fact that the worst
abuse takes place when a woman leaves her abuser. If the
abuser has previously just screamed at her, he now threatens to beat her; if he has previously destroyed her property,
he now threatens to kill her; if he has previously threatened
to kill her, he now may very well try and, in many cases, he
may very well succeed: over 50 percent of women killed in
the United States each year are killed by their husbands or
ex-husbands.

Women who have walked out on abusive husbands can
request police protection to return to their home and collect their clothes and personal belongings. One woman told
me she felt she would not need the police, since she chose
to go back to their apartment while her husband was at
work. What she hadn't counted on was that, anticipating her
move, he waited inside, grabbed her as she entered, covered
her mouth so she couldn't scream, and beat her till she was
almost unconscious. What saved her life, she feels, was the
sound of her body as he banged it against the wall, which
led a neighbor to call the police.

If a woman announces to her husband ahead of time
her intention to leave him, while he may not resort to physical abuse, he will intensify his nonphysical abuse. Since she
has probably made similar threats before, he has learned
that by throwing a greater scare into her he will succeed in
frightening her enough to change her mind. "I'll kill you if

you ever leave" is the most common threat, but there are others as well:

"You try to leave, and I'll take the kids where you'll never see them again."

"Don't try to go to your mother's, because you'll find her dead if you do."

"You're so crazy, you'll be on the streets if you try to go it without me."

In many cases the threats hold a woman captive forever, but as safe alternatives open up, more and more women venture the risk and escape. Some leave with no more than the clothes on their back, fleeing alone or with children, to whatever safety they can find, with whatever precautions they can make. They keep their new address secret; they change their job; they put their children in a different school; they alert their friends to keep silent. Still, a thwarted man determined to regain his power can call forth incredible inner resources.

One man called ten elementary schools in the city, asking for permission to pick up his daughter, giving the excuse that his wife had been in a serious accident, until he got the school in which his daughter was newly enrolled. Meeting her at school, he learned her new address and was waiting on the doorstep with her when his wife returned from work. Although she tried to get the police to arrest him for kidnapping, she had no case, since he was the child's father and had equal custody rights until she went to court.

A woman named Mildred Coe thought she had really found a way to hide by having the bank where she was a teller transfer her to another branch in a nearby town. Her husband, not to be outwitted, however, on learning that his wife was no longer at the same workplace, took a chance that her old boss might know where she was. Phoning him, the husband said—apparently convincingly—that he was from the Internal Revenue Service and had to clear up a matter with Mrs. Coe. Did the boss know where she could be reached? Of course he did, and after calling the new bank, where the receptionist who answered gave him the bank's address and even directions to get there, Mr. Coe walked up to Mrs. Coe's window and in front of transfixed staff and customers screamed, "You cheating goddamn whore, you bitch, I'll get you."

In many cases, if a woman is not married to her abusive mate, the house or apartment in which they live is hers; she owns it and pays the rent or taxes. When she decides she has had enough of his battering, therefore, since she can stay by law, her job is to get him out. When he won't leave, she may do what a woman at court told me she did the other day—threw his clothes on the street and changed the door locks while he was out drinking with his buddies. Unfortunately, he kicked the door down when he came back drunk and in a rage would have kicked her down as well if she had not escaped next door to a friend's house. In court the next day, the judge ordered him to vacate immediately.

One of the saddest cases I remember is an older woman whose hard-earned money at two cleaning jobs had enabled her to buy the house she and her husband lived in, which she had put in both their names. As they aged, he grew more and more abusive, and after forty years or so, she wanted him out of her life. Since she would not oblige him by vacating the house into which she had put her own money, and he wasn't about to give up either free lodging or free slave service, she felt trapped until she heard about Family Court, which had the authority to order him out. The hope of attaining abuse-free peace with which she entered court faded quickly when the judge issued an order that her husband could not harass, assault, or threaten her but would not put him out of the house. Even though she herself had bought and paid for the house—and only from a sense of equality had listed it in joint ownership—the judge turned a deaf ear to her pleas, insisting impatiently that the order would protect her. Not surprisingly, it has not protected her, and unless she leaves—with no job now and no place to go— she is doomed to live with her abuser until one of them dies.

What really threatens an abuser is not only his woman slipping away from his control but also his woman finding another man. "Andy won't let me get on with my life," Rebecca, an attractive young woman with three children, told me the other day. Divorced three years ago, she had allowed Andy, her estranged husband, to see the children as often as he wanted, ignored his legal ploys to delay final- ization of the divorce, and wasn't even too concerned about harassing phone calls and the negative things he said about her. She met and developed a relationship with a new man, was building a new life.

However, when Andy began hearing the children talk about "Tom" and saw Tom at her house once or twice when he returned them from a visit, Andy's behavior became more extreme and aroused Rebecca's alarm. One day he stood in front of her house, banging on the door and screaming; another time he sent his girlfriend to the front door to shout obscenities at Rebecca when she answered. His abusive behavior proceeded to accelerate. When, no longer content to shout from the street, he began pounding on her windows and cursing, the children became hysterical and ran upstairs with the report that he had said he was going to kill Tom. At that point she went to court for a protective order.

Some abusers use their children to spy on their mother, getting them to relay information on whom she is seeing and what she is doing when they have visits; others use them as emissaries to beg their mother, "Please let Daddy come back to us." Almost all of them play on their children's sympathy, arousing pity against a cruel mother who tells lies and doesn't want them to see Daddy. It is not unusual for children to become so upset over being emotionally dragged away from their mother, like a rope in tug-of-war, that they begin acting out with nightmares, crying, and a slump in school; many require therapy. In my experience, far more mothers show concern for their children by keeping their hostile feelings to themselves than estranged fathers do.

Shelters and safe houses exist to protect women when protective orders can't. Although there are not nearly enough of them to house the thousands of women in danger—only about five hundred at this time—hospitals, social agencies, and women's groups continue to open new ones as they get funding. While both offer protection, safe houses and shelters are somewhat different: the former are homes where women can find temporary sanctuary under the care of empathetic non-professionals, while the latter provide professional counseling services as well. Since many of the counselors have themselves been battered, they are in a position to offer unique help to meet the unique needs of the women who flee to them.

An abused woman is wise to assess her options and think through a plan of escape. Without this, if in the midst of a battering attack, whether physical or nonphysical, she suddenly knows she can take no more and runs for the door, she faces greater danger.

First, she will enrage her abuser even further. Seeing his control ebb as she tries to leave, he will take harsher measures to keep her. Among those measures have been beatings so severe as to maim her permanently, leave her unconscious, or kill her. Threats, even the most outrageous ones, often turn into reality at this point: from time to time the newspaper reports on men who followed their fleeing wife to her parents' home and murdered the whole family.

Second, if the woman has children, her spontaneous flight will most likely include them, but how? Will she grab them from bed or crib or television? Will she call them to follow her? Either way will traumatize them and will escalate her husband's rage. Since the children are his strongest weapon, he will wield it with force, even against them, striking where it hurts the most: "Try to go with your mother, and I'll kill you too." In the face of that, a woman will often concede her hustand's victory and stay, or leave without her children. Many women who have chosen the latter alternative have regretted it later when in a custody suit the judge berates them for abandonment.

Third, a woman who flees her abuser in the heat of an incident without a predesigned plan has to decide where to go and how to get there when her mind is in a state of chaos. Unable to think clearly, she acts in panic, making herself even more vulnerable to her abuser's control. "I didn't know what to do," a woman told me after she had run from the house and her husband had locked the door, "so I just sat on the steps and cried all night."

Planning Ahead

When a woman plans ahead in the cool, clear moments when she is alone in the house, she affords herself a far greater chance of escaping to safety than if she runs on impulse:

Getting Advice

She can begin by phoning a domestic violence hot line, where a trained volunteer will help her clarify her concerns and needs and will guide her to the proper source for help.

If she feels in immediate danger, the volunteers will call the police. If she has been injured, they will call an ambulance. If she is confused and distraught, they will call her in for counseling. If she wants to leave, they will help her make arrangements. With each question they ask to clarify her needs both for her and for them, they turn the decision over to her by repeating, "How can I help you?"

This kind of guidance enables a woman to assess her needs and options so that she can make workable decisions for her and her children. If she tries to reach for a phone in the middle of a battering bout, from what I hear in court, her husband will probably tear the phone from the wall and might even throw it at her or hurl it through a window. In the calm of another day she can not only speak to the person on the hot line in safety but also receive suggestions with a clear mind. The hot-line number in most states is listed under "Domestic Violence" in the "Community Services" section at the beginning of most phone books.

Finding a Place to Go

Whether she reaches for help from a hot line or outlines a plan herself, a woman's first need is a place to go. If family and friends are not a possibility, she may turn to a shelter or a safe house for a temporary haven until she has time to formulate a permanent alternative to her abusive home. If she knows the name of a local shelter or safe house, she can speak to someone at the administrative office and make an appointment to see her. Since it is essential that addresses remain secret to keep out the abusive men from whom women are seeking protection, she will be able to contact only the administrative office at first, whose number the hot line will give her.

Find a Way to Get There

Once a woman determines where she is going, she will have to figure out a way to get there. If she has a car, whose key her husband has not hidden and whose tires he has not flattened, or if her friends or family can pick her up, she has no problem. If, however, she must rely on public transportation to a shelter, a safe house, or someone's home, she should be secure about where she gets it, how often it runs, and how much it costs. A call to the city's transit company will answer her questions.

Planning for Expenses

In making her escape plan, a woman needs to consider money. If she has her own bank account, all she needs is her checkbook; if she and her husband have a joint account, she will need to draw out enough money to tide her over till she arranges for an income. With no funds of her own, unless she has a job or another source of income, she will have to go to the Department of Social Services to apply for government assistance—welfare, food stamps, and housing—a tedious process with which the shelter personnel will help her if she has been able to find a space there.

Deciding When to Go

Next the woman has to decide when to make her break. Since her years of abuse will culminate at the point of her leaving if her husband knows, she has to keep her plans secret from all but the one or two who are to help her. Then, when he is away from the house and she is sure he will remain away for several hours, she should quickly pack up her clothes, any legal documents she has, and the few personal keepsakes she can carry and go. A woman who came to court one day for a protective order showed me all the legal papers she had stuffed into her pocketbook—lease, bank books, car registration and insurance, receipts, etc.— "because the kids and I aren't going back there till he's out." I have spoken to women who left notes behind explaining their reasons for leaving and to women who left without a word. Which is more effective depends on what she writes in the letter and, perhaps even more, on what he reads into it.

Planning for the Children

The last and most important part of the woman's plan is her children. If they are young, experience has taught many women not to alert them ahead of time because no matter how forcefully she explains the need for secrecy they are apt to let it slip. One little boy, determined to obey his mother, decided to reinforce their secret by fooling his father and told him, "We're not going to leave you tomorrow." Although teenagers are clearly capable of keeping the secret, it may cause them such guilt that it is kinder not to make them carry it within them much in advance.

The logistics of leaving are carried out most effectively when all the children are home and the husband is away. If this situation never positions itself, the woman has a problem to solve. While preschool children pose no difficulty, since she can carry them with her—although not all shelters and safe houses accept children—she has to decide what to do about children in school. If she leaves them, they are a target for their father's harassment, and through them he can discover where she is. If she takes them, she disrupts their education until she can place them elsewhere. Chapter 14 will discuss how the school can help.

It is not easy for a woman to leave her home, even when it has isolated her in hurt and humiliation. It is still her home, built on love, shared with a belief in permanence, endured through her tears with hope. "I thought taking my husband's abuse was the hardest thing I ever had to do," Lucy told me once, adding, "but I didn't know what hard was until I decided to leave." It is frightening to face an unknown future; it is risky to face what might be murderous consequences. Yet if she stays, she tells her man it is all right to batter her, and to inflict abuse on her children as well. The consequences of staying are just as frightening, just as life-threatening to the soul and possibly to the body.

CHAPTER 14

"What if he keeps after me?"

Protection for Women Who Leave

"IT'S HARD TO BELIEVE," Maria told me while waiting for the judge to call her case, "but the day after we were married, Danny began telling me what a dumb bitch I was. He had been so nice up till then." I didn't find it hard to believe it because I had heard the story before. Wasn't it Groucho Marx who said he had no friends because he couldn't respect anyone low enough to want him for a friend? Abusive men seem to share Groucho's feeling that any woman dumb enough to marry them isn't deserving of their respect.

It took Maria four years to convince herself that since she couldn't remake Danny into the man she had married— or *thought* she had married—she was going to get on with a life of her own. When she first threatened to leave him, he cut up her pajamas; she was angry. When she threatened a second time, he took their baby from the crib and drove off with her for thirteen hours; she was scared. So the third time, she omitted the threat and took off while Danny was at work, a suitcase in one hand, the baby under her arm. "Free at last," she sighed.

Maria was wrong. That was nine years ago, and there hasn't been a day since when Danny hasn't continued his nonphysical abuse of her, defying court orders, escaping police, shrugging off the days and weeks in jail (for contempt of court, not for abuse) to which the court has sentenced him. He has violated the U.S. mail by sending obscene letters and postcards, screamed vulgarities into the telephone, tracked down her unlisted numbers, kicked in her front door, dragged her into court on a sexual molestation charge and her mother on assault, refused to pay child support, lied on his tax return, and fought the divorce on grounds that she was crazy.

In the light of what other abusers have done, Maria considers herself lucky. When one woman left, her husband had her arrested for stealing his car; another had a key made for the door lock she had taken the precaution to change and while she was at work moved out all her furniture. Many pick the children up at school under false pretenses and run off with them; others track the woman down and assault her— cut up her face, shave her head, beat her up; some, like the husband of Anne Scripps Douglas, kill her. A Milwaukee man stabbed his wife to death in the very courtroom where she was applying for an order of protection.

Since abuse rises from a need for control, a man is most challenged when the woman in his power breaks away. Up until then he has been able to keep her in submission by destroying her self-image and threatening her physical, psychological, social, and economic welfare. Suddenly she leaves, and although she may not speak a word, her actions flaunt his powerlessness. That being the one state he cannot endure, he goes to whatever lengths necessary to regain his control over her, a fight to the death if need be—her death. That is why more women are killed after they leave their abusers than while they remain in thrall.

Merely relocating in what the woman perceives as a secret place will not assure her safety. Her abuser can trace her through her car, her driver's license, her social security number, her place of work, her friends, the children's school, etc. One man reported his wife missing, then went to the police just as they located her in hiding in her mother's house. "Hold on a minute," the officer said as he spoke to the woman on the phone. Then, handing the phone to the man, he explained cheerily, "Here, I have your wife on the phone right now."

Another man tracked down his wife through their son's friends, whose names he knew through the little boy's conversations. Phoning the school, he obtained the children's telephone numbers on the pretense of giving his son a surprise party and then called each home repeatedly until he located his son. Through him he discovered the new address. Many women must feel as the wife in this case did when she told me, "If he would apply his brains to something constructive instead of hounding me, he'd solve the world's problems." He's not interested in solving the world's problems, though; he just wants her back where she belongs—under his domination.

Just as the woman who decides to remain with her abusive mate must find some means of protection, so must the woman who decides to leave. Having him arrested is one way. Although some nonphysical abuse practices are criminal, as discussed in Chapter 10, few police will arrest a man for them; and when they do, few judges will follow through with a jail sentence. The father of a young woman I know tried repeatedly with no success to get one of the district attorneys to prosecute his daughter's husband because of increasing harassment—from obscene phone calls to stalking and crawling into her house through a window; he refused "because that wasn't enough."

The alternative, which most women turn to, is an order of protection. A woman may apply for this through either Family Court or Criminal Court, the purposes of which differ: the purpose of Family Court is to protect the abused; the purpose of Criminal Court is to prosecute the abuser. She may seek protection from one court and prosecution from the other simultaneously.

Getting an Order of Protection

Most abused women decide to take their case to Family Court, where they undergo a somewhat similar process in most states:

1. They first describe to a court clerk or probation officer the most recent abusive event that made them seek court protection and fill in details of their history of abuse. They then indicate the specific kind of protection they would like the judge to order. In the court where I work, they can check as many of the following as they feel are necessary:
   • Not to harass, threaten, or assault
   • To vacate the premises
   • Not to drink or take drugs on the premises
   • Not to come to the house under the influence of drugs or alcohol
   • Not to take the children without supervision

2. They file the report of their complaints and their protective needs with the court clerk.

3. They wait until called by a judge.

4. In court the judge asks them to confirm their complaints as presented in the report and gives them an opportunity to add whatever else they want. The judge then decides what specifics to grant in the way of protection. Since it is literally the women's day in court, they are allowed to offer further explanations and arguments to convince the judge of greater protection if they do not consider it adequate. In most cases the judge issues them a temporary order of protection listing some restrictions, though not always the ones the women have requested.

5. They return to the clerk's office and await their papers, which in most courts include a copy of a temporary order for them to keep; a copy of the temporary order to be served to the respondent, their abuser; an affidavit of service to be signed and notarized by the person who serves the papers; and a report for them to leave at police headquarters for filing.

6. In three or four weeks they must return to court, either bringing the affidavit of service or having mailed it earlier, and face their abuser often before the same judge as before. Respondents are allowed to answer women's charges in one of three ways: they may admit to them and accept the protective order with no further discussion; they may deny them but agree to accept the order anyway; or they may deny them and refuse to accept the order.

7. If they accept the order, the respondents and the petitioners will both pick up permanent orders of protection, valid for a year.

8. If they refuse to accept the order, they will be given another court date to appear for a fact-finding hearing.

Since both the petitioner and the respondent are entitled to attorneys at the fact finding, many courts assign
a free court-appointed attorney to either party whose
income is deemed insufficient to pay.

9. At the fact finding the judge will hear evidence from
both sides, either in person or through their attorneys,
after which the judge will decide in favor of either the
petitioner or the respondent. Attorneys usually advise
women to photograph evidence of abuse, whether a telephone pulled from the wall, a kicked-in door, or a black
swollen eye. Although judges will not usually admit evidence from taped phone calls, transcriptions of harassing calls may help women's lawyers strengthen their case.
If the judge decides in the petitioners' favor, the abusers
depart with a court order to leave the women alone or
face a possible jail sentence; if the judge decides in the
respondents' favor, the abused women leave with no protection and the abusers with the freedom to continue
their abuse.

The Obstacles

The process may appear routinely easy; however, each step
requires patience, entails frustration, and often arouses fear.
As a result, while some women carry the process through to
its conclusion, many others who undertake the first step—
filing for a temporary order—find reasons to abandon the
effort and return to their abusive status quo:

Waiting for a Court Date

The first obstacle is the long wait to actually get into a courtroom. Courts being heavily overcrowded and the calendar
filled minute by minute, judges see in order cases that have

been previously scheduled or those that arise from emergencies. Since the woman applying for an order of protection has just walked into either probation or the court clerk's office to file, she has not been previously scheduled and must wait until the judges have completed those cases on the calendar. This may take three hours, an entire morning, and there are instances when judges are so busy that, unable to fit her in, they have her return after the court reconvenes in the afternoon or even the next day. Since a woman's scheduled return is on the court calendar, her wait is usually shorter, although it is not uncommon for a woman with a 9:00 A.M. appointment to see a judge no sooner than 11:00. Both parties for a fact finding face a similar situation.

Waiting with Children

The waiting room itself poses another difficulty, especially for a woman who has had to bring a young child or two or three along with her, since few courts have a supervised center where mothers may leave children. The court waiting room is noisy and congested, with police and probation officers, lawyers, court assistants, petitioners, and respondents walking back and forth, calling cases, talking, crying, and at times fighting. Some court waiting rooms have a few books and maybe a chalkboard for children, but with the books soon torn and the chalk broken, children are left on their own, often being spanked or yelled at to stop hitting, stop playing with the water fountain, stop crying. It is a long, dull wait for those children and a tense one too if their father and mother are both there, separated by barbed-wire fences of anger.

Taking Time Off from Work

A working woman has an even harder time. If she tries to keep her abusive relationship a secret, her inventiveness is tested in trying to devise reasons for her repeated absences.

If she explains to her employer that she is going to court at
9:00 and should be back in an hour or so, she will be a nervous wreck as the minutes tick by. More than one woman
has told me she would be fired if she wasn't back on time,
and although the court clerk will give her a letter of explanation, she continues to worry.

Facing a Judge

The very act of being before a judge is frightening for
most women, even with the court assistant close by for moral
support and a whispered word when needed. Under stress,
some women forget what they intended to say, weakening
their case and even communicating erroneous information.
For instance, the judge was warning a woman of the legal
danger of forbidding her ex-husband visits with her two
daughters when I had to interrupt with the explanation that
the ex-husband was not the father of the children; in her
anxiety she had forgotten. One woman neglected to let the
judge know her husband was a drug addict when he was
deliberating whether to make him vacate or not, and
another, whom the judge was berating for waiting a month
before coming to court, didn't think to explain that she had
been in the hospital.

Receiving Minimal Protection

Some judges are loath to order a man out of his home, even
when the abused woman describes threats he has made and
the fear in which she lives. "I'll order him not to harass,
assault, or threaten you," I hear them say, "and if he does,
you come back and file a violation." Case dismissed. The
judge turns to the next case, and the woman goes home in
fear for her life or, not daring to run the risk of going home,
seeks shelter elsewhere, leaving her home and possessions
to her abuser. One more case of the victim paying the price
for the crime perpetrated against her.

Finding Someone to Serve the Papers

One of the greatest problems a woman has to deal with when she receives her temporary order of protection is the matter of service. Until she arranges for someone to serve the papers to her abuser, they do not take effect. The server must be over eighteen years old and cannot be the woman herself or a future witness in any of her hearings. The server has to hand the papers to the respondent in person and can't mail them or slide them under the door, although he or she is permitted to lay them on the floor if the respondent refuses to accept them. The server must subsequently swear before a notary that he has personally served the papers and return the notarized affidavit to the court or to the woman to bring on her next court appearance.

If the woman has no one to serve the papers, some courts will order the police to do it, or the woman may pay a marshal or sheriff. Still, problems exist: not all cities allow the police to serve papers, and those police that do often take a long time, since drugs, robberies, and homicides take precedence over wife abuse; paid law officers cost more than many women are able to pay. The biggest problem in many cases, however, is tracking down the abuser so as to serve him with papers. He may have left town or gone into hiding with friends; he may have quit his job or enlisted his co-workers to lie for him should the server appear. I have known men to wear false mustaches or shave off their real ones to escape service or to hide under large brimmed hats like an animated cartoon. One man even disguised himself with a woman's wig.

Unless the man is served the temporary order and unless the court has in hand a notarized affidavit to that effect, the woman is not allowed in court to follow through for a permanent order. If she has been unable to locate him, the judge may give her a postponement, after which, if she has still not found him, the judge may allow the temporary order to be mailed or may on rare occasions issue a permanent order anyway. If a man is known to deliberately avoid service, a judge may occasionally allow the order to be mailed by certified mail.

Just as often a man who has received a copy of the temporary order may choose not to appear in court for the scheduled hearing, and the woman finds herself alone, unable to proceed. Knowing the judge will set another date, men are apt to use repeated postponements as a way to further harass their mate. However, even judges lose patience and often issue the permanent order despite the man's absence.

The Emotional Barriers

Although some women give up their hopes of court protection in the face of this long line of difficulties, others, willing to struggle through them, give up for other reasons. One is fear.

Fear

Just as batterers become enraged when their mate leaves or threatens to leave, they are apt to react even more so when served with an order of protection. They see their control slipping away not only to the woman who dares escape it but now to the justice system as well. Since at the time of service the order is still only temporary, they may use the three weeks prior to the next court hearing to stage a power act that will make her change her mind. Stalking her, they send the message "You'll never get rid of me." Harassing her, they say, "This is only the beginning." Threatening her, they warn, "Wait till I really do it." One man mailed a threatening letter that ended "If you think you're going to raise my kids under court protection, you're wrong, DEAD wrong." She was frightened and dropped the protective order. He was still in control.

Hope

Hope is a second reason women sometimes drop the idea of a protective order. The husband who has isolated them, humiliated them, driven them half crazy, and left them penniless suddenly wins what one woman called "The Husband of the Year Award." Pulling the right strings, he moves her like a marionette in the direction he wants, which is away from the court and, he expects, back to his subjugation. "He's changed," women say, making the miracle happen in their mind because they desperately want it in their life.

Some women follow through on their temporary order to the point of appearing with their mates on the scheduled return date and then, while in the waiting room before being called, change their mind and leave. I see them talking, playing with their child like a happily married couple in a sitcom, and then I see them leave together, smiling— she with new hope, he with the same old success. One woman explained to me before she left with her seriously abusive husband, "He says, 'How can we make our marriage work with this hanging over my head?'" I say, How can she make their marriage work with abuse hanging over her life?

Trapped Again by the Man's Deceit

A third reason for lack of follow-through on a protective order is the manipulative deceit of the abused woman's mate. Since nonphysical abuse is greatly a matter of manipulation, the abuser can put his already-honed skills to use in persuading his mate not to secure a permanent protective order against him. I have run across men who tear up the temporary order when they receive it, then track down hers and tear that up too; men who say the court phoned to postpone the scheduled return date so that when she fails to appear the judge drops the case; men who swear they were never served the papers, despite the notarized affidavit, which they contend was forged. Unless the woman has enough insight to see through his trickery and enough will to counteract it, the court will cancel her temporary order.

The consequence of not appearing in court for the scheduled hearing at which the issuing of a permanent order of protection is decided is most often further abuse and the woman's realization that she has made a serious mistake. As a result, she returns to court to reapply for protection and begins the whole process again. This time, however, the judge, reading in her file that she had failed to follow through on a previous application, is somewhat less than empathetic and often downright angry. I have heard a judge question the woman, scold her, and even tell her what she did was "just plain dumb." Recently a judge berated a woman for failing to follow through when her husband was sent to a drug rehabilitation center for six months, despite the fact that he could not possibly have appeared in court, nor could he have abused her. Most often a male judge will sigh, shake his head, and, like the chauvinist father figure he often is, visibly resign himself to her incompetence.

A common ploy men use when served with an order of protection is to come immediately to court to file for one of their own, counterclaiming their mate abused them. In some cases the woman may have tried to shout him down when he was berating her; she may have kept money from him because he was spending it on drugs; she may have spied on him and the girlfriend he slept with to get evidence for a divorce; she may even have hit him when he came at her with his fist. Since no one is denied an opportunity to seek protection, the man goes through the same process his wife just completed and waits to appear in the same court the next day.

In an attempt to limit time and harassment, the court clerk schedules their return dates together, and I have seen some hot fireworks in the courtroom. With anger exploding, I have seen men scream at their wives, rise, and shake their fist threateningly; I have seen them argue heatedly with the judge, their voices rising in rage. I have seen judges quickly threaten arrest for contempt and police rush to hold men down in their seats. And when a six-foot man complains that his five-foot wife shoved him against the wall or scratched his arm, I have seen judges smile.

I am not arguing that women never abuse their men; they do. There are nagging wives and penny-pinchers who snatch the week's salary; there are women who scream in jealousy and belittle their men in disgust; there are even women who assault them. However, because of the disparity in male-female strength and size, because of the disparity in the male-female power structure, and because of the disparity in male-female abuse statistics, I am not going to make a case for abused men. A few exist, but over 95 percent of the abused are women.

Men also use another turning-the-tables ploy that strikes a woman where she is most vulnerable, her children. The child protective services in all states urge citizens to contact them when they suspect or know of child abuse, and they are obliged to follow through on any report to determine whether the allegations are founded. Knowing this, an abuser, enraged at having been served with an order of protection, will often report his woman to CPS, bringing on an investigation. Frequently children are taken from their mothers and placed in foster homes while the investigation continues, resulting in trauma for both mother and children and satisfied revenge for the father.

Anne FitzSimmons of the White Plains Police says, "An order of protection is only as strong as the value system of the person against whom it is issued." So after all the work and waiting, the woman who finally receives a permanent order of protection may not be protected after all. If her abuser respects or simply fears the law, he pays attention to the restrictions detailed in the order and behaves himself as required. If, however, he has no respect for the law and no fear that he can't outsmart it, he will continue his abuse as before, probably with even greater intensity.

Even so, the order has a claw that can lash out at an abuser through the police. If the man breaks any part of the order and the woman calls the police, they may—and in many states, they *have to*—arrest him. If he has fled before the police arrive, the court may issue a warrant for his arrest. In either case, the woman may file a violation order and return to court. If the police have the abuser in custody, he will appear in court with her, handcuffed, the next day; if the police are looking for him, he will be brought in when he is found. Although Family Court has the power to sentence him to jail for six months, the judge rarely does, giving him warnings and further restrictions on his behavior instead. The Criminal Court judge, on the other hand, dealing with more violent cases, is likely to send a consistent violator to jail.

There is no sure way to protect a woman who lives with an abuser, and—sad to say—there is no sure way to protect a woman who leaves. A man abuses a woman because abuse works: it succeeds in getting him what he wants—power and control. In the same way, a man will obey a protective order if it gets him what he wants. If he wants to keep his job and knows his wife will have him arrested for violating the order, he will obey it. If he wants to lure his wife back—or, in rare instances, genuinely change and *win* her back—he will obey it. If he wants to be a good father to his children, he will obey it. If his wife moves away and it's too much trouble to pursue her, he will obey it. If he has another woman to abuse and finds one at a time is enough to satisfy him, he will obey it.

However, if his determination to regain the power and reassert the control a woman wrested from him overrides all other concerns, he will not obey it. Nothing and no one will protect that woman—not the police, not the court, not a jail sentence. Because he can't live as a loser, he won't let her live as a winner.

CHAPTER 15

"Will he ever change?"

Treatment for Abusers

IN MAY OF 1994 Admiral Mike Boorda, newly appointed chief of naval operations after the Tailhook sex scandal, expressed his faith that it would never happen again. "I think our culture is different," he said. Congresswoman Patricia Schroeder responded with doubt that navy culture has changed, and Senator Barbara Boxer months later said, "The military needs to be realistic and admit there is a problem" (*The New York Times*, May 23, 1994). In fact, a study reported in the same article indicated that one in every three military families has suffered some kind of family abuse. Since it focused only on physical abuse and the overwhelming preponderance of nonphysical abuse among the general public is acknowledged, it is horrifying to consider what that statistic might be among the military.

Most people working with battered women doubt that American culture has changed either. Battering has not abated. Rape continues. Men still exchange sexually demeaning jokes and buy *Penthouse* and *Playboy*. Rock videos titil-

late with violence against women. The film industry grows
rich on macho heroes. And only recently a men's counselor
told me that a judge who gave a batterer extreme leniency
whispered knowingly to him, "We know the trouble—she's
not giving him enough sex."

Stephen Dill, who with Gordon Duggan runs batterers'
workshops in Putnam County, New York, believes that "as
men we are all on the continuum of abuse" and that until
the belief system of our society changes, neither the navy
nor America will see a diminution, much less an end, to
abuse. To underscore the deep-seated male view of women,
he points out how often a male employer in firing a woman
for incompetence says, "I'll never hire another woman" but
in firing a man, never even thinks, "I'll never hire another
man." Along the same line, most of us while on the road
have heard our husband or some other man shout, "Dumb
woman driver" but never identify an equally errant male as
"Dumb man driver." In fact, I heard a man curse the "woman
driver" in front of him one day and then whiz past only to
discover it was a man. Unchagrined, he growled, "Well, he
drives like a woman!"

The Virginia Slims ad may have proved that women need
no longer smoke cigarettes behind closed doors, but abuse
professionals feel we certainly haven't come such a long way
in matters that really count. The first steps toward ending
abuse have to be taken, everyone agrees, through education.
Twenty-five years ago few people understood the hazards of
smoking (except the cigarette executives, it appears) until
the American Cancer Society spent millions of dollars to educate the public through media campaigns and to prepare
materials for use in schools. Today, despite a recent rise in
teenage girls' smoking, an overall decrease is apparent. Similarly, no one paid much attention to intoxicated drivers
until the parents of children killed—they call it *murdered*—

by drunken drivers formed MADD, Mothers Against Drunk Driving, and sent a blitz of advertisements across the country. As a result, new legislation has been passed, more is being demanded, and *designated driver* has become a household phrase.

Abuse prevention activists are pressuring local, state, and national governments to wage a similar bombardment to educate the public in two directions. One is to reach adults—first with basic information on what constitutes abuse so that no man will ever again say, "It's only my wife" or "What's all the fuss about? I didn't lay a hand on her"; and second with a realistic picture of the destructive effects of abuse on a woman and the legal effects on the man who abuses her. While the goal is admirable and the program would undoubtedly effect some change, results would be limited. As Lisa Frisch of the New York State Office for the Prevention of Domestic Violence explains, a man can understand it all intellectually and still act from a deep-rooted need for control that only intensive therapy can reverse.

The other direction is to reach children before their stereotypes are fixed in society's concrete—to discuss the interdependence and equality of men and women and to explore constructive ways of expressing the anger and need for control that leads to abuse. School programs of this kind are growing, sponsored by local governments and by women's shelters. My Sister's Place in New York's Westchester County runs two-day programs in schools throughout lower Westchester, of which *The New York Times* reported that in every class children could name neighbors who were abused and at least one knew of a woman murdered by her husband. Education will bring awareness, but whether it will bring change will take years to tell. "Progress is being made, but in itsy bitsy baby steps," claims Thea DuBow of My Sister's Place (quoted by Louise Wollman in the *Scarsdale Inquirer*).

To stop men from battering, it is essential to understand
why they do it, and the explanations of professionals differ
widely from those of the men themselves. The following list
of reasons was compiled by the Virginia Peninsula Council
on Domestic Violence, a copy given to me by Judge Allbritton of Clearwater, Florida's, Family Court. Although we have
discussed many of these points in previous chapters, because
the list incorporates the understanding of most people who
work in the field, I am including it here as a contrast to the
reasons batterers themselves give.

The Batterer: Why Does He Batter?

1. Exaggerated need to control/dominate. Defines manhood in terms of dominance and control over others,
   especially females.

2. Violence is an accepted part of male upbringing in our
   society—and most others.

3. Learned response to stress.

4. Extreme emotional dependence upon victim. Relationship addiction.

5. His violence gets results—if only temporarily. He "gets
   his way."

6. The violence "feels good"—if only temporarily.

7. Lack of conflict negotiation skills. Lack of cooperative
   decision-making skills.

8. Expresses anger as aggression. Expresses most emotions,
   such as hurt feelings or sadness, as anger.

9. Accepts abuse as normal due to childhood experiences.

10. Does not see himself as responsible for his own behavior. Feels other people or events provoke him and are therefore responsible. Feels the abuse is justifiable. Blames the victim. Externalization.

11. Objectifies women—it's OK to hit an object.

12. Views relationships in terms of a hierarchy of power. Sees women as "second-class citizens." Believes in a decidedly patriarchal social and personal structure. Quotes the Bible to substantiate his belief that women should be submissive to men.

13. Self-pity and self-deception. Denies the abuse. If he acknowledges the abuse, he denies the pain that results from the abuse.

14. Poor impulse control/poor anger control.

15. Pathological jealousy.

16. Low self-esteem.

The Abusers' Claims

While people who work with abusers recognize all sixteen of these factors as contributing to abuse of women, the abusers themselves identify the motivation for their actions quite differently. Only on number 10 do they agree, insisting, "It's not my fault." For an article entitled "Why Do Men Batter Their Wives?" (included in *Feminist Perspectives on Wife Abuse,* edited by Kersti Yllo and Michele Bograd) the author James Ptacek conducted interviews with batterers to elicit reasons for battering firsthand. He found that the explanations for their behavior split into two groups—excuses and justifications—and concluded, "The batterer appeals to standard rationalizations in an attempt to make sense of or to normalize his behavior."

Almost all the women I work with, whether battered physically or nonphysically, corroborate the findings of Yllo and Bograd, reporting that their husbands explain their actions not as abuse but as uncontrollable outbursts. "I just lose it" is the common phrase. The authors of the study found that a third of respondents in their study shrugged off responsibility for their loss of control by attributing it to drugs or alcohol, which is a guilt-free cop-out for them and an obvious evasion, since professionals generally agree that neither causes abuse. The remaining two-thirds blamed a buildup of frustration for which they needed an outlet, another cop-out because, as pointed out earlier, they selectively released frustration where it would do them no damage, on their wife. On June 22, 1994, *The New York Times* reported on a study led by Dr. Neil S. Jacobson that corroborates the fact that many men not only batter with "cool control" but also actually feel better while doing it. They fall back on the loss-of-control rationale because it enables society to exonerate them and at the same time enables the men to exonerate themselves.

A second excuse men give for their abusive behavior is the familiar turnaround that blames the victim: "It's her fault; she provoked it." Even men who never physically abuse their wives—and that is the majority of abusers—shed personal responsibility by saying she brought it on herself. "If somebody gets antagonistic, you want to defend yourself," a man in the study explained. Since self-defense is acceptable even in a court of law, men are readily able to excuse their abusive behavior with a clear conscience; only probing by a highly skilled and highly patient professional may bring to light previous actions of their own that provoked their wife's antagonism in the first place.

While some men batter their women guilt-free by directing the blame elsewhere, others delude themselves into not even acknowledging it as wrong. I saw a man in court tell a judge in all innocence, "I barely touched her" when his wife had black-and-blue marks up and down her arm. Women frequently come to court for protection against abusers who threaten to beat them up or kill them if they repeat an action that can be as harmless—to anyone but an abused wife—as phoning their mother. When confronted with their threat, men who have mentally tortured their wives for years can laugh it off with "I was only kidding."

The Yllo and Bograd study reports a different kind of justification that 78 percent of abusers used, which Stephen Dill and Gordon Duggan see in the men's workshops they conduct and which I also hear in court: the woman's failure as a wife. If she doesn't do what she's supposed to do—and by that an abuser means what he wants her to do—he considers it his right to punish her. "How else is she going to learn?" a man once asked me with assured self-righteousness. How else indeed! He disciplines his dog and his children when they misbehave; why not his wife—when she disagrees with him or doesn't want to have sex or asks for more money or visits a friend or forgets that he doesn't like broccoli? So self-convincing is the man's skill at justifying his abuse that even when his wife struggles to please him by always agreeing and having sex on demand and not asking for money or visiting friends and never serving him broccoli, he will find a score of other areas in which she fails. And he will know he is right in punishing her.

The Prognosis

With abusers' defenses entrenched so solidly against reality, it is little wonder that the prognosis for cure is not encouraging. With nine out of ten batterers regarding their behavior as acceptable, according to Linda Rouse in *You Are Not Alone,* that leaves only one who admits what he is doing is wrong and who therefore might change. Even the best of treatment programs, which most professionals agree is the Domestic Abuse Intervention Project in Duluth, Minnesota, reports that 40 percent to 60 percent of the men it treats return to abusive behavior within five years. Joan Zorza of the National Center on Women and Family Law holds an even dimmer view: she sees at least half of treated male abusers returning to their abusive behavior.

The rate of cure depends on more than the program in which the batterer is treated, however. Jeffrey Edelson and Richard Tolman report in *Intervention for Men Who Batter* that a successful outcome, which they find ranging from 53 percent to 85 percent among different programs, depends on several factors:

- Whether the man had been arrested and mandated to enter a treatment program

- Whether he was separated from the woman he abused

- Whether he neither drank excessively nor took drugs

- Whether he contacted a counselor for help when he felt himself slipping back into abusive behavior

- Whether he was not a narcissistic personality but rather could extend himself empathetically into the feelings of others

I feel other factors are equally influential in determining the success rate of treatment. One is the abuser's attitude toward women. If, after treatment, he continues to hold the male chauvinist view that women are inferior and there-

fore deserve to be dominated, that they are a man's property to be used as he wills, and that they behave only when
hurt and intimidated, there is no hope for change. If, however, a program is able to turn his thinking around, he may
begin to check his abusive behavior. More important, if it is
able to uproot the unconscious drive that obsesses him with
a need for power and control over women, it may eliminate
his abusive behavior entirely. Since, according to Edelson
and Tolman, it is more difficult to cure a wife abuser than
a child sex abuser, expectations of people who run treatment
programs for the former, despite their hard work and earnest
commitment, are not high.

Another important factor in the success rate is the
strength of a man's resolve to change. If an abuser agrees
to treatment as a means of exerting control, of manipulating a woman into doing what he wants, there is little chance
of success. She may, for instance, threaten to call the police
or get a protective order against him, or she may start to
leave as he is cursing and humiliating her, and he, having
played out the scene numerous times before, makes his usual
promises. This time, however, since they don't work, he goes
a step further. "I'll change, I promise," he pleads contritely.
She has heard that before and doesn't even turn around.
"I'll enter the treatment center you told me about." She hes-
itates, her hand on the phone or the doorknob. "Tomorrow,"
he adds. She stops.

"Honest?"

"Honest." She turns around, and tomorrow he signs up
for the program.

Whether he drops out after the first meeting or stays
through the entire program under pressure, however, there
is little hope for change because he didn't enter it with the
hope for change. He didn't even want change; his wife did.

A man can overcome abusive behavior if he really wants

to keep his wife—keep her not out of fear but out of love. Just as Alcoholics Anonymous can restore a person who, having hit rock bottom and seen his or her life in shambles, is desperate enough for help to admit aloud, "I am an alcoholic," so an abuse intervention program can restore an abuser. Like an alcoholic, however, he must stop playing mind games and hear himself admit, "I am an abuser."

In a book called *The Sexist in Me*, author Kevin Powell gives a powerful firsthand account of his abuse of his girlfriend. After she left him, he realized that unless he changed his attitude toward women he would never be able to sustain a serious relationship, which he wanted. With effort and determination and with reluctance, he relinquished the machismo that had protected his ego for a lifetime and was able to relate to women as equal human beings. It wasn't easy, because like all batterers he didn't know sexual equality, only sexual control.

An abuser in an intervention program confessed, "When I leave the treatment center, I feel less like a man." Eventually, unable to overcome his feelings of inadequacy without resorting to the drug of control, he dropped out of the program; and later, I heard, his wife dropped out of their marriage. The crippled little boy in Menotti's *Amahl and the Night Visitors*, finding strength in the stories the Wise Men tell, dares to drop his crutch and, with no assurance other than his faith, takes a first unsupported step. In the same way an abuser must drop his crutch of phony manhood and dare to walk side by side with his woman as a real man.

There is no standardization of treatment for abusers because there is no agreement on what the treatment should be. Some believe in what Edward Gondolf of the Domestic Violence Study Center of Indiana University of Pennsylvania calls the *social service approach*, others in what he refers to as *social action*. The main difference between the two is that the former treats wife abuse as a relationship problem between husband and wife, while the latter treats it as a power problem in which the man dominates the woman through either physical or nonphysical methods of control.

Treating Abuse as a Relationship Problem

When abuse is viewed as a short circuit in the relationship between a man and a woman, it is the relationship that must be healed. This is attempted in a number of ways:

1. Working with the Abuser and His Woman Together

Advocates of couples counseling believe that abuse is attributable to both members of the relationship; as they see it, something in the dynamics of the marriage has gone wrong. The therapist's job, therefore, is to have husband and wife confront the problem together to discover what she does to incite him, what he does to incite her, and how communication breaks down, enabling abusive behavior to replace it. Counselors using this approach lay the blame on neither the man nor the woman but consider each of them an equally contributing factor.

Although couples counseling was used extensively in the past, recent studies indicate that not only does it fail to halt abuse, but also in many cases it actually increases it by encouraging the abuser to shrug off responsibility. One couple I know who went for counseling—the woman with a bachelors degree, the man with a master's—were told that the reason for the husband's abuse was that she was not intelligent enough for him. The counselor based his decision on what the overbearing man told him about his wife's "stupidity" and what the frightened wife did in response— giggled and apologized. As a result he increased his controlling behavior, using the counselor's determination as reinforcement. She eventually left him and today has a master's degree and an interesting job; he has been unemployed for two years.

Many therapists, however, still have faith in couples counseling or what they call the *codependency approach* to ending abuse. They feel that the feminist approach, which is built on the principle of the woman as blameless victim and the man as perpetrator, oversimplifies the issue by assigning good-guy and bad-guy roles. Sheila Beisel, a New Jersey therapist, believes that the codependency approach treats the woman more like an adult than the feminist approach does, since it enables her to assume some responsibility for the abusive situation instead of putting her off on the sidelines.

2. Enabling the Man to Vent His Hostility

David Adams of Emerge, a Boston-based treatment center for male abusers, calls this approach the *ventilation model.* Believing, as Freud propounded, that repressed anger, like stew in a pressure cooker, explodes without a release valve, advocates of the ventilation approach provide that release. They create a situation in which couples are urged to let off steam in a so-called fair fight in which one is not allowed to bully the other. Although they are not allowed to hit, they can scream and name-call, curse and belittle, all in the cause of getting rid of feelings that might lead to further abuse if taken home. In one case a man spat at his wife; in another he worked himself into such a rage that he punched her, knocking out a tooth, before the counselor could intervene.

One reason this approach fails is that it legitimates the verbal abuse the man has been hurling at the woman all along, the situation that brought them to the counselor in the first place. Since, according to Emerge's David Adams, men are more apt than women to use verbal abuse without regard for the other's feelings, the ventilation approach, while granting free expression with impunity to the former, cuts more deeply into the already-bleeding wounds of the latter. The man returns home with license to intensify his nonphysical abuse; the woman returns home more hurt, more frightened, and more abused.

3. Undergoing Traditional Psychotherapy

Developmental psychologists outline behavioral patterns along which children normally grow, passing from stage to stage to acquire the mental, social, and emotional maturity of a healthy adult. When destructive parenting practices or possibly other environmental factors interfere with this normal development, the child, deprived of the fulfillment of his needs that would normally nurture him through the succession of stages, becomes what we think of as an unhealthy adult. In batterers the symptoms of this sickness appear, according to many psychiatrists, as a sense of worthlessness and emotional impotence.

Therefore, when an abuser enters into psychiatric treatment, he, under the guidance of his therapist, digs into the dark of his subconscious to bring to light painful past experiences that have destroyed the self-esteem with which children are born. Was he himself abused? Did his parents reject him? Was he neglected? Abandoned emotionally? Was he overprotected? These are the questions to which he and his psychiatrist strive to pull up answers from the deep well of repressed memories in the belief that by understanding his past experiences he can deal with them constructively. He can expect to rebuild his self-image, aware that the failure was not his as a child but that of the people who caused him to accept it as his.

All this is true. Psychoanalysis and/or psychiatric treatment can go far in helping an abuser change his attitude toward himself and, as a result, his relationship with women. However, as the sole intervention treatment in cases of abuse, it falls short on two scores. First, it takes a long time, usually years; I know a man who after ten years is still in therapy. While a man is uncovering his repressed past to find the child he was, his wife continues to take abuse from the man he still is. While therapy may eventually enable the man to change his abusive behavior, during the lengthy process his wife will have to endure the humiliation and fear that sent him into treatment in the first place.

The second shortcoming of traditional therapy as a cure for abuse lies in its focus. So intent are both the man and his therapist in turning up the hurts of the past that they all but forget the hurts of the present, which they have come together to prevent. In an article entitled "Rethinking Clinical Approaches" (*Feminist Perspectives on Wife Abuse,* edited by Kersti Yllo and Michele Bograd), David Adams quotes a study of fifty-nine battering prevention programs of which, in defining their primary goal, only 14 percent said "having the abuser take responsibility for his violence"; 90 percent, on the other hand, said "increased self-esteem." Most people who work with abusers—and certainly the women they abuse—feel treatment goals should be the other way around.

4. Reshaping Abusive Behavior

Years ago B. F. Skinner introduced behavioral psychology as a contrasting method of treatment to psychotherapy. While the latter deals with the inner person—his or her experiences, attitudes, and emotions—the former focuses solely on the actions of the outer person. Many abuse intervention programs use behavioral techniques in their treatment in two main ways. First, they enable a man to recognize what triggers his abusive behavior: Is it drinking or drugs? Is it suspicions of infidelity? Is it stress over money or his job? Is it a put-down by his wife? His children's commotion? Too much of his in-laws? His wife's arguments? The behaviorist instructs the abuser to keep a journal, not just day by day, but hour by hour or minute by minute if necessary, until he can identify the specific incidents that set him off. Often they are revealing, as in the case of a man who found that whenever their daughter captured his wife's attention he screamed obscenities at his wife and threatened to take the child to his home in another state.

The second technique behaviorists use is teaching abusers new ways of responding to the triggers that set them off. An abuser lacks coping skills, they believe, and, in his inability to react appropriately, lashes out with either physical or nonphysical violence in the same way a small child hits and screams before acquiring more socially acceptable ways of getting what he wants or more tolerance in adjusting to not getting it. He is taught how to compromise, how to talk through a conflict, how to excuse himself from a potentially explosive scene, how to manage his anger and relieve his stress.

While it is valuable for men to alert themselves to the triggers of their abuse and to develop skills for coping with them, intervention programs that rely solely on these behaviorist methods cannot solve the problem. Abusers want control, and men abuse because abuse gives them control. Knowledge of what makes them abusive and of new ways to

behave doesn't give them control. So even with new understanding and new skills, they will continue to do what works,
and what works is abuse.

Treating Abuse as a Power Problem

Any kind of treatment for batterers is relatively new, since
battering itself has been acknowledged only recently, and the
four methods of treatment just discussed were the only ones
that intervention programs could turn to, since no others
were known. Today, however, a new approach has been developed based on the belief that no amount of couples counseling, anger venting, therapy probing, or behavior reshaping
can end abuse without altering the abuser's fundamental attitude toward women. Some, but unfortunately not all, of the
batterers' programs work toward that end.

There are in the country about two hundred batterers'
groups composed of a small minority of men who are court-
mandated to attend, an equally small number who attend
from a desire to change, and the majority of men who are
coerced to attend by their wives, families, or a social service
agency. With so few truly self-referred, it is not surprising
that the dropout rate is anywhere from 60 percent to 75
percent, especially among those who attend reluctantly and
expect immediate love and praise from those whose pressure
they caved in to. In short, the man who abuses because it
gets him the control he wants attends a treatment group to
maintain that control. With the instant rewards not forth-
coming, he drops out. Groups are working hard to lower
their dropout rate. In Quincy, Massachusetts, for instance,
men are expelled from the group if they merely show up
for meetings and do not participate actively. The Quincy
Court demands active participation, viewing mandated treat-

ment as "a substantive obligation, not a simple matter of attendance."

The first men's group in the country was Emerge, which opened its doors to batterers in 1977 at the urging of local women's shelters, whose counselors realized that not until men reversed their sexist views would women feel safe. Ever since, the goal of Emerge has been to end abuse by ending sexism. The Men's Domestic Violence Program of Putnam County, New York, like other effective men's programs, describes its objectives in terms of the Emerge goal: "We do this by providing a supportive atmosphere where men learn about their social causes, the cultural conditioning and their own personal history . . . the roots of domestic violence, its negative consequences for the family, its illegality, ways of avoiding violent situations, and what help is available in the community."

Most counseling groups work toward effecting three major changes in batterers:

The first and most immediate change required is for the abuser to ensure the safety of the woman he has injured and intimidated. This may entail his moving from the home they share until he completes the counseling program or under-taking drug or alcohol treatment or cooperating with her in obtaining an order of protection, a violation of which will send him to jail.

Second, group counselors realize that an abuser must change his sexist attitudes, and since, like most other abusers, he enters treatment in strong denial of any wrong-doing, he can't even acknowledge sexism. In fact, according to Linda Rouse in *You Are Not Alone*, nine out of ten men see no reason to change their abusive behavior, which they excuse or justify as "no different from every other man." As a result, the first hurdle they have to overcome before hope for change even arises is to be able to admit they are abusers. With that admission they can begin to understand their methods of control, with the resultant pain it inflicts on their wives and the sexist attitudes from which it stems. By the end of the course, which usually runs for about six months with weekly meetings, the man is expected to face up to the fact that he alone is responsible for his abuse, not only of his wife but of all women because, as he has treated his wife, so has he treated all women as lesser human beings.

The third change men have to undergo in treatment groups is developing coping skills to replace violence, and not only developing them but also using them. This entails learning alternative methods of expressing anger and giving testimony in the counseling group to the actual use of them. It further entails developing the ability to communicate, so the abuser must learn to hear while listening and to speak truthfully while talking.

Although men who lead batterers' groups claim few major victories, they feel "It's the best we have to date." Despite a large rate of dropout and recidivism, they remain hopeful, aware that for every man who stops battering there is a woman, along with her children, who stops living in fear. Even more discouraging than the low success rate of treatment is the even lower percentage of abusers who enter treatment centers in the first place. "If we can get them here, maybe we can help them," a counselor told me. "If they won't come, there's no hope."

A woman who came to court one day had tried to get her husband into counseling, a skinny little woman with four-month-old twins, whose husband, a security guard, had abused her brutally, but nonphysically, for three years. Isolated from her family, taunted for being a "dumb hillbilly," deprived of enough money to buy simple necessities for the babies, and told repeatedly that she was crazy, she developed asthma. Annoyed, her husband drove her from the house, yelling obscene names after her as she left with the babies. Although for over a year she had pleaded with him to seek help to save their marriage, he had refused on the grounds that she was the one who needed it, not he. Would counseling have changed him? There is no guarantee, and the odds are not good, but it might have. Without it there were no odds.

Since counseling by itself has produced only mediocre results, a few communities had the idea of pulling together men and women from diverse agencies to help them develop more extensive programs. Two in particular have such hopeful prospects that cities across the country have copied them. Both programs include batterers' groups, but only as one part of a multifaceted approach to the problem.

One of the programs is the Quincy, Massachusetts, Model Domestic Abuse Program, which operates under the four goals stated in its manual:

1. To protect and empower women who seek legal assistance

2. To encourage battered women to seek legal assistance

3. To control batterers and hold them accountable for their abuse

4. To prevent domestic abuse by redefining it as a serious crime in the minds of the public and the criminal justice community

Created on the belief that the criminal justice system is the cornerstone on which abuse prevention is founded, the Quincy program coordinates the efforts of the social service agencies with those of all divisions of the criminal justice system, requiring continual communication among them. It begins with the Quincy Police Department, which unlike many in other cities has a strong commitment to intervention in cases of abuse: extensive police training, detailed policies and procedures, mandatory arrests with a woman's safety the primary concern, and careful follow-up.

Next, the district attorney's office becomes involved with specially trained lawyers and counselors to inform and support the woman throughout the court procedure and afterward.

The court as well is brought into the process in a new way. Instead of the long wait and absence of privacy of most courts, the Quincy program has established a separate waiting room and an all-female staff for abuse victims in addition to giving priority to abuse cases and scheduling two special sessions each day.

While most communities close the books on an abuser after a woman receives a protective order, the Quincy program puts him under surveillance by the probation department. Officers monitor his movements, keeping in close contact with his friends, relatives, and the agencies dealing with him.

In Quincy the abuser is required to enter a treatment program and, as pointed out earlier, to become an active participant in it. In addition to the usual treatment methods, counselors keep in close touch with the abuser's mate and with the police, probation, and court should the abuser shows signs of further abuse.

Even the sheriff's office plays a role in the comprehensive Quincy Model Domestic Abuse Program. Instead of merely being used to serve abusers with a woman's order of protection, they inform other agencies of the release of any abuser from jail and even provide his woman with an alarm alert if the man appears dangerous.

DOVE—Domestic Violence Ended—is the woman's shelter in the Quincy program, which provides emergency housing, counseling, legal help, activities for the children of residents, tutoring if they are afraid to go to school, and teachers to help women prepare for the high school equivalency exam.

Although Quincy admits that its program has discovered no cure for abuse, it points with hope to comparative statistics:

- No court-involved woman has been killed in a domestic abuse case in nearly six years.

- More women are seeking protective orders and are following through on them.

- More men are completing treatment programs.

- Judges are giving stronger sentences and longer probation to abusers.

- Quincy feels, and it certainly appears, that there is cause for hope.

A different kind of program, called Coordinated Community Responses, was designed and set in operation in the early 1980s. The Community Involvement Program—CIP—in Duluth, Minnesota, has become a paradigm for programs in other cities in a growing number of states and in more than twenty other cities in its own state. Linda Frisch of the New York State Office for the Prevention of Domestic Violence says that they are striving to adapt the Duluth program throughout New York State.

In an article entitled "Coordinated Community Responses" (*Women Battering: Policy Responses*, edited by Michael

Steinman), Jeffrey Edleson found from his study that CIPs develop from three main assumptions:

1. That no one has a right to use violence except in self-defense

2. That abuse originates in society's acceptance of it as a man's right to dominate

3. That social systems must protect women by confronting men and changing the acceptability of abuse, both socially and legally

The core of a CIP program is a group of advocates from whom branch contacts with agencies and systems coordinated to deal with abuse offenders. It is the advocates who work to establish mandatory-arrest policies, to clarify with prosecutors what constitutes abuse, to urge women to obtain orders of protection and support them through the process, to set up court-ordered treatment programs for men and see that they complete them, and to provide shelters for women. In addition, advocates keep in close touch with the abused women and their children, offering counseling and other services they may need.

Although evaluators differ in determining the success of CIP programs, most agree that they effect lower rates of recidivism. As Jeffrey Edleson concludes, "The experience of Minnesota's intervention efforts indicates the importance of building networks not only within specific criminal justice systems but also across the state and with legislative bodies."

While the focus of both Quincy and CIP efforts has been mainly on physical abuse, it must be remembered that years of nonphysical abuse have usually preceded it. It is up to the courts and the advocates who influence them, therefore, to look beyond the bloody nose and black eye of the woman before them and recognize the invisible wounds inflicted by the emotional and psychological and social and economic battering the women have endured unseen.

When programs begin to address nonphysical abuse with the concern they express over violence today, they will begin to minimize the physical abuse to which it inevitably escalates.

CHAPTER 16

"So why don't I feel happy?"

Building a New Life

WHEN ELLIE AMES finally left Roger, she expected a lifetime of rainbows and song. Like a Grimm's fairy tale heroine, she had escaped from the den of the ogre into the pure fresh air of freedom, where she saw herself living happily ever after. Reality, however, provided a different ending to her story. She felt as miserable as she had while living with Roger. "It was awful," she says today. "The sun could be shining, and the children doing well in school and my friends standing by with support, and it made no difference. I was mean and ugly and mad. It didn't make any sense." Ellie was wrong: it did make sense.

A battered woman lives with stress so great that it may terrify and render her powerless, effecting the extreme shock experienced by soldiers in battle, Hiroshima victims, holocaust survivors, and children held hostage. Under ordinary stress the mind and body arm themselves for fight or flight: adrenaline rushes in with a charge of energy, and perceptions heighten to take a stand against immediate danger.

The media periodically report stories of people lifting steel beams to free a man trapped beneath a steel girder or breaking a professional runner's speed record to save a child from an oncoming car—that's the protective mechanism of fight. We see on television with amazed horror Bosnian families who have been in hiding for a week or more without food or water and Rwandans, babies on their backs, children in tow, walking a hundred miles to the hoped-for safety of the Tanzanian border—that's the protective mechanism of flight.

However, when circumstances make both fight and flight impossible and a person is powerless in the face of danger, the result is trauma. A woman, kept captive by the locks and keys that bolt doors or by the manipulative skills of her husband, battered by fists or by threats and humiliation, cannot flee and cannot fight, or the battering will increase. She is trapped in inevitable destruction, like a rabbit in the headlights of an oncoming car, a mouse cornered by a cat, a woman in the grip of a rapist. Traumatized, she surrenders, mind and body.

That's what happened to Ellie, and it is why she continued subjecting herself to Roger's abuse until her family offered her a way out: she could live with them, and her mother would care for the children until Ellie got a job that could support them. One day while Roger was at work, she took the children to her mother's, returned home to pack up a few things, and walked out the door, as she put it, "free." The first night, the family sat around the dinner table with a new thank you in the grace her father said, with smiles and hope and a bottle of champagne to celebrate.

After dinner, Ellie put the children to bed, kissed her parents good night, then went to her room and cried.

Tears of joy, her mother explained that night and the next day and the next, but Ellie began to cry a different kind of tears. She was angry. She snapped at her parents, didn't want to see the children, lay in bed all day, and worst of all, couldn't get Roger out of her mind. No one understood why, especially not Ellie. "Forget it," her mother advised. "It's over."

"So why don't I feel happy?" she asked, but neither she nor her mother found an answer.

There is an answer, though, discovered in the 1970s by psychiatrists, among whom was Dr. Robert J. Lifton working with a group of Vietnam veterans who had suffered trauma during the war and continued to have recurrent feelings of terror along with inexplicable explosions of rage. Finding an amazing similarity in their symptoms and those of men traumatized by the horrors of entirely different experiences, psychiatrists came to the conclusion that the men suffered from a psychic illness that they called *post-traumatic stress disorder*. In 1980 the American Psychiatric Association officially recognized PTSD.

It is only recently, however, as a result of feminist efforts, that PTSD, formerly diagnosed as a disease attributed to the male experience of war, has been recognized as a disease suffered by battered women as well. Since an abused woman's trauma extends over a longer period of time than the year-long tour of duty in Vietnam, psychiatrists describe it as complex trauma, more closely resembling the experience of prisoners of war. Having been rendered helpless by prolonged abuse in the face of fear for their safety and sanity, like released prisoners of the North Vietnamese, they become veterans of their personal imprisonment and succumb to its ravages. Release provides no freedom, escape no safety.

Ellie and tens of thousands of women battered physically or nonphysically suffer from post-traumatic stress disorder without knowing it. They know only that they are miserable; their friends and family know only that they are different. Professionals describe PTSD in three major categories:

1. Hyperarousal, in which the woman is constantly on the alert for danger, can't sleep, is ill tempered, and flies into sudden rages

2. Intrusion, in which she relives her abusive relationship in unshakable memories and nightmares

3. Constriction, in which she no longer feels any emotion and cuts off social contacts and activities

Ellie experienced all three categories, her family walking on eggs in fruitless attempts to ease the irritability and explosions of hyperarousal and she suffering in silence as the intrusion of recurring memories tortured her one day and the constriction of deadness enshrouded her the next. In this way she kept the trauma alive, unable to lay it to rest in the peace of her past.

About half of battered women who suffer from complex post-traumatic stress disorder fall into a clinical depression, which is not to be confused with "the blues" or grief. The former is simply a temporary low mood swing that can be brought on by fatigue or the weather or missing a loved one, while the latter is the result of a serious loss that can be worked through in a series of stages. Clinical depression, on the other hand, is a specific illness that stems from not fully understood genetic and environmental

sources and for which scientists continue, not fully successfully, to seek cures.

Millions of Americans suffer from depression, about a
third of all women at some time in their life, many of whom
are experiencing the aftershock of abuse. Physicians and
psychiatrists attribute the following symptoms to depression:

- Inability to sleep

- Pervasive sadness

- Loss of energy

- Withdrawal from the world

- Weight loss

- Lack of interest in sex

- Inability to concentrate

While some symptoms of depression resemble those of
complex PTSD, the overall feelings of the two differ: PTSD is
like streaks of lightning electrifying a woman; depression is
a heavy, wet blanket suffocating her. PTSD creates such
intense pain that a woman may feel that only alcohol or
drugs can spare her; depression so paralyzes and deadens
her that she need take only a small step into suicide.

PTSD, which can easily turn the lives of family members
upside down, may not even be evident to strangers; for
instance, I see women in court who have left abusive mates,
usually angry, sometimes in tears, and there is no way of
knowing which are suffering from PTSD. On the other hand,
just last week a woman brought her sister, who had left her
husband and moved in with her, to court for an order of
protection. One look diagnosed the sister's depression: she

was dirty, her hair snarled as if uncombed for weeks, a vacant stare in her eyes. "She won't feed the baby," the woman said, "or even change into pajamas to go to bed." Years of abuse had turned her into the walking dead.

Depression, although not always curable, responds well to treatments that modern science offers—usually drugs such as Prozac or lithium—that, like insulin for diabetics, enable sufferers to carry on normal lives. Therapists who treat complex post-traumatic stress disorder, on the other hand, tend to avoid drugs, concentrating instead on interpersonal therapy, which entails a great deal of pain.

Healing abuse is like healing a sore, which is red and raw at the wounding; it hurts. White blood cells rush to a sore area to heal it, and if it has festered, collections of them form in pus to do their work. Sealed, the bacteria multiply, so you keep the sore open, cleaned with antiseptic and draining.

The sore is the bleeding hurt of abuse. The body's protective white blood cells are the fight response that has enabled the woman to escape from her abuser. The collections of pus are defense mechanisms that obliterate her memories of pain. Uncovering and draining those memories, bringing them into the light of her consciousness, is the work the woman must do.

How she does this depends greatly on the intensity of her trauma and the depth to which she has repressed it. Some women find they are able to pour out their abusive experiences to a close friend; others write about them through a stream of consciousness; some paint or compose music to express their feelings. Many women undertake counseling and join groups to share their problems with other abused women; a few whose memories are too deeply interred to be dug up turn to hypnosis or psychodrama under the care of specialized therapists. Whatever method they use, the aim must be to bring the experiences of their abuse into the open, because until they face them and let themselves feel the pain of them, the women will not heal. Repression only increases the festering.

In being asked to reexperience the abuse she suffered, a woman usually begins by giving a blow-by-blow description—what her mate said to her, what he did to her, and what she did in response. This, however, is mere storytelling; in fact, as a woman relates and relates again the horrors of her experience, the story unfolds as though on tape—word for word the same, expressionless. She is not reexperiencing; she is merely recounting.

A trained counselor, aware of this, urges her further to talk about herself, not about her abuser. "What were you feeling?" she asks.

"I felt he was cruel," she might answer. "I felt he was a bully and enjoyed flexing his muscles on me." When she has finished analyzing her abuser and interpreting his motivations, the counselor will point out that what she has just done is explained what she was *thinking* about her abuser during their time together.

"But what were you *feeling*?" she will ask again.

Thoughts are not feelings. The former rise from the mind, the latter from wherever the source of emotions lies— the heart, we like to believe, though science points less romantically to a localized spot of the brain and the hormones secreted by glands. Although it is therapeutic to face the details of her abuse and to share her thoughts about them, she will not heal until she can face her feelings as well. Thoughts are easy to bring back because they keep their distance from a woman's vulnerability; they are "out there" while she remains "in here," safe behind the ramparts and the castle moat of nonfeeling.

But she must feel. An effective counselor helps her knock down her defenses—to stop denying the feelings, stop repressing them, stop escaping them. To feel the pain of them as she felt during the months or years of suffering abuse. What does she have to experience—not relate or think but *experience?* What does she have to feel?

First anger, which is nearest the surface—anger at her mate for turning her into a submissive slave, anger at herself for acquiescing, and anger at the world for standing by while it happened.

Then shame—shame over relinquishing the sense of self in which she took pride, shame over abandoning her values, over demeaning her self-esteem, over ceding her will.

Also guilt—guilt that she had brought the abuse upon herself by not knowing how to build a good marriage, guilt over marrying her abuser in the first place and enduring the intolerable situation for so long.

Finally sorrow—sorrow over the marriage she might have had and never did, sorrow that the spasmodic glimpses of the husband she loved couldn't last to become the husband she had.

The Process of Restoration

An old Yiddish proverb says, "The greatest pain is that which you can't tell others." It is on the wisdom found there that the healing of abuse is based. When a woman is finally able to reexperience her pain, she can begin to restore what her abuser stole from her through isolation, disempowerment, and fear for her sanity. The process goes through three main stages.

1. Reestablishing Social Contacts

A woman cannot heal herself in isolation. It was, after all, isolation that enabled her mate to take control of her life.

Without the outside world against which to measure her own world, she had no way to evaluate her relationship, no one against whose judgment she could compare her own, no social norms of husband and wife along which to graph her line. Therefore healing has to come from breaking forth from the pupal shell in which she has been sealed and emerging like a butterfly into a community of people.

It is toward this end that self-help groups have formed throughout the country, enabling women to establish contact with other abused women and, as a result, to accept one another's experiences as a reality testing of their own. Family and friends also play an important role in leading a woman back into the social world, for in their support she rediscovers the safety her abuser denied her and the sense of belonging he distorted into ownership.

2. Regaining Control

When a woman is able to relive the hurt of her abusive years, she begins to take back control of her life. By admitting the feelings into her consciousness, she holds them in her power, like a team of horses with the reins in her grip, able to canter or trot or gallop at her command only, unable to charge or run away. By confronting her feelings, she can keep them in place: her anger—she can know it is justified and hold it back from revenge; her shame—she can subdue it with pride in her courage; her guilt—she can heap it, along with responsibility, on the shoulders of her abuser; her sorrow— she can know it is real and work through her mourning until she distances the pain.

3. Answering "Why?"

Everyone who has been hit by unpredictable suffering eventually asks the same question: "Why me?" Why am *I* the one who got cancer? Why was *my* child killed by a drunk driver? Why did lightning strike *my* house? And, keeping in mind what she remembers as the happy marriage of her parents and friends, "Why did this happen to *me?*"

From the start humankind has tried to find a reason for its cruelties and injustices, relocating its source over time from God to Kismet, from the psyche to the genes, and still the question persists. Thornton Wilder wrote a Pulitzer Prize–winning novel called *The Bridge of San Luis Rey* in which the narrator, Brother Juniper, attempts to explain why five people were caught on a bridge when it collapsed, plunging them to their death. "Either we live by accident and die by accident, or we live by plan and die by plan," Brother Juniper concludes after his six-year study. His answer is that there is no answer; suffering happens because it happens.

That's the answer an abused woman must eventually come to terms with. She may know that her husband suffered abuse as a child, realizing that it often perpetuates itself; she may know that she mistook his need for control as strength and admired him for it; she may know that her mother warned her and that her friends expressed doubt, but she will never understand why they met in the first place and fell in love and married. She may figure out *how* she got into an abusive relationship, but she will never understand *why*, nor is it important. When the escapee from abuse can stop wasting her energy on "Why me?" and start planning "Now me," she is well on the way to a new life.

The founding fathers of psychiatry, Sigmund Freud and Alfred Adler, agreed that one of the cornerstones of mental health is commitment to work, on which much of an abused woman's healing builds. It is not surprising, therefore, that many women who have survived the ordeal of battering become activists in domestic violence prevention programs—shelters, lobbying groups, educational outreach. I met one who had enrolled in law school "so I can give women like me a better deal than I got." With firsthand experience and a sense of mission, these women continue to heal themselves while alleviating and helping to heal the pain of others.

Other women embark on a new career as a way to start a new life. "I've got eight years ahead of me, but I've always wanted to be a doctor," a woman told me the day she left her husband and got an order of protection so he wouldn't harass her in her new home. I see her now sitting by my side in the crowded court waiting room, peeling one by one the layers of fear that had encased her during three years of marriage. Determined to break her spirit, her husband had made her drop out of college and become his virtual slave and, though never laying a hand on her, had so isolated her from support that his threats landed like physical blows. I want to think of her now as a junior in a premed program, confident and proud of herself. I wonder. I hope.

Most women who leave abusive mates are not in a financial position to spend eight years in preparation for a profession. Some will finish high school or take courses in a community college. Others will stay home to raise their children—a new career because they will do it alone, often dependent on public assistance. Still others will take whatever jobs they can get and build a new home, hard earned but independently theirs.

While women are eager to undertake new work after growing through the trauma of abuse, many remain too vulnerable to recommit themselves to love for years, if ever. Fourteen years after Joan's divorce from Irwin, with a master's degree, a challenging job, a commitment to hospital volunteer work, and her children successful in school, she has taken her place securely in the outside world. However, in the inside world—her inside world—she remains fearful, unable to enter into a new relationship.

Joan is not alone; many women, able to adore their children, love their parents and siblings, and enjoy friends, shy away from a new intimate relationship. Like Joan, they may declare, "I don't ever meet a man I can fall in love with" when what they really mean is "I never let myself fall in love with a man I meet." They make excuses, find fault, deny their feelings—use all mechanisms available to prevent reopening the wounds of their abusive marriage. This is sad, since scars have covered them over, and it is only the woman's fear of herself that refuses to heal.

"How can I trust love again when I goofed so badly last time?" a divorced friend asked me once. The answer, I think, lies in taking a closer look at love. What is it? Carol married Ted because he was a macho hero; Terry married John because he was going to war; Joan married Irwin because he was a symbol of rebellion; Ellie married Roger because it was the proper thing to do. Was it love? Many other girls marry because they are pregnant or want to become pregnant or hate their parents or want to quit school or don't want to find a job. Is that love?

Maybe the abused woman should give up the idea of discovering what love *is* and define it by discovering what love *isn't*. It isn't the possessiveness, the domination, the tyranny, the calculated manipulativeness of her former husband, the abuser. It isn't the humiliation, the fear, the sense of worthlessness, the dependence, the pain he made her feel. Love nurtures; it doesn't hurt and belittle. Love makes two people want to "protect and touch and greet each other," as the poet Rainer Maria Rilke wrote. Love realizes that a man and a woman are equals.

A woman who has been in an abusive relationship knows all too well that the only touch and greetings she got from her husband were cruel and the only protection her own prayers. Like my friend, therefore, she "goofed" not in love but in the misinterpretation of love. Accepting this, she may realize she can love for the first time and can commit herself to a relationship for the second.

Is a woman ever fully healed of the ravages of abuse? She won't forget them any more than she will forget the contracting pains of birth, but in remembering she won't suffer the agony again. She won't erase the wounds of abuse like pencil marks on paper, but she will feel stronger from the scar tissue covering them. Being healed is like Gordon Allport's definition of maturity: it's the process of becoming, not arriving (*Becoming*). In her book *I Can't Get Over It*, Aphrodite Matsakis, a psychologist specializing in post-traumatic stress disorder, outlines some of the milestones a woman will pass as she works her way through the process:

- Less frequent reliving of the abusive experience—fewer nightmares, less fear, increased self-confidence, greater skill in taking charge of her affairs

- Feeling less the helplessness of a victim and more the strength of a survivor

- Enjoying life more—friends, activities, nature

- Learning to laugh again, to have fun, to play

- Changing from the rigidity that kept her life together to the ease and spontaneity of freedom

- Turning anger and vengefulness into righteous indignation that motivates a mission to help others

- Feeling kinship not only with other battered women but with all people who suffer

As I read this list, I long for the day when all the battered women I know or have met or have not met pass these milestones and become whole women again, and I long for the day when a worldful of people can understand what abuse is, bloodless abuse with invisible wounds whose festering poisons and pain destroy. Even men bear unseen scars from this abusive world; by allowing themselves to touch those scars, perhaps they will recognize the weapons that inflicted them and throw away the weapons with which they inflict their women.

Psychohistorians tell us that over the years child-rearing practices have improved. In a way they are right: what used to be legal—infanticide and sexual and physical abuse—are now illegal. Parents still kill their children, exploit them sexually, and beat, starve, and imprison them; only now since the law has stepped in, if they are found out, they are tried in court. Children are put in foster homes, and parents in extreme cases go to jail.

Since a large percentage of abused children grow up to be abusers, methods of child rearing play a major role in producing nonabusive men. The new woman who becomes whole as she passes the milestones of healing can take the first step toward a new world by raising her son to become the new man.

- Let her listen to him, hear him, and accept what he feels as his truth . . . not disparage him as she was disparaged but reinforce him as she was not reinforced . . . let her love him unconditionally and let him know it.

- Let her guide him, not control him, so he keeps his independent self . . . not punish him for failures but support him for daring to try . . . and help him learn from his mistakes through creative discipline, not punishment.

- Let her play with him so he will learn the fun and the give-and-take of being alive.

- Let her love him not for what he accomplishes but for who he is.

The little boy she mothers in this way will be the man who finds power within himself, so he won't have to seek it by imposing it on his mate; he will be assured of his own self-worth, so he won't have to degrade hers; he will be an equal in life's game, so he will share it equally; being loved by his mother, he will know how to love a woman. The little boy she mothers in this way will not be an abuser, but like Mahatma Gandhi will look on his wife "not as the husband's bondslave, but his companion and his helpmate, and an equal partner in all his joys and sorrows—as free as the husband to choose her own path."

In the book *The Wizard of Oz,* Dorothy is hurled through a cyclone, tracked down by monkey captors, imprisoned by a witch, manipulated by a weakling in the guise of a powerful wizard, and finally abandoned in a topsy-turvy land. Only when the Good Witch of the North explains the power of the red shoes is Dorothy able to escape. Although unintentionally, author Frank Baum has described in metaphor the plight of a nonphysically battered woman—hounded, enslaved, manipulated, cut off from family, driven crazy in a senseless world. Since not every battered woman has magic shoes to free her from the mess, however, it is up to every citizen to urge every leader in our power structure to provide them.

With the explosive revelation of O. J. Simpson's alleged history of wife abuse, the world has been forced to take a hard look at the blood of physical battering and the panic of nonphysical battering that long preceded it. "Maybe wife-beaters will never again feel quite so secure. Maybe judges will not be as quick to give them a 'sentence' that amounts to a knowing wink," wrote A. M. Rosenthal in the June 26, 1994, edition of *The New York Times.* Maybe.

"He'll get a light sentence this time too because he's a celebrity," I heard repeatedly in the weeks following the crime. If he is found guilty, it is true that he may get a light sentence, but if he does, it won't be because he's a celebrity; it will be because he is an abuser. Until now that's what judges have been giving abusers—light sentences. Maybe Nicole Simpson's years of suffering will make a difference. Maybe the face of abuse has imprinted itself indelibly on our collective mind, and we will not forget.

The good sign is that we can no longer sidestep belief: abuse exists, not among *them* but among *us.* In a little book with big thoughts called *I May Not Be Totally Perfect, but Parts of Me Are Excellent,* Ashleigh Brilliant writes, "Believing is seeing—I wouldn't have seen it if I hadn't believed it." O. J. Simpson has made us believe abuse; now we can see it and do something about it.

At the end of *Gaslight,* Joseph Cotten, a newspaper reporter who saves Ingrid Bergman, stands with her looking out into the night as her abuser is led away. Aware that she is traumatized by what her husband has done to her and that she will continue to suffer from aftershock, he says to her, "It will be a long night, but it will end. It's starting to clear. In the morning when the sun rises, sometimes it's hard to believe there ever was a night."

Since few battered woman have a Joseph Cotten to save them, our nation must acknowledge them and give them the wherewithal to save themselves—housing, skills, jobs, child care, emotional support—so that they can be independent. Then we will be able to say to battered women: Yes, the night will end . . . Yes, the sun will rise again.

Help Lines

IF YOU IDENTIFY WITH any of the abused women in this book, you may be an abused woman too. If any of the abusive situations seem like home, you may be living in one. If you consider yourself the only woman in the world trapped in abuse, you are probably too ashamed to tell anyone. And if you believe it's all your fault, you are wrong.

Professionals say that if you think your man is abusing you, chances are he is. With that in mind, the National Coalition Against Domestic Violence reaches out to American women through an extensive network of national, state, and local offices and hot lines with information and help. Take advantage of it: pick up the phone and call or mail a letter today:

> National Office
> P.O. Box 18749
> Denver, CO 80218
> (303) 839-1852

State Coalitions Against Domestic Violence
(with information on local shelters, offices, and hot lines)

Alabama
P.O. Box 4762
Montgomery, AL 36101
(205) 832-4842

Alaska
130 Seward Street, Room 501
Juneau, AK 99801
(907) 586-3650

Arizona
100 West Camelback, #109
Phoenix, AZ 85013
(800) 782-6400, (602) 279-2900

Arkansas
7509 Cantrell Road, Suite 213
Little Rock, AR 72207
(501) 663-4668

California (Central/Northern)
619 13th Street, Suite I
Modesto, CA 95354
(209) 524-1888

California (Southern)
P.O. Box 5036
Santa Monica, CA 90405
(213) 655-6098

Colorado
P.O. Box 18902
Denver, CO 80218
(303) 573-9018

Connecticut
135 Broad Street
Hartford, CT 06105
(203) 524-5890

Delaware
507 Philadelphia Pike
Wilmington, DE 19809-2177
(302) 762-6110

District of Columbia
P.O. Box 76069
Washington, D.C. 20013
(202) 783-5332

Florida
1521-A Killearn Center Boulevard
Tallahassee, FL 32308
(800) 500-1119, (904) 668-6862

Georgia
250 Georgia Avenue, S.E.
Suite 308
Atlanta, GA 30312
(800) 643-1212, (404) 524-3847

Hawaii
98-939 Moanalua Road
Aiea, HI 96701
(808) 486-5072

Idaho
200 North 4th, Suite 10
Boise, ID 83702
(208) 384-0419

Illinois
937 South Fourth Street
Springfield, IL 62703
(217) 789-2830

Indiana
2511 East 46th Street, Suite N-3
Indianapolis, IN 46205
(317) 543-3908

Iowa
Lucas Building, First Floor
Des Moines, IA 50319
(515) 281-7284

Kansas
820 SE Quincy, #416B
Topeka, KS 66612
(913) 232-9784

Kentucky
P.O. Box 356
Frankfort, KY 40602
(502) 875-4132

Louisiana
P.O. Box 3053
Hammond, LA 70404
(504) 542-4446

Maine
P.O. Box 89
Winterport, ME 04496
(207) 941-1194

Maryland
11501 Georgia Avenue, #403
Silver Spring, MD 20902
(301) 942-0900

Massachusetts
210 Commercial Street, 3rd Floor
Boston, MA 02109
(617) 248-0922

Michigan
P.O. Box 16009
Lansing, MI 48901
(517) 484-2924

Minnesota
1619 Dayton Avenue, #303
St. Paul, MN 55104
(612) 646-6177

Mississippi
P.O. Box 333
Biloxi, MS 39533
(601) 436-3809

Missouri
331 Madison
Jefferson City, MO 65101
(314) 634-4161

Montana
1236 North 28th Street, #103
Billings, MT 59101
(406) 256-6334

Nebraska
315 South 9th Street, #18
Lincoln, NE 68508
(402) 476-6256

Nevada
2100 Capurro Way, Suite E
Sparks, NV 89431
(800) 500-1556, (702) 358-1171

New Hampshire
P.O. Box 353
Concord, NH 03302
(800) 852-3388, (603) 224-8893

New Jersey
2620 Whitehorse Hamilton Square Road
Trenton, NJ 08690-2718
(800) 572-7233, (609) 584-8107

New Mexico
P.O. Box 25363
Albuquerque, NM 87125
(800) 773-3645, (505) 246-9240

New York
Women's Building
79 Central Avenue
Albany, NY 12206
(800) 942-6906 (English),
(800) 942-6908 (Spanish),
(518) 432-4864

North Carolina
P.O. Box 51875
Durham, NC 27717-1875
(919) 956-9124

North Dakota
418 East Rosser Avenue, #320
Bismarck, ND 58501
(800) 472-2911, (701) 255-6240

Ohio
4041 North High Street, #101
Columbus, OH 43214
(800) 934-9840, (614) 784-0023

and

P.O. Box 15673
Columbus, OH 43215
(614) 221-1255

Oklahoma
2200 Classen Boulevard, #1300
Oklahoma City, OK 73106
(800) 522-9054, (405) 557-1210

Oregon
520 NW Davis, Suite 310
Portland, OR 97209
(503) 223-7411

Pennsylvania
6400 Flank Drive, #1300
Harrisburg, PA 17112
(800) 932-4632, (717) 545-6400

Puerto Rico
Calle San Francisco 151-153
Viejo San Juan
San Juan, Puerto Rico 00905
(809) 722-2907

Rhode Island
422 Post Road, #101
Warwick, RI 02888
(800) 434-8100, (401) 467-9940

South Carolina
P.O. Box 7776
Columbia, SC 29202-7776
(803) 254-3699

South Dakota
3220 South Highway 281
Aberdeen, SD 57401
(605) 225-5122

Tennessee
P.O. Box 120972
Nashville, TN 37212-0972
(800) 356-6767, (615) 327-0805

Texas
8701 North Mopac, #450
Austin, TX 78759
(512) 794-1133

Utah
120 North 200 West, 2nd Floor
Salt Lake City, UT 84103
(801) 538-4100

Vermont
P.O. Box 405
Montpelier, VT 05601
(802) 223-1302

Virginia
2850 Sandy Bay Road, #101
Williamsburg, VA 23185
(800) 838-8238, (804) 221-0990

Washington
200 W Street SE, Suite B
Tumwater, WA 98501
(800) 562-6025, (206) 352-4029

West Virginia
P.O. Box 85
Sutton, WV 26601
(304)765-2250

Wisconsin
1400 East Washington Avenue, #103
Madison, WI 53703
(608) 255-0539

Wyoming
341 East E Street, #135A
Casper, WY 82601
(307) 235-2814

U.S. Virgin Islands
8 Kongens Gade
St. Thomas, VI 00802
(809) 776-3966

and

P.O. Box 2734
Christiansted
St. Croix, VI 00822
(809) 773-9272

Index